TALKING
PICTURES

TALKING PICTURES

HOW TO WATCH MOVIES

ANN HORNADAY

BASIC BOOKS

New York

Basic Books
Hachette Book Group
1290 Avenue of the Americas, New York, NY 10104
www.basicbooks.com

Printed in the United States of America
First Edition: May 2017
Published by Basic Books, an imprint of Perseus Books, LLC,
a subsidiary of Hachette Book Group, Inc.

The publisher is not responsible for websites (or their content) that are not owned by the publisher.

Print book interior design by Amy Quinn

Library of Congress Cataloging-in-Publication Data
Names: Hornaday, Ann author.
Title: Talking pictures : how to watch movies / Ann Hornaday.
Description: New York : Basic Books, 2017. | Includes
    bibliographical references and index.
Identifiers: LCCN 2017009751 | ISBN 9780465094233
    (hardcover) | ISBN 9780465094240 (ebook)
Subjects: LCSH: Motion pictures. | Motion pictures—Anecdotes.
Classification: LCC PN1995 .H66 2017 | DDC 791.43—dc23
LC record available at https://lccn.loc.gov/2017009751

LSC-C

10 9 8 7 6 5 4 3

For Dennis
who helps me see the world
anew every single day

CONTENTS

INTRODUCTION

THERE ARE A FEW INEVITABLE questions film critics face when we stagger our way into the sunlit world outside the darkened theaters in which we spend so much of our time. The first, almost always, is, "Film critic, wow, how did you get that job?" (Implied follow-up: "How do I go about getting paid to sit around and watch movies all day, too?")

The answer, in my case, is: pure accident. I did not grow up a congenital movie geek. If anything, I was a bookworm, avoiding my family's usual weekend pastimes of board games, cards, and watching Iowa college football on TV to burrow into *Harriet the Spy* and, as a teenager, *On the Road* and *Zen and the Art of Motorcycle Maintenance*. I went to movies, sure: *Fantasia*, *Mary Poppins*, and *Oliver!* as a little kid; *Young Frankenstein* and *Blazing Saddles* as a fourteen-year-old (I can still remember the frisson of hearing Robert Redford's "Oooooh shit" when my friends and I saw *Butch Cassidy and the Sundance Kid* as easily scandalized youngsters). I credit one of my formative cinematic experiences to a favorite babysitter who took me to see the melodrama *Dark Victory* at the Varsity Theatre next door to Drake University, purely for the camp value of Bette Davis voraciously devouring the scenery as a rich party girl elegantly succumbing to a brain tumor. But I didn't eat, sleep, and breathe movies like so many contemporaries who would become my colleagues in the field.

Instead, I came to reviewing as a writer: after graduating from Smith College with a degree in government, I moved to New York to become a journalist. I worked at *Ms. Magazine* as a researcher and, for two wonderful years, as Gloria Steinem's administrative assistant. It was Gloria who urged me to become a freelancer, because she had found the freedom and variety of freelancing to be both fulfilling and fruitful in discovering her own voice as a young writer. By the time I summoned the courage to take her advice, a handsome New York–based movie magazine called *Premiere* had come into being. I began writing about filmmakers for their Cameo section—edited with superb taste by the poet April Bernard—where I wrote short profiles of the documentarian Albert Maysles, the costume designer Ellen Mirojnick, and the casting director Margery Simkin, among others.

Within a few years, I was writing film-related stories for *The New York Times* Arts & Leisure section, for which I interviewed the documentarians Joe Berlinger and Bruce Sinofsky, the experimental filmmaker Jem Cohen, emerging directors Noah Baumbach and Ang Lee, and a then little-known actor named Stanley Tucci.

This is all by way of explaining that, with the exception of a year spent studying filmmaking and cinema history at the University of Georgia under the auspices of a Pew National Arts Journalism Fellowship, I've learned my craft on the job, as well as through frequent visits to my local video stores (remember those?). By the time I was invited to be the film critic at the *Austin American-Statesman* in 1995, I had watched enough movies—and had learned enough from their makers—to feel confident that I could evaluate films knowledgeably and fairly. What's more, my background as a non-expert allowed me to approach movies more like my readers, who even in our movie-mad culture only go out to see an average of five or six movies per year.

Still, I'll never forget the paralyzing experience of sitting down to write my first official review—of *To Die For*, Gus Van Sant's based-on-a-true-story satire about murder, self-deception, and postmodern celebrity starring Nicole Kidman. I had adored the movie, of that I was certain. The question was: Why? As I stared at the cursor insistently blinking back at me in the *Statesman* newsroom, my mind was as blank as the computer screen. How on earth could I explain to thousands of readers—of wildly divergent ages, backgrounds, tastes, and temperaments— what made this movie so brilliant? How could I quantify the ways in which Kidman delivered such a shrewd, well-judged performance, or prove how Van Sant interpreted Buck Henry's stingingly funny screenplay so adroitly?

Luckily, I had received some advice just before moving to Austin that helped me forge ahead, counsel that has held me in good stead throughout the intervening twenty years. At one of several going-away get-togethers, my dear friend and fellow journalist David Friedman took me aside to share some wisdom he himself had received years before, when he became the television critic at the *Philadelphia Daily News*. "Before you write any review," David told me, "ask yourself three questions: 'What was the artist trying to achieve?' 'Did they achieve it?' And 'Was it worth doing?'"

I later learned that David was paraphrasing Goethe, who had similar advice for evaluating a piece of theater. No matter: those three questions have served as something of a north star throughout my career, as I've tried to write reviews that go beyond mere subjective, thumbs-up-thumbs-down opinion and instead judge movies on their own merits, to help readers put them into context, and, if they should decide to see the film in question, to prepare them for the encounter—without including pesky spoilers and time-wasting synopses.

After working in Austin for two delightful years of music, movies, and Tex-Mex (enriched by director Richard Linklater's Austin Film Society, whose screenings of vintage repertory and avant-garde contemporary cinema helped enormously in my continuing film education), I went to the *Baltimore Sun*, and from there to the *Washington Post*. In all three newsrooms, I've sought continually to improve my understanding of filmmakers' artistic aims and the challenges they face, as well as the assumptions and expectations of viewers with dauntingly diverse opinions as to what constitutes a "good movie." An *Iron Man* and *Dark Knight* fanatic may have no intention of attending the latest Nicole Holofcener comedy of manners, but being a critic requires that I evaluate each of those movies in a way that's useful both to its natural constituency and to general audiences who simply want to keep abreast of what's happening in pop culture. And who knows? On the strength of one of my reviews, someone might decide to take a flier on a film they never would have considered before, and emerge a newly minted fan.

EACH MOVIE IS ITS OWN animal, with its own genre DNA, tonal quirks, and artistic and intellectual aspirations. Just as it's not fair to subject a period Western to the same standards as a post-Soviet Romanian family drama, it's not useful to expect a movie that simply sets out to be a slick piece of mainstream entertainment to traffic in lofty ideas about meaning and existence (although slick entertainment and deep meaning aren't at all mutually exclusive). But it *is* reasonable to expect that all these films will be original, well-crafted, and smart, and that they won't pander or condescend to their audiences. No matter what expectations they're seeking to fulfill, all films have an essential grammar in common: a lexicon of visual, aural, and performance conventions that link them to each other, or, when those conventions are cleverly subverted, constitute an invigorating break. The job of the critic is to recognize these connections and disruptions, not in order to be pedantic or superior to the reader, but to open up interpretive possibilities that will enrich the viewing experience, or at least provide some thought-provoking reading.

Still, the question lingers: What makes a movie "good"? And, conversely, what makes a movie "bad"? As a way of exploring the answer, in 2009 I embarked on a series of articles intended to help readers analyze and evaluate films in the same ways I do when I sit down to watch them. Called "How to Watch a Movie," the series explored various categories of filmmaking production and how the average movie-watcher can recognize fluency, ambition, and excellence when they've seen it. Returning to my roots as a reporter, I interviewed directors, screenwriters, producers, actors, sound technicians, cinematographers, and editors about their crafts and about what they wished audiences appreciated more about their work. How do we know when a movie's been well-written, aside from some memorable lines and a shock ending? How can we tell if a film's been well-edited? What exactly is cinematography, and how does it affect the viewer's visual and emotional experience? How does a virtuosic screen performance differ from one on stage or TV?

The series inspired me to write *Talking Pictures*, which is designed to guide readers through a medium that, as it morphs into an ever more constant presence in our lives, has called upon everyone to be their own most trusted film critics. Fans deliver instant reviews on Twitter to their friends, collectively deciding a movie's fate in 140 characters or less. Friends gather over a glass of wine or an espresso after a film, trading opinions on the screenplay or a star's performance. Extras on DVDs and streaming platforms have introduced consumers to information and background knowledge once reserved for archive-dwelling historians. The days of passive viewing are over. We're all experts now.

More than ever, viewers care deeply about what they're seeing and want to bring a critical eye to a medium that, uniquely, is simultaneously an art form, a mass entertainment medium, and a complex, rationalized industrial practice. They want the means and language to make sense of the sounds, stories, and visual images they encounter on screens that seem to proliferate with each passing day.

As many observers have pointed out, film is an amalgamation of almost every mode of expression—painting, theater, dance, music, architecture, photography, and writing. At their most analytically attentive, viewers must be aware of how each of those disciplines is informing what's happening on the screen, as well as its physiological, psychological, emotional, and even subconscious effect. That's a lot to take in for audiences, let alone tease apart while powerful images and sounds are washing over them.

And, make no mistake: that sensory baptism is vitally important. Although this book is intended as a primer in evaluating movies, the best way to appreciate them is through complete surrender. At its best, cinema should resemble a kind of dream-state that we enter collectively and experience personally. If we're constantly deconstructing an actor's performance or scrutinizing the lighting or production design of particular scenes, then either we're not letting the movie "in," or it wasn't made well enough to achieve that complete, almost cellular merging with our own consciousness that defines cinema at its most powerful and immersive.

The first duty of the critical viewer, then, is a mental one. You must cleanse your mind of any defenses, biases, or lingering distractions that might get in the way of succumbing entirely to the work on offer. Ideally, the movie will cast enough of a spell that you won't be tempted to engage in mental box-checking or second-guessing while it plays. If that's the case, your "critical mind" won't turn on until the end credits begin to roll. If the movie isn't working, for whatever reason, then you'll most likely begin your analysis while still in the theater, trying to figure out what's going wrong and where, and what the filmmakers might have done to create a more rewarding viewing experience.

Talking Pictures is meant to be useful in both circumstances—as a guide for appreciating movies more fully when they succeed, and for explaining their missteps when they fall short. The book is structured roughly according to a film's production—starting with the script, then moving to casting and production design, cinematography, and so forth. I've saved the chapter on directors until the end, because—ideally, at least—it's the director whose guidance and creative vision most influence the entire film, from the first day of shooting through the final edit. (Admittedly, when movies are mega-budgeted, big-studio blockbusters, the directors' roles become murkier; often they're at the mercy of studio executives who dictate casting and plot elements.)

In every chapter, I've tried to include examples of movies that capture the principles and best practices of a particular cinematic discipline; readers will note that most of them are culled from Hollywood's "Golden Age" from the 1930s through the 1950s, and from the 1970s through the present moment, a period that coincides with my most memorable filmgoing experiences as a fan and as a critic. I've included two or three leading questions viewers can ask themselves after they've seen a movie to ascertain whether it succeeded in particular craft areas.

Certain titles will keep popping up throughout *Talking Pictures*, from wartime dramas such as *The Best Years of Our Lives* and *The Hurt Locker* to wry "serio-comedies" like *The Graduate* and *You Can Count on Me*, from taut thrillers, including *All the President's Men*, *Michael Clayton*, and *Children of Men*, to such classics as *Do the Right Thing* and *GoodFellas*. These are all personal favorites of mine, and each exemplifies discrete areas of the craft— script, acting, design, camerawork, sound—as well as the kind of unifying directorial vision it takes to make them work as a beautifully integrated whole. And at the end of each chapter, I've included a "mini-canon" of movies that exemplify the best in each discipline.

Readers will also notice that certain words recur throughout the book—adjectives like "seamless," "expressive," "authentic," and "specific," and phrases like "emotional connection," "genuine feeling," "service to the story," and "building a world on-screen." In speaking with the hundreds of artists, technicians, and craftspeople who have been my unofficial tutors over the past quarter century, it's become clear that the ones at the top of their respective games keep these ideals foremost in their minds during the creative process, whether they're scouting a location, assessing the proper neckline for a seventeenth-century ball gown, choosing a camera lens, or preparing a monologue for a pivotal scene. It never ceases to amaze me to what lengths writers, actors, directors, designers, and technicians will go in order to finesse every single detail. The least the rest of us can do is notice. With luck, that's precisely what this book will help you do.

CHAPTER ONE

···· THE SCREENPLAY ····

When people say a movie is well-written, they usually mean they enjoyed the snappy dialogue or
appreciated a diabolically clever plot twist. But a
screenplay is responsible for so much more than that. Why
do we love a certain movie? Because we liked the story it
told, what happened, where it went, and how it got there.
Most often, we loved the characters—even when we didn't
exactly *like* them, or even understand them.

When those elements are in place, it's because they
were put there by a screenwriter, usually after months,
maybe even years, of difficult, unheralded work. The
screenplay serves as the founding document of every film,
laying out not just plot and dialogue but also structure,
internal "rules," the inner lives, motivations, and believability of the characters, and such intangible values as tone
and theme.

The script is the chief reference point for the director and all the creative collaborators on a film, who use it
when they're planning everything from costumes and sets

to lighting schemes and camera angles. The better written the script, the more focused and consistent the craftspeople can be in creating a compelling and credible world
on-screen.

A screenplay written with authority, detail, and specificity allows the actors to sink completely into their roles
without being nagged by questions about motivations or
inconsistent behaviors. Everything they need to know
about the characters they're bringing to life is right there
on the page. George Clooney once told me that the importance of the screenplay hit him after he received the
poorest reviews of his career for *Batman & Robin*. From
that moment on, he said, script came first when deciding
what projects to do. Tellingly, his next three films were
the smart, well-crafted *Out of Sight, Three Kings*, and *O
Brother, Where Art Thou?*, which together vaunted Clooney into the ranks of handsome movie stars who are also
serious actors of discerning taste. The moral of the story?
"You cannot make a good film out of a bad screenplay,"
Clooney said flatly. "You can make a *bad* film out of a
good screenplay, I've seen that happen a lot. But you can't
do it the other way around."

In the 1980s and 1990s, a raft of screenwriting work-
shops and how-to books emerged touting particular versions of writing "rules." Some were based on a three-act
structure with carefully timed "plot points" (Act One:
Setup. Act Two: Conflict. Act Three: Resolution). Others relied on the classic "hero's quest" popularized by the
mythologist Joseph Campbell. Regardless of what ru-
bric individual screenwriters follow, most contemporary
Hollywood films adhere to the classical model of narrative,
one based on linear forward movement, with every inci-
dent, encounter, and reversal of fortune driving inexorably

toward a conclusion that, if all has gone according to plan, will be both surprising and satisfying to the audience.

Hewing to those principles, a serviceable screenplay will move a largely predictable story along at a decent clip, hitting all the usual "beats" before reaching its foregone conclusion—i.e.: boy meets girl; boy and girl fall in love; obstacles arise; boy and girl overcome them to get together in the end.

An exceptional screenplay, to paraphrase the writer-director Billy Wilder, grabs viewers by their throats and never lets them go. It leads us along a path that we have no choice but to follow, doling out just enough information at each moment to keep the audience interested in what happens next—and never alienated, bored, or fatally confused.

Put simply, it's the screenplay that answers the first question all critical filmgoers must ask themselves: <u>What kind of movie were the filmmakers trying to make?</u> An action-packed, escapist spectacle? An action-packed, escapist spectacle with a deceptively smart subtext about modern life? A meditative chamber piece about the evanescence of love? A stylish, sophisticated romantic comedy? The aspirations of every film lie in the screenplay, which, if it's been competently executed by the creative team, will result in exactly what the originator intended, whether it's an intellectually demanding work of art or high-gloss entertainment.

PUTTING US IN THE PICTURE

Did the movie define a specific world from the outset, vividly and with efficiency?

Were we on board and oriented within the first ten or twenty minutes?

Within the first ten minutes, a well-written movie will teach the audience how to watch it.

Whether viewers are learning dense historical background during a film's opening credits sequence (which may or may not have been specified in the script), or observing as the film's protagonist performs her morning ablutions at the start of the first act, this is where we garner crucial information about the characters, the story's physical setting and time period, and its pacing, mood, and tone. Think of the initial tour through Rick Blaine's Café Americain in *Casablanca*, the scene of private detective Jake Gittes comforting a distraught client in his Los Angeles office at the beginning of *Chinatown*, or diminutive FBI agent-in-training Clarice Starling dominating an arduous cross-country obstacle course in *The Silence of the Lambs*.

Each of those scenes conveyed volumes in relatively little time about what and who the movie was about: intriguingly flawed characters and wartime intrigue set against an exotic World War II no-man's-land; an atmospheric riff on 1930s and 1940s pulp detective fiction; a determined, physically tough heroine proving herself within the male-dominated world of criminal justice. The opening sequence determines whether the audience will "buy in" to the protagonist's journey, and whether he or she is appealing or beguilingly complex enough to follow to the ends of the earth (or at least the end of the film).

Once the audience is hooked, over the next ten to twenty minutes the story's context and general mood should be pretty well set up, the main characters introduced, and their relationships to one another clearly established. From here, everything else should flow in such a way that the viewer can look back at that first section and realize that even the biggest whopper of an ending was completely supported by the early material—maybe even preordained.

The classic example of earning the audience's allegiance early is the masterful opening sequence of *The Godfather*, set at a sprawling, lavish wedding reception. During the film's opening scene, we meet mob boss Don Vito Corleone as he receives a supplicant in his sepulchral home office. Seven minutes later, we're plunged into the lively rites and rituals of a traditional Italian wedding; we're introduced to key members of his organized-crime family, and finally, twelve minutes into the sequence, meet Michael Corleone, a returning World War II hero who wants nothing to do with his family's morally dubious business. Luckily, Michael has brought an outsider to the affair—his future wife, Kay—who knows nothing of mob life; she is the audience's proxy, learning about a culture that is as alien to us as it is to her. When she expresses shock at a particularly violent example of the Corleone way of doing things, Michael looks at her soulfully and says: "That's my family, Kay. That's not me." Francis Ford Coppola's screenplay—adapted from the Mario Puzo novel—has elegantly set the gears of the film in motion within its first twenty minutes, driving us toward an ending where those words will prove to be either prophetic or cruelly ironic. What's more, by conveying the characters and environment of Michael and his family so clearly and economically, Coppola has made sure we'll eagerly tag along on whatever journey they take.

For a particularly invigorating example of scene-setting, look at the first page of writer-director Tony

Gilroy's screenplay for the 2007 legal thriller *Michael Clayton*: "It's 2:00 a.m. in a major New York law firm. Ten floors of office space in the heart of the Sixth Avenue Canyon. Seven hours from now this place will be vibrating with the beehive energy of six hundred attorneys and their attendant staff, but for the moment it is a vast, empty, half-lit shell. A series of shots emphasizing the size and power of this organization; shots that build quietly to the idea that somewhere here—somewhere in this building—there's something very important going on."

Boom. We're in.

Screenwriters are word people. But the best ones know they're working in a visual medium, and they think and write accordingly. Although the visuals of a movie are ultimately the director's responsibility, the initial concept begins at the screenplay stage, when it's incumbent upon the writer to relate the story by outlining potent images that convey as much information as possible with as few words as possible, rather than through a series of static conversations explaining what's happening and why. Most scripts adhere to the one-page-per-minute rule, meaning that typical feature-length screenplays are between 90 and 120 pages; the beauty of Gilroy's *Michael Clayton* script is that it conveys an enormous amount of information about his characters and their environments economically, not with novelistic density, but almost poetically. Not all scripts need to be written with such voice and detail: although that kind of descriptive specificity can be enormously helpful in terms of visualizing the story, in the hands of a gifted director a spare, more schematic screenplay can allow plenty of room for creativity and interpretation.

As viewers, most of us will never know how much of what transpired on-screen, and how it looked, was specified in the script. As a rule, the best screenplays are exact and closely observed in terms of settings and characters. But they don't suggest particular camera angles, edits, or stylistic flourishes, those choices being the purview of the director and his or her creative team. Indeed, screenplays with long, descriptive passages can be a turnoff to filmmakers who are looking for a compelling story and vivid characters to bring to life in their own way, rather than being railroaded by an overeager writer—who, in most instances, won't be involved once the production is under way, and who may well be rewritten by a raft of "script doctors" as well as the director and even the film's star.

But sometimes, even the smallest details that we would assume are the choices of the director or editor first appeared in the screenplay. The pink underwear Scarlett Johansson wore in the opening shot of *Lost in Translation*? Specified in the script. The hamburger phone in *Juno*'s retro-tastic bedroom? Written into the script. The famous "match cut" in *Lawrence of Arabia*, when a lit match is juxtaposed with a rising sun over the desert? The same. It is the screenplay that defines the world we will inhabit for the next two hours—and it's initially up to the writers and their words to make that world vivid and alive enough for us to move right in.

NO PLOTS PLEASE, JUST STORIES

Did the story "want" to be a movie?

Was the movie simply an illustrated plot, or was the story intrinsically visual?

If it wasn't a conventional story, did it take me on a journey or plunge me into an unfamiliar environment?

I hate plots. I love stories.

The movies you saw once and barely remember were, most likely, mechanically executed plots. The movies most critics and fans recognize as classics are great stories, from *Casablanca* to *The Godfather* to *Fargo*. Plot gets the protagonist from point A to point B. A good story moves the protagonist through a journey that feels simultaneously personal and universal, both spontaneous and organic. Plot is what happens. Story is meaning. Plot is mechanics. Story is emotion.

There's a truism in Hollywood that there are only a handful of basic movie plots; it's the detail, depth, and ingenuity of the screenplay that turn them into unique stories. The tale of a reticent hero who reluctantly saves the day was just as galvanizing in *Captain Phillips* as it was in *Casablanca*. A vulnerable stranger's arduous journey home made for epic, emotional drama in *The Wizard of Oz*, *E.T. the Extra-Terrestrial*, and *12 Years a Slave*, albeit within radically different contexts. The monster vanquished in *Jaws* was just as daunting as the ones in *Gravity* and *The Revenant*, even if the monster took the form of a giant fish in one film, and outer space and nature itself in the others.

You'll notice that most of the movies I just mentioned were book adaptations, which suggests how difficult it is to come up with genuinely original stories. Hollywood has always depended on previously produced work from which to cadge narratives and characters—right now, the studios are mining comic books, old television shows, and even their own archives for properties to remake. If it worked once, they figure, it'll work again; and often, previously produced works bring their own built-in audiences in the form of rabid fan bases.

The studios' simplistic reasoning has met with notoriously spotty success: for every well-executed commercial hit, such as the Disney/Marvel *Avengers* franchise, there are countless duds on a par with *The Lone Ranger, Battleship*, and the latest *Ben-Hur* reboot. In most cases, when adaptations fall flat on-screen it's because the screenwriters simply lifted plots and characters instead of mining the source material for emotion, subtext, metaphor, and even poetry. Their efforts result in banal, one-dimensional versions of otherwise deep and textured creative works. This is why there's never been a truly successful adaptation of *The Great Gatsby* or a Philip Roth novel, and why no one should attempt to adapt J. D. Salinger's fiction: as tempting as their characters and settings are, it's the literary voices of their authors that make them great art.

The ubiquity of screenwriting formulas has resulted in a plethora of busy, by-the-numbers movies that fulfill the requisite needs of script structure (a hero with goals, complications, and setbacks, ultimate triumph), but achieve very little else. These are the movies that come and go without being noticed throughout the year, so interchangeable that they're barely worth naming. More often than not, they're quickly produced rip-offs of better, more successful movies: the buddy-police comedy *Let's Be Cops* tried to cash in on the genuine humor of *21 Jump Street*, for example; ditto their female-driven counterparts, *Hot Pursuit* and *The Heat*.

Although both *Let's Be Cops* and *Hot Pursuit* featured terrific actors, they were so slavishly plotty—making sure to put the character into lots of "hilarious" scrapes before tidily lifting them out—that they felt derivative and stale

rather than delightful and amusing. Every genre has conventions to obey: in every romantic comedy, for example, the star-crossed lovers will encounter obstacles before
they inevitably end up together. The well-written film,
however, will subvert its formula or get to even the most
predictable outcome in novel ways. If, toward the end of
a rom-com, the couple in question breaks up out of nowhere simply so that one of them must then run through
an airport to propose, that is the sign of a patronizing and
manipulative screenplay, cobbled together for the writer's
convenience rather than to serve the well-established motivations and needs of the characters. "The first time the
couple meets, first they're really snarky with each other,
and competitive, and they put each other down, and ten
minutes later they're in love," said the writer-director
Kenneth Lonergan about another hackneyed romantic cliché. "But most girls I ended up with I got along pretty
well with from the beginning. The tensions came from
other things. And those tensions are there for anyone to
mine who wants to pay attention to them."

For a story to work, it must feel new and surprising, even if it's hewing to old forms. The narrative arc
of *Gravity*, in which Sandra Bullock played an astronaut
who becomes stranded after the destruction of her space
station, is as simple as a story can get (it's basically a classic "escape from the haunted house" yarn, set in space).
But as elaborated by writer-director Alfonso Cuarón and
his son and cowriter Jonas Cuarón, Bullock's character's
fight for survival included inspired moments of wit and
self-reflection, and, ultimately, a moving symbolic rebirth.
The outlines of Solomon Northup's kidnapping and even-
tual escape from slavery were broadly familiar in *12 Years a
Slave*, but John Ridley's screenplay gave them immediacy

and fine-grained singularity, resulting in a film that felt like something we'd never seen before. One of the things I admire the most about writer-director John Carney, who made the winsome musical *Once*, as well as *Begin Again* and *Sing Street*, is that he tends to avoid the standard pat ending where the central couple ends up together. Even within the reassuring genre of romance, he injects a welcome note of ambiguity and uncertainty.

Sometimes, a movie doesn't even need a story to work. Some of my favorite movies are by filmmakers who were—and remain—far less interested in conventional narrative than in characters, atmosphere, and mood. The Italian director Michelangelo Antonioni was the master of this meditative form of filmmaking, as was Robert Altman; similarly, the writer-directors Richard Linklater (*Slacker, Before Sunrise*, and its sequels), Sofia Coppola (*Lost in Translation*), and Terrence Malick (*The Tree of Life, To the Wonder, Knight of Cups*) often eschew conventional notions of three-act structure and familiar, what-happens-next forward movement to explore human behavior and environments. All of them work from screenplays, even if they're simply rudimentary outlines, like the "roadmap" of scenes Linklater gave his nonprofessional cast for *Slacker*, or the pages of "suggested dialogue" Natalie Portman, Cate Blanchett, and others received while filming *Knight of Cups* (the film's star, Christian Bale, was reportedly never given a script, Malick preferring that he be left to his own spontaneous improvisational devices).

Jem Cohen, whose work I discovered when he was making music videos and concert films for R.E.M., has forged a brilliant career making nonnarrative essay films that, through Cohen's thoughtful juxtaposition of images, introduce spectators to his restless, ruminative view of a world he finds simultaneously strange and intimately familiar. Cohen's 2012 film *Museum Hours*, about a woman on a visit to Austria who strikes up a tentative friendship with a guard at the Kunsthistorisches Art Museum in Vienna, is his most conventionally narrative movie to date, but its searching, open-ended quality surely has something to do with the fact that he never produced a completed script for the film, something he said "would have been antithetical to the film, a betrayal." Rather, he wrote out only a few dialogue-heavy scenes; for the rest, he gave his lead actors, Mary Margaret O'Hara and Bobby Sommer, one or two lines that they could then "riff" on. The result is a film that feels very much like a walk through an unfamiliar museum or city—and the tour, though conditioned and gently guided by the design of the spaces themselves, also encourages the viewer to be open to unexpected delights and discoveries.

After being assaulted by over-plotted, Hollywood-machined movies for most of the year, I applaud the efforts of any filmmaker willing to explore something different from the usual three-act narrative with the cinematic medium. As Cuarón himself once told me, film is in danger of becoming merely a "medium for lazy readers"—the big-budget version of a simplistic, easy-to-digest pop-up book. A good story is a wonderful thing, but it doesn't have to be the only thing. Whether a film is a deep dive into a particular environment, an open-ended journey with no fixed "ending," or a tautly structured journey from A to B to C, it was most likely first conceived by a writer with a particular story to tell—even if it wasn't a conventional one.

WHAT MAKES SAMMY RUN?

Were the people in the movie complex, unpredictable, believable?

Did I care about them?

Did they change or stay the same?

Bad movies are about characters. Great movies are about people—even when they aren't exactly human.

One of the great pleasures of interviewing the director Guillermo del Toro is getting a firsthand look at the sketchbooks he carries with him everywhere, pages spilling over with his handwritten notes and detailed drawings of the fantastical creatures that, one day, might end up in one of his films. The notebooks aren't just for visual ideas, he insisted when I spoke to him about his 2006 fantasy-drama *Pan's Labyrinth*. They help him design complete, complex characters. "Everything counts" when he's conceptualizing the people who populate his films, he told me, right down to whether "the character buttons his shirt all the way up, or unbuttons four buttons, or unbuttons six buttons. All of that is screaming to the other characters who that character is."

More often than not, if we care about what's happening in a movie, it's because we care about the characters. Most crucially, we care about the protagonist, the lead character who serves as the audience's main guide through the film. And like the bones of a good story, a strong protagonist is established early in the film, signaling his or her core personality traits and desires through action, dialogue, and personal environment.

Although viewers rarely get to read screenplays before they see the movies, they can often tell when a character hasn't been thoughtfully conceived or fleshed out in the script. When a screenwriter trots out one more square-jawed former Navy SEAL who's unwillingly pressed back into service to save the day, or a hooker with a heart of gold, it's no wonder the actors playing them deliver trite, clichéd performances: trite clichés were all they had to guide them.

Consider how characters from the instantly forgettable romantic comedy *He's Just Not That Into You* are introduced in the script: Gigi, "pretty and approachable," Conor, "cute but holding on to his frat boy roots," and Anna, "hot in an earthy sort of way." There's not much there to help the actors inhabit their characters. Now read how Lonergan introduces Sammy Prescott, Laura Linney's character in the tender and bittersweet brother-sister drama *You Can Count on Me*: "She is a nice-looking young woman of a neat appearance, saved from primness by an elusive, pleasantly flustered quality. An unsuccessfully neat person. She is dressed in office clothes—white blouse, dark skirt, high heels, light raincoat over everything. She picks out a couple of weeds and then bows her head and closes her eyes."

Sammy may not have been conventionally heroic or larger-than-life, but she was complicated and enigmatic enough to pique my interest, which grew throughout the first several minutes of *You Can Count on Me*. She was revealed to be not just an unsuccessfully neat person, but the harried single mom of a bright eight-year-old, an optimistic but put-upon employee of a controlling new boss at a small-town bank, and, far from prudish, someone who enjoys sex, a glass of wine, and the occasional illicit cigarette. In other words, Sammy was a charming, well-meaning, utterly intriguing bundle of contradictions. "An unsuccessfully neat person." And exactly what Linney played in the film.

I was far less interested in—and convinced by—Leonardo DiCaprio's character in *The Revenant*, which, even though it was based on the true survival story of trapper Hugh Glass, strained credulity, in part because of the filmmakers' efforts to soften and "humanize" Glass's character. Presumably believing that audiences wouldn't sympathize enough with a protagonist whose desire for revenge was motivated purely by being left for dead by his fellow trappers, Alejandro González Iñárritu and his cowriter Mark L. Smith gave him a lyrical, heartstring-tugging backstory involving a Native American family and lots of gauzy, sentimental flashbacks.

The term for this kind of character-gilding is "stakes," wherein screenwriters invest their stories with more urgency, and their protagonists with more "relatability," by creating dramatic, morally sympathetic reasons for their actions. If his wife wasn't in the building being threatened by a terrorist madman, John McClane would be just an off-duty cop doing his job in *Die Hard*; if it was his neighbor's sixteen-year-old son who was kidnapped in *Taken*, instead of his daughter and her best friend, Liam Neeson's vicious vengeance trip would look like vigilante overkill. This gambit not only allows the movie to derive lurid titillation from the sadistic violence it pretends to decry, but it's lazy characterization, giving the protagonist instant, unimpeachable motivation for embarking on a series of otherwise morally unspeakable acts.

The best good guys aren't perfect—how boring would that be? And plenty of them aren't just imperfect, but downright wicked. Whether it's Dirty Harry or Travis Bickle in *Taxi Driver*, audiences will hang in with even the most difficult antihero so long as his flaws are not born of inherent evil but rather of simple human frailty. One of the finest filmmakers of antihero-driven movies is Alexander Payne, whose films *Citizen Ruth*, *Election*, *About Schmidt*, *Sideways*, and *The Descendants*—all of which he wrote or cowrote—frequently revolve around prickly, self-centered, often downright unlikable characters. At their most disagreeable, though, they're still worthy of the viewer's time and emotional investment, because their flaws and mistakes are the result of all-too-human vulnerability. Payne may look askance at their foibles, but he never looks down on his petty, selfish, emotionally off-plumb characters; instead, he seems always to view them with humor rather than scorn, compassion rather than contempt.

Aaron Sorkin, who has brought some notoriously unlovable real-life and fictional characters to life in his work, told me he writes his most unsympathetic characters "as if they're making their case to God as to why they should be allowed into heaven." But by that same token, even the most antisocial bad-good-guy should undergo some meaningful transformation by the end of the movie, even if it's the barely perceptible result of some unresolved inner conflict. Not only does even a slight change give the story dynamism and a sense of forward movement, but it allows viewers to feel reassured, maybe even hopeful, about their own fears, struggles, and failings.

The writer-director James Cameron is highly accomplished in many things, including the conception and orchestration of dazzlingly impressive visual spectacles; his writing, however, is usually rife with clichés and over-statement, especially when it comes to his characters. The 1997 blockbuster *Titanic* was enormous fun to watch, but its story was corny and contrived, and his characters were too often human billboards for Good and Evil—especially when it came to bad guy Cal Hockley, a snobby philistine played by Billy Zane, who was so obviously the villain of the piece that he might as well have twirled a waxy mustache à la Snidely Whiplash throughout.

By contrast, Karen Crowder, Tilda Swinton's ambitious corporate executive in 2007's *Michael Clayton*, was anything but a standard-issue baddie. Karen's complexity is clear from her first introduction in Gilroy's script: "Karen Crowder sitting fully dressed on the john. She is Senior In-House Counsel for the largest agricultural/chemical supply manufacturer on the planet. She is hiding here. She is trying to fight off a panic attack using a breathing exercise she read about in an airline magazine."

And so, after the film's tense opening montage (set to an enigmatic, foreshadowing verbal aria delivered by Tom Wilkinson's bipolar attorney), we meet Karen nervously gathering her wits in an office bathroom, a twisted knot of mounting anxiety and dread. Throughout the film, Gilroy imbues Karen with ever more complex layers of self-doubt and quivering desperation, rather than the brittle, shark-like amorality we've come to expect from similar big-business villains. Like Sorkin, Payne, and all great writers, Gilroy harbors some sympathy for even his most loathsome characters, knowing that without it, not only would he not be interested in them, but we wouldn't, either. In other words, he treats his characters like people.

AN ALTERNATE UNIVERSE

Did the movie obey even the most fantastical rules it set up?

For a movie to work, we must believe it—down to the last word, glance, tie clip, and teacup.

In a medium as powerfully realistic as cinema, credibility may be the most cardinal and unsung virtue. Credibility—or lack thereof—is a reflection of the screenwriter's understanding of human nature, how in tune the screenwriter is with human flaws, foibles, and behavior, both rational and irrational. Most often, credibility comes down to specificity—the writer's command of telling details that spell the crucial difference between the merely passable and the most memorable and lasting.

On typical big-budget blockbusters, as many as half a dozen screenwriters—credited and uncredited—have been known to take a whack at the script, one writer punching up dialogue here, another juicing up the love interest there. Too often, the committee approach winds up sapping the movie in question of the very thing a great screenplay should create: authenticity.

This is especially true of the scripts for effects-driven summer action movies and sequels, which seem mostly to exist as scaffolding for things that go *boom*; if you've ever wondered why movies like *Twister*, *Armageddon*, *Deep Impact*, *The Day After Tomorrow*, and *San Andreas* bear such an uncanny resemblance to one another, it's simple: too often (but thankfully not always), their chief role is to deliver visceral mayhem and spectacle, not memorable stories or complex, layered characters. So we get movies that have been reverse-engineered to deliver the requisite number of "whammies" (industry parlance for action sequences like car chases or explosions), but not to provide much by way of nuance, detail, or complexity. In other words, we get lots of plot, but no story; characters, but not people; thrills, but no feeling. No credibility.

Of course, the team approach doesn't always result in impersonal dreck. Plenty of good, even great movies have been the result of more than one writer. Most of the best (and funniest) lines in *Casablanca* were put there by screenwriters Julius and Philip Epstein; cowriter Howard Koch supplied the political idealism; Casey Robinson was responsible for developing Ingrid Bergman's love-torn heroine Ilsa Lund; and the setting, characters, and much of the plot originated in a play by Murray Burnett and Joan Alison. *Iron Man*, a noisy summer blockbuster if ever there was one, was cobbled together by four screenwriters—who produced a smart, witty script that resulted in one of the most refreshing and satisfying examples of the genre.

Still, as a general rule, the fewer the writers, the more singular and sharply defined the sensibility of the film. Mark Boal, a reporter-turned-screenwriter who wrote *The Hurt Locker*, returned again and again to elaborate thumbnails he'd created about the psychological states of his core characters, a group of Iraq War bomb technicians. His punctiliousness paid off in the final version of the film, which possessed impressive credibility even when it took dramatic license with literal truth. Working with director Kathryn Bigelow, he said, "We painstakingly fleshed out every nook and cranny of the action sequences in order to make them feel realistic. In the right context, a detail that normally doesn't seem suspenseful can be suspenseful, like putting on a bomb suit. . . . You know there's a reason you're seeing all this. You're just not sure why."

After years of puzzling over why I've never loved the films of Alejandro González Iñárritu as much as so many of my colleagues, I've decided that credibility might be the chief problem. With very few exceptions, I've found his films to be handsomely made and well-acted—but also pretentious, superficial, and contrived, molded and shaped less out of the organic needs and motivations of their characters than the filmmaker's ambition to impress viewers with deep observations about interconnectedness and man's inhumanity to man. When I read an interview with screenwriter Guillermo Arriaga, who wrote Iñárritu's *Amores Perros*, *21 Grams*, and *Babel*, I figured out the problem: Arriaga rarely does research or outlines for his scripts; nor does he spend much time developing backstories for his characters. Often, he doesn't even know how his stories will end while he's writing. I believe this lack of detail has resulted in a lack of credibility in his films, which, despite Iñárritu's obvious visual gifts, I never quite bought. (I had the same problem with *The Revenant*, which Arriaga didn't write, but which suffered when it took on the contours of an utterly preposterous tall tale instead of the stark, realistic historical drama it set out to be.)

Even the most outlandish fantasy must follow the same rules of believability in order to create a seamless space allowing viewers to suspend their disbelief. Part of the brilliance of *Groundhog Day*—which is taught in many screenwriting classes and seminars as a supreme example of comic structure and character development—is how its supernatural premise is firmly grounded in day-to-day reality. There is no "magical" moment to account for Bill Murray's Phil experiencing the same day over and over again; it's his own selfishness and immaturity that keep him in the time loop, which will only stop once he has grown up and become a decent human being. Similarly, the romantic relationship between a man and his computer's operating system in the techno-romance *Her* by the end of the movie feels utterly believable, even unremarkable, because writer-director Spike Jonze has created a world that, while vaguely futuristic, feels lived in, familiar, and completely plausible. We've all seen movies that didn't work, for reasons we can't specify; there was nothing blatantly objectionable about them, they just didn't ring true. Chances are that the script never achieved the kind of hard-won credibility that only months, often years, of reflection and research can achieve.

HARDEN IT UP AND MOVE IT ALONG

Did the movie flow?

Did I care what happened next?

Was I surprised?

We all know the sensation of walking out of a movie we thoroughly enjoyed. All the pieces fit. It moved at the right clip. It zigged and zagged in just the right places. We didn't see the Big Plot Twist marching down Main Street. It just . . . *felt* right.

The ineffable quality of feeling right—and, alternatively, that gnawing discomfort when a movie feels frustrating and off—is usually a function of structure, which is all the more crucial to a film for being invisible. The best stories feel natural, each scene and conflict leading logically and gracefully to the next, with an air of both inevitability and utter surprise. Just as it takes all day to achieve the Meg Ryan "I woke up this way" tousled hairstyle, it takes months of painstaking work to write a script that, once realized on-screen, feels fresh and spontaneous. Not only every scene but every moment within each scene has been labored over and honed so that each dovetails perfectly into a whole with nary a discernible joint or flaw.

The most conventional movie structure is linear and chronological: events transpire, one after another, over a period of time, finally reaching their natural and satisfying conclusion. But it's always interesting to watch a filmmaker play with established structural conceits, whether in such real-time dramas as *Rope* and *High Noon*, which take place within the same time frame as their running times, or fractured narratives that run backward (*Memento*), take dramatic leaps forward (*Boyhood*), or seemingly radiate in multiple directions at once (*Pulp Fiction*).

One of the finest recent examples of how structure can make or break a movie is *The Social Network*, about Facebook founder Mark Zuckerberg. The standard approach to such a film would have been a modern-day Horatio Alger tale about a gifted Harvard student who, through pluck and ingenuity, harnessed computer technology and changed the world as we know it. Instead, screenwriter Aaron Sorkin crafted a prismatic view of Zuckerberg, portraying him from the perspectives of the friends and competitors he accumulated on his journey. The result is a fascinatingly ambiguous portrait that was open to competing interpretations and reflective of contemporary history that is still in the process of being settled. Similarly, for his screenplay for *Lincoln*, Tony Kushner made the brilliant decision to narrow the focus of the film—which director and producer Steven Spielberg had always intended to chronicle Abraham Lincoln's entire presidential administration—to one specific period: when he battled to pass the Thirteenth Amendment abolishing slavery. The film didn't play like a soft-focus historical biopic, but became a swift, urgent political drama with startling contemporary resonance.

Structure is also a matter of correct pacing. Let's say that a movie has successfully hooked you within the first twenty minutes. You care about the protagonist, you're fully on board with her aspirations and vulnerabilities and the stakes of her quest, you're rooting for her to succeed and can't wait to see how it all pans out. And then— quicksand. Suddenly, the story turns turgid, with scenes piling on top of one another with little or no forward momentum.

You've entered the dreaded Second Act Slump, the bane of the screenwriter's trade and the filmgoer's backside. One of the most common problems of otherwise decent movies is uneven pacing, especially saggy, baggy middle sections in which precious focus and momentum are lost, leading to fatal confusion in the audience about what the characters are doing and why we should care. When the main protagonist who is struggling to find her way out of a loveless marriage gets into an altercation with a mall cop and has to figure out how to pay her fine for twenty minutes. When the male hero goes to a bar instead of chasing the girl, and spends ten precious minutes conversing with his friends before they convince him he's in the wrong place. When a character appears out of nowhere, only to disappear—for no particular reason in either case. A bad second act is usually a matter of the screenwriter reverting to rote or unconvincing obstacles for the protagonist to overcome before reaching his or her goal, or throwing in way too many such setbacks and developments for the audience to remain oriented. Flabby, over-busy second acts—where characters seem to be doing stuff just for the sake of doing stuff, or where obstacles and opponents seem to emerge out of nowhere purely to give the protagonist something to do—were what made the three *Star Wars* prequels *The Phantom Menace, Attack of the Clones,* and *Revenge of the Sith* pale so dramatically in comparison to their predecessors in the series, which were far more streamlined, motivated, and coherent. They're what make a promising movie run out of steam midway through, or compel you to sneak out for popcorn or mentally review your grocery list. They're among the toughest things for a screenwriter to fix—and too often they're not, which accounts for the number of forgettable, utterly dispensable, below-average movies that flood the multiplex every weekend.

Pacing is a function of several craft areas in the filmmaking process—especially editing, which we'll explore in a later chapter. But it should start with a screenplay that keeps the story moving at an engaging, even suspenseful, clip, providing just enough information to keep the audience curious but not hopelessly confused.

Robert Towne's screenplay for *Chinatown* is often taught in film schools for precisely this reason. In *Chinatown* Towne so judiciously doles out information about the detective Jake Gittes and the wealthy Los Angeles family he's investigating that he keeps viewers engrossed and surprised up until its final, shocking conclusion. Every scene in *Chinatown* has a purpose, whether it's to advance the story, reveal something about one of the characters, or set something up that will later pay off. In *Manchester by the Sea*, his searing portrait of Lee Chandler (Casey Affleck), a man suffering the aftermath of an unspeakable tragedy, Kenneth Lonergan creates an almost origami-like structure of unfolding revelations as we discover what happened to Lee several years earlier. Lonergan didn't create that structure to keep viewers curious—although we are—but because Lee himself is trying desperately to keep his own memories and engulfing shame at bay. "It's a simultaneous process where, if you happen to hit it right, the structure of the movie is dictated by the personalities of the characters, and vice versa," Lonergan explained. "And that's when it seems to feel good."

When a movie doesn't unfold smoothly—when instead its journey from point A to points B, C, and D feels plodding or too pat, critics will criticize it for being "episodic"—meaning that the scenes butt up against each other in ways that feel disjointed and choppy, awkwardly stopping and starting rather than seamlessly flowing together. Another word for the problem is "schematic," which refers to artificial characters and situations that are obviously invented purely for expedience's sake, either to cover up fatal plot errors or to spell out the movie's deeper subtexts. It's probably not fair to blame *Forrest Gump*'s structure on the screenplay, since it was adapted from a novel, but Robert Zemeckis's film has always been a chief offender in this area for me, its conceit—of a slow-witted naïf bumbling his way through the most memorable events of the mid-twentieth century—clearly meant to be fable-like, but feeling increasingly forced and patronizing in its tiresome this-happened-then-that-happened execution. Although the structure of the romantic comedy *Four Weddings and a Funeral* is purposely episodic, using those five events to tell the story of a purportedly ill-fated but star-crossed couple, Richard Curtis's script brims with so much wit, and his

I mean, I agree but it has potential guilty pleasure movie

characters are so vividly drawn, that it feels unforced and of a piece; by contrast, his movie _Love Actually_ felt jam-packed with inauthentic incidents and conflicts that played out as convenient excuses to tie everything up with a neat bow.

Most screenplays strive to obey the rules of classical storytelling, efficiently setting up the action, introducing complications, developing character and story, and reaching a satisfying climax. It's that middle part—introducing complications and developing character and story—that can be tricky, as the writer tussles with moving his or her characters forward without allowing the machinery to show. There's a term for a particularly expedient form of problem-solving in this regard: _deus ex machina_, wherein a person or thing conveniently emerges from out of left field, at just the right time, either to save the day or to spin the protagonist on to another leg of his or her journey. Most screenwriters know better than to resort to this kind of cheat, which was brilliantly satirized in Charlie Kaufman's script for _Adaptation:_

Along with the _deus ex machina_, exposition—dialogue that explains a character's history or emotional subtext—is a cardinal no-no in the screenwriting trade. Mike Myers parodied this problem in _Austin Powers_ with the character Basil Exposition, but it persists every time a rumpled "expert" emerges in a disaster movie to explain exactly what's going to happen and why it's very bad. (For a recent example, look no further than 2016's _The Accountant_, in which J. K. Simmons delivers a particularly windy expository monologue at a crucial point in the film, ruining what could have been a better-than-average action thriller.)

Exposition is certainly problematic in terms of credibility: Has anyone ever actually uttered the words, "I made insert-name-of-dish-here, it's your favorite"? Do we really need an on-screen title saying "Paris, France" superimposed over a shot of the Eiffel Tower? But it also plays havoc with pacing, particularly when characters stop the action to talk about something they already know, simply for the benefit of the audience. Some exposition is unavoidable, but the most adroit writers handle it with ingenuity and grace—such as Sorkin's famous walk-and-talks, in which characters engage in rapid-fire repartee while walking briskly down a corridor, enlivening what would otherwise be a static two-shot of blah-blah-blah. Humphrey Bogart reportedly quipped, "If I ever have exposition to say, I pray to God that in the back of the shot they've got two camels fucking." Walk-and-talks are Sorkin's camels.

Closely related to exposition is the gnarly challenge of evoking or explaining the past without flashbacks or narration. There are plenty of movies that have benefited from narration—*Sunset Boulevard*, *Double Indemnity*, *Badlands*, and *Into the Wild*, to name a few—but in general it should be avoided if at all possible. Ideally, flashbacks should be used only to illuminate characters—their unspoken motivations, emotional worlds, and psychological flaws—rather than move the story forward. As a narrative device, they should be used when the information they contain can't possibly be conveyed in any other way—or when the filmmaker purposefully wants to establish aesthetic distance between the audience and what's on-screen. Examples of great flashback scenes include Martin Scorsese's *The Last Temptation of Christ* and Spike Lee's homage to it in *25th Hour*; long, elaborate, and detailed enough to be movies-within-a movie, both of these flashbacks express the enormous material and emotional stakes of protagonists facing dramatic moral choices. Similarly, the prologue in *Up* stands as a masterpiece of compressed,

poetic storytelling, portraying a couple's romance, marriage, and entry into lonely old age with breathtaking
economy and feeling.

Whether it's straightforward and literal, or oblique and
nonlinear, a well-structured screenplay, if well executed by
an attentive filmmaking team, will result in a movie that
engages the audience from start to finish, leaving them
feeling satisfied, with no nagging questions about what a
particular scene had to do with the story, or whether an
encounter with a particular character was included for the
sake of convenience rather than authentic behavior and
motivation. A poorly structured ninety-minute movie can
feel like an interminable slog, whereas a well-structured
three-hour epic whizzes by; conflicts that are introduced
midway through a poorly constructed story will feel arbitrary, even nonsensical, whereas in a well-structured story
they will feel of a piece with the settings and characters
that have already been established. We all have experiences at the movies when something either fits together
nicely or seems to fall apart: more often than not, the difference lies in their structure.

PUTTING WORDS IN THEIR MOUTHS

Did the characters converse or did the actors recite?

Did their words sound spontaneous? Practiced? Witty?
Mannered?

Whether natural-sounding or stylized, did the characters' language fit the setting, story, and aesthetic approach of the film?

"Round up the usual suspects."
"The cat's in the bag and the bag's in the river."
"Leave the gun. Take the cannoli."
"You had me at 'Hello.'"
Of the chief pleasures of watching movies, hearing a great line is among the most delicious.

Screenplays are much more than just dialogue. But you can't have good screenplay without good dialogue. And "good," in this case, doesn't mean the perfect, plummy speeches that trip off the actors' tongues with over-practiced ease (although that can be a lot of fun, as any Preston Sturges or Howard Hawks movie will show you). Dialogue establishes character, credibility, and the tone of a movie. So if it doesn't fit—if it's too glib, or too full of stammers and stops, or too strenuously clever—it will throw the entire enterprise off. Dialogue needs to be convincing, whether it's the florid, operatically profane prose-poetry found in a Quentin Tarantino script, or what sound like the improvised "uhms" and "uhs" of low-budget American filmmaking aptly dubbed "mumblecore."

Paul Schrader, who wrote *Taxi Driver* and *Raging Bull*, among many other films, once said that a good drama "should have about five good lines and about five great lines. Any more than that and it starts to become word-heavy and unrealistic. You're listening to all the words and you're not watching the movie." Most great movies contain memorable lines, but the best are more than a collection of quips. Instead, the words the characters say should be minimal, not explaining or restating what's already being shown on-screen, but providing an extra layer or counterpoint to the scene.

Good dialogue is believable, in that the characters must speak naturalistically and seemingly spontaneously, without theatrical pronouncements and speechy declamations—and it must be economical. The best dialogue, to paraphrase the great writer Ernst Lubitsch, allows the audience to add two and two to get four: it's subtext, not text. It subtly leads the viewer to understand something otherwise unspoken about the characters that the characters may not even be aware of themselves. It's the teasing verbal volleys between James Stewart and Grace Kelly in *Rear Window*, and Mary Tyler Moore's clipped, fake-cheery rejoinders to her alienated son in *Ordinary People*. It's Robert De Niro and Al Pacino talking in a coffee shop about dreams, women, and the predations of age in the climactic scene in the crime thriller *Heat*. None of the characters in these sequences was talking about what they *seemed* to be talking about; it was all under the surface, illuminated but not spelled out by their words (except, of course, in the balcony scene in Woody Allen's *Annie Hall*, perhaps the finest paean to subtext ever committed to film).

For Kenneth Lonergan, dialogue is almost entirely and only about subtext, which is why he often insists on directing his original scripts. In fact, Lonergan's scripts are distinguished by the kinds of scenes that conventional screenwriters are taught to leave out, because they don't "advance the plot" or provide "character beats." In Lonergan's films, these interstitial moments—which would be so deadly dull or perfunctory in other writers' hands—become the dramatic meat of life. "It feels like nothing's happening," explained Casey Affleck, who starred in *Manchester by the Sea*:

> It feels like you've spent two hours listening to people argue. So many of the scenes have a lot of conflict in them, but the conflict is almost never about what the

movie's about in any way. It's always people arguing about did you put the food in the freezer, where are the car keys, all this stuff. And in some cases, with a different writer, that's all it would be about. It wouldn't add up to anything. It would be a slice of life. In this case, you're following along these people and their sometimes petty conflicts, sometimes bigger problems, but you never feel like you're being led. But at the end, you do arrive somewhere and you feel like you got there on your own, but you didn't.

Early in *Manchester by the Sea*, Affleck's character, Lee Chandler, tensely confers with a doctor and a nurse in a hospital corridor; the audience can almost see the gears of his mind turning as he asks questions, listens to the responses, and decides what to do next. Just in those quotidian details, viewers see Lee come into focus as a character carrying an unknown but terribly oppressive burden; the mystery of his affliction will drive our interest and sympathy for the rest of the movie. And it's all accomplished in subtext.

"If you swipe away all those mundane details, you have to provide what's often a very false conflict," Lonergan said, explaining his frequent focus on supposedly "un-dramatic" moments. "That's why so many movies, I think, are overwritten, because there's this anxiety to put into dialogue what everybody can see for themselves. Why does the main character have to sass the boss? Why is the friend a jerk? It's this very easy conflict that you've seen a million times."

In those movies, the dialogue worked in tandem with the visual elements—the actors' physicality, their costumes, and their personal environments—to express what was going on. But far too many contemporary films consist of static scenes of two people talking to each other in front of a variety of attractive backdrops, reducing them to soap operas with movie stars, punctuated every ten minutes by something blowing up if they're action flicks, or a raunchy sight gag or sex-related stunt if they're R-rated comedies. If the writer can't clarify the characters and their motivations without resorting to dialogue-heavy talking-head scenes, that's a sign of a poor script. (For examples of scripts that brought subtext to the surface rather than artfully burying it, see *Gladiator* and *Revolutionary Road*, both of which contained painfully obvious dialogue; or George Lucas's horribly wooden verbiage in the aforementioned *Star Wars* prequels.)

It's not that there haven't been great films consisting of people simply talking—*My Dinner with Andre* is still the classic of the form, and the recent film *Locke*, with Tom Hardy, was similarly gripping. *A Man for All Seasons, 12 Angry Men, The Social Network*: All of these films were expressly constructed around dazzling dialogue that was exquisitely acted, staged, and edited to possess the accelerated feel of a thriller, rather than a verbose set piece.

Even filmmakers devoted to dialogue-driven movies—writer-directors like Woody Allen, Kenneth Lonergan, Richard Linklater, Nicole Holofcener, Wes Anderson, Quentin Tarantino, and Joel and Ethan Coen—are never content simply to film their characters as an inert collection of pictures of people talking.

These movies are meant to be heard and seen, imparting as much information visually as they do aurally. As Linklater explained to me, "It's not really about the specific words, it's about what comes through the actors. It's about the ideas." And conversing about ideas is a contact sport: dialogue isn't just the stuff the characters say, it's the action itself, with all the dynamism and forward thrust the term implies. Every word counts, each has been chosen and curated with care, and each contains multitudes of unspoken meanings.

WATCH YOUR TONE

What mood was the movie in?

Was it meant to be amusing? Serious? A combination of both?

Were the filmmakers sympathetic toward their subjects? Inside their heads, or observing them from a more critical distance?

<u>Tone might be the most important, and difficult, part of the screenwriter's job. And it's almost impossible to define.</u>
In the early 1960s, when Stanley Kubrick and Terry Southern contemplated the nuclear standoff between America and the USSR during the height of the Cold War, as adapted from Peter George's novel *Red Alert*, they imagined it as a dark, absurdist political satire, which became *Dr. Strangelove or: How I Learned to Stop Worrying and Love the Bomb*. At the very same time, screenwriter Walter Bernstein adapted the similarly themed book *Fail-Safe* as a sober, almost documentary-like thriller. A young person diagnosed with cancer was a tragedy in *Love Story*, but the same subject matter made for a rueful blend of observant humor and touching drama in the wonderful buddy

movie _50/50._ Each approach was perfectly suitable for the
material at hand, and each film succeeded in sustaining its
respective tonal values up until the end.

Tone is ultimately executed by the director, by way
of his or her taste and sense of proportion and judgment.
But it begins with the screenplay. Is the film meant to be
irreverent, affectionately teasing, mockingly cruel? Sophomoric and broad, or self-aware and sophisticated? Is it
dramatic, bringing the audience to a cathartic conclusion
by way of a slow burn and subtle, buried signals? Or is it
melodramatic, with lots of stylized language and multiple
emotional outbursts? If the movie seeks to balance drama
and comedy, is the mix smooth and natural, or awkward
and intrusive? If it's a science fiction film or a Western or a
detective story, does the movie aspire to be a classic within
its canon, or is it "playing" with the genre, tweaking or
critiquing its most cherished conventions?

One writer might choose to represent the savagery
and inherent insanity of American slavery through the
exaggerated vernacular of a spaghetti Western, as Quentin Tarantino did in *Django Unchained*, while another pre-
sents it as a meditatively paced, deeply immersive drama,
as in *12 Years a Slave*; one writer makes space explora-
tion a knotty, existential conundrum (*Interstellar*), while
another makes it a funny, optimistic story of adventure
and rescue (_The Martian_). In recent years, an unplanned
pregnancy has been the fulcrum for at least three comedy
scripts—*Knocked Up*, _Juno,_ and *Obvious Child*—each completely different from the others in perspective and, most
crucially, tone.

Tone is how Sofia Coppola captured the hushed
strangeness of two jet-lagged denizens of a quiet Tokyo
hotel striking up a tentative friendship in *Lost in Translation*,

and how, in *You Can Count on Me*, Kenneth Lonergan managed to write a movie that was several things at once, including funny and sad, touching and surprising, human-scaled but just heightened enough to be rivetingly dramatic. Tone can be found in the diligence and restraint that pervade the journalism drama *Spotlight*, in which cowriter and director Tom McCarthy, working with Josh Singer, decided to propel the narrative of a historic *Boston Globe* investigation not through moments of big scoops and high-fives, but through the mundane details of the reporting process.

For filmmakers, the most important aspect of their craft might be the most difficult one to refine and master; for critics, it's nearly impossible to describe or quantify. "Tone is the hardest thing to explain to someone," the writer-director Jason Reitman once told me. "It's like how you know you're in love with somebody."

Sometimes we know tone when we see it; more often, we know it when we *feel* it, picking up on the subtle signals the filmmaker conveys with every word and glance, every visual and sonic cue. Tone is the emotional pitch of a movie, its mood and gestalt; it's the governing aesthetic principle that, depending on whether it's skillfully sustained, determines what filmgoers will get out of a movie above and beyond the basic storyline—or whether they'll get anything out of it at all. Tone might be made up of what we see and hear, but it takes the form of what we sense.

WHAT'S IT ALL ABOUT?

Was the movie about more than just what happened?

Am I still thinking about it?

Did it have something to say about history, contemporary life, human nature, hope, or despair?

There's what happens in a movie, and then there's
what the movie's really *about*.

Some films aspire simply to provide a few diverting
hours of escapist entertainment, unconcerned with deeper
questions of meaning and morality. Others, even in the
guise of superficial spectacles, seek to engage questions
that go further than the rudiments of the superficial story,
whether through subtext, metaphor, or subtle visual cues.
One difference between those two levels of aspiration is
theme.

On the surface level, *High Noon*—in which Gary
Cooper plays a sheriff trying unsuccessfully to enlist his
community in a battle against an encroaching band of
criminals—is a classic Western about an honorable law-
man doing right by his small town; look deeper, though,
and it's an indictment of political cowardice in the face of
populist demagoguery. On one level, *RoboCop* is a tough,
wryly funny action thriller about a Detroit cop who's—
cool!—part robot. On a deeper level, it's about human
nature, the paternalistic, corporate social control of late
capitalism, and the cultural construction of masculinity.
Boogie Nights is an affectionately lascivious glimpse of por-
nography workers in 1970s Los Angeles, crammed with
period music and detail; on another level it's about finding
oneself through tribal affiliation, how values and concepts
of identity shift with changes in technology, and the romance and fragility of the cinematic medium itself. All of
these meanings are conveyed underneath what's being said

or explicitly shown. A good script allows viewers to provide as much meaning through their own imaginations as through what occurs on-screen.

The best movies grapple with big questions and profound emotions above and beyond the stories they tell. Far more than an accumulation of plot points or character behaviors, they possess an added layer of ambiguity—or even unease—that still fascinates long after the credits have rolled. If you wake up still thinking about a film you saw the night before—wondering about the characters, puzzling over an unresolved mystery—it's because a skillful screenwriter planted those seeds so deeply into the narrative that they were naked to the human eye. It's only in the fullness of time that they come to their most rewarding, and enduring, fruition.

BECAUSE SO MANY THINGS CAN change during a typical film production, it's impossible to know with any certainty how much of a particular movie is the result of the screenwriter's intention. Still, if a film works at all, it's most likely because it began with a good script. If the film you just watched brought an entire world to life— one you've never seen, one that couldn't possibly exist, or one you feel like you live in every day—that's because a writer conjured it with vivid detail and revealing background. If you're thinking and talking about the characters days later—whether they're culled from comic books, real-life historical events, or pure imagination—that's because a writer invested them with the behavioral contours and emotional complexity of real, recognizable people. If you're delighted, amused, moved, haunted, or troubled, it's because a writer took enormous care to make sure that

you would be. If you kept watching and caring what happened next, it's because a writer wrote a script that was a
compulsively readable page-turner. If you fell through the
looking glass, even for a little while, it's because a writer
crafted and polished it with no cracks or jagged edges to
get snagged on.

RECOMMENDED VIEWING ··

Casablanca (1942)
The Godfather (1972)
Chinatown (1974)
Annie Hall (1977)
Groundhog Day (1993)
Manchester by the Sea (2016)

CHAPTER TWO

············· # ACTING ·············

We know it when we see it: Daniel Day-Lewis
transforming himself to play a peroxided London punk, or an Irish artist with a crippling dis-
ability, or an American oilman at the turn of the century.
Helen Mirren thoroughly banishing her off-screen persona
and becoming Queen Elizabeth. David Oyelowo inhabiting Martin Luther King Jr., even though he bears no obvious physical or vocal resemblance to the civil rights leader.
Or Vivien Leigh, Gregory Peck, and Audrey Hepburn,
respectively, bringing Scarlett O'Hara, Atticus Finch, and
Holly Golightly to such vivid life that they feel like people
we know as intimately as our own friends and family.

Acting might be the most deceptively difficult aspect of
filmmaking, because its best practitioners make it look so
easy. After intensive intellectual, emotional, and physical
work, the actor must make his or her performance look
effortless and unplanned—even when delivering the same
line in take after take, expressing the same devastating emotions on command, accessing intimate, vulnerable feelings

in front of dozens of technicians, banks of hot lights, and that ever-present confessor and judge, the camera.

In many ways, acting is the most fundamental element of cinematic grammar. After all, capturing human performance was the first thing pioneers like Thomas Edison and the Lumière brothers did when they invented motion pictures in the late nineteenth century. As an essential building block, acting often seems to be the point of modern movies, which even at their most simplistic and visually inert can still provide opportunities for actors to deliver emotionally powerful, memorable performances.

How do they do it? That is what fans and critics, mere mortals, continually endeavor to discern and explain. This story may be apocryphal (the best ones usually are), but Spencer Tracy—the acknowledged master of naturalism in front of the camera—is supposed to have said, "It's simple. You come to work on time, know your lines and don't bump into the furniture." Surely there's more to a great performance than Tracy's offhand pragmatism—which was, no doubt, something of an act itself. But what is it? More to the point, how do we put "it" into words?

The actor's job is to deliver the dialogue written in the screenplay, and to inhabit his or her character so convincingly that viewers will be able to immerse themselves completely in what's transpiring on-screen. While the director can certainly help guide a performance, it ultimately comes down to the myriad choices an actor makes in creating a character—the command of the external and internal details that accrue into a complex, credible, compelling person—that constitute a performance. When those choices are judicious, original, and believable, the audience perceives them as a seamless, spontaneous whole. When the choices fail, we see inconsistency, overacting, an actor shamelessly begging to be liked, or allowing vanity to get in the way of complete submersion into a role. Apart from speaking and behaving—knowing one's lines and not bumping into the furniture—the actor's primary function in the collaborative undertaking of a film is to be an emotional instrument within a calibrated, collaborative whole. If even one player is poorly tuned or out of step, the entire movie can feel off-key.

THE EYES DON'T LIE

Did the actors disappear completely into their roles?

Were their gestures and vocal cadences natural, or were they forced and exaggerated?

Did the actors ask for the laugh, or for the tea?

> *The most important thing about acting is honesty.*
> *If you can fake that, you've got it made.*
>
> —George Burns

In the opening moments of the 2007 drama *The Visitor*, the actor Richard Jenkins stands at a living room window, nursing a glass of red wine, staring into the middle distance. As scenes go, it's a brief and seemingly uncomplicated one. A man stands, looking out a window. Nothing happens.

And yet, everything happens. Or at least everything the audience needs to know about Jenkins's character,

Walter Vale. He's alone. Isolated. Depressed. He's craving connection but can't break through. It's all there, in the way he stands, the way expression barely plays across his face, and especially in his eyes—eyes in which swim oceans of pain, loneliness, grief. A few seconds later, he's taking a disastrous (and very amusing) piano lesson, and the audience realizes: we may not know Walter Vale yet, but we want to. What's more, within a few scant minutes, we've come to care about him. A lot.

Standing at that window, Jenkins is showing viewers only the most visible piece of the scaffolding actors build to prepare for a role. He has developed layers of inner and physical life for his character that he brings to even the most uneventful moments, becoming the primary vessel through which viewers connect to the movie's ideas, feelings, and themes.

The same craftsmanship that Jenkins brought to *The Visitor* was also on display in *Spotlight*, in which Mark Ruffalo, Liev Schreiber, Michael Keaton, and Rachel McAdams portrayed a group of *Boston Globe* reporters investigating the Catholic Church. Although the actors in the ensemble drama spent weeks, sometimes months, doing individual research into their characters, ultimately they came together in a way that felt organic, un-showy, and rivetingly dramatic. "I think it's having a very good sense of where they're coming from and where they're going, and exactly where they are at that moment in time," explained Tom McCarthy, who wrote and directed *The Visitor* and *Spotlight* (and, not incidentally, who is also an actor). "They all do it differently, but they're all processing [each] scene on multiple levels."

Schreiber, who played *Globe* editor Marty Baron, "has this wonderful moment in one of the penultimate scenes,"

McCarthy added. Another character is "going on and on about URLs and putting an article online, and you can just see Liev and he's like, 'Uh-huh, yeah, great.' He's hearing it, because he knows on some level it matters, but it doesn't have his full focus. And it makes such sense for that character at that moment in time. And he has no idea he's doing that."

At its finest, screen acting exemplifies an almost super-human balance between expressiveness and restraint—enough transparency to allow an audience to connect with you almost immediately, tempered by enough inscruta-bility to make them curious about what you're going to do next. Watch an actor's face when her character isn't talking. Does a little light go out? Or is she paying atten-tion to her fellow actors with the same focus and intensity she brings to her own lines?

The difference may not be readily apparent to viewers, but they will sense it. "I know when I've done bad work, there are certain essential things I haven't done," Dustin Hoffman told me over a four-hour lunch across the street from his Los Angeles office. "The most essential thing is, I'm not behind it. If it's not me behind it, then it's bull-shit. Then it's just a character. The work that you're doing, whether it's the limp or the way you're talking or what-ever, you're behind it. . . . You're not there to play a prick, you're there to show the prick that's in *you*."

Because actors bring so much of their own identities to the roles they play, it's tempting—and lazy—to accuse them of playing themselves. (When *Klute* was released in 1971, a critic dismissed Jane Fonda's performance as just playing herself. "What was she supposed to do?" the film's director, Alan J. Pakula, later quipped. "Use things from Barbra Streisand?") Part of the actor's job is to fuse her persona with that of the character she's playing: the question shouldn't be whether an actor is playing herself, but whether she has allowed vanity, questionable choices, or distracting mannerisms to get in the way of a full characterization.

"The eyes don't lie," the acting coach Larry Moss said regarding credible performances. And he's right: whether it's Saoirse Ronan's wordless expression of longing and loneliness in the romantic drama *Brooklyn*, Mark Ruffalo's lovable lost soul in *You Can Count on Me*, or the way Tom Cruise changes his expression from gung-ho aggression to stone-cold rage in a pivotal interview scene in *Magnolia*, so much of what makes good acting compelling can be found in an actor's simplest, most direct gazes. "When you look in the eyes of a great performer, you see the depth of their whole life," Moss continued. "Their history, their desires. I think that's what made James Dean so extraordinarily transparent. With great actors, you can almost see their heart beating, and sense unconscious conflicts even they don't sense."

When viewers don't believe a performance—when they find themselves slipping out of the reality on-screen, or even scoffing at what's being presented—it's likely because they've "caught the actor acting," meaning they've perceived him or her playing to the audience rather than playing the truth of whatever the movie is asking us to believe. It's just this kind of approval-seeking obviousness that actors sought to erase in the 1950s when they embraced the Method, a theory of acting that prizes psychological realism over mimicry, and an idiosyncratic, even flawed performing style over technical perfection. For a master class in both approaches, watch Elia Kazan's filmed adaptation of *A Streetcar Named Desire*, in which the epitome of Method acting, Marlon Brando, stars alongside Vivien Leigh, who trained more traditionally at London's Royal Academy of Dramatic Arts. Leigh reportedly felt out of place among her costars, all of whom had trained in the Method and had appeared on Broadway in the play—a sense of alienation that likely informed her characterization of the too-fragile-for-this-world Blanche DuBois, making her performance accidentally Method in its own right. In any event, she won an Oscar for the role, underlining the fact that the means an actor uses to transform into a character are far less important than the end. (Having invoked Dustin Hoffman and Vivien Leigh, I can't resist sharing the oft-told anecdote about Hoffman's experience filming *Marathon Man* with Leigh's husband, Laurence Olivier. After Hoffman told Olivier that he hadn't slept in seventy-two hours in order to prepare for a scene, Olivier supposedly replied, "My dear boy, why don't you just try acting?")

As counterintuitive as it sounds, the genre that might rely most heavily on not catching the actor acting is comedy—which, as most actors will tell you, should never be played for laughs.

A beloved story has circulated in theatrical circles for years: The actor Alfred Lunt complains to his wife, Lynn Fontanne, that he didn't get the expected laugh in a play when he asked for the tea. Her withering reply: "That's because you asked for the laugh and not the tea."

The actors who have delivered the greatest comic performances, from Charlie Chaplin to Robin Williams, share one quality: each would have been just as at home in a drama, because all of them asked for the tea. One of the regrettable side effects of the current trend of R-rated comedies is that they depend so much on slapstick and raunchy shock value for their humor, making it difficult for actors to deliver the kind of nuanced, emotionally contradictory performance reminiscent of Jack Lemmon or Marilyn Monroe at their most sublime. One notable recent exception was Amy Schumer in the 2015 film *Trainwreck*, in which she impressively switched gears midway through the ribald sex comedy to portray a young woman mired in confusion and grief at the sudden loss of her father. (Her costar in that film, Bill Hader, is another example of a performer who brings as much dramatic depth and poignancy to his comic characterizations as to his dramatic ones.)

"In a comedy film, 'trying to be funny' is certain death," Michael Caine wrote in his book *Acting in Film*. "The history of the cinema is littered with great comics who failed on the screen largely because they weren't actors; they could not be real up there."

Just as we go to the movies for laughs, we also go for tears. There's nothing more cathartic than watching a pro in a full-tilt, floor-pounding, curtain-shredding catharsis. But, as the acting teacher Sanford Meisner advised his students, they couldn't cry, scream, or otherwise start chewing scenery until they'd done everything possible to hold it back. Otherwise, what the actor creates is emotionalism, not emotion. There's a scene in *Babel* when Brad Pitt, playing a man whose wife has just been critically injured in a faraway country, phones his children at home in America. His attempts to hold back his tears while his son tells him about his day are devastating, precisely because he doesn't allow his emotions to take over. Robin Wright delivers a similarly small-canvas tour de force of restraint in *Nine Lives* when her character runs into an old boyfriend during a supermarket run. Shock, curiosity, fondness, pain, and regret all play across her face in a scene wherein she manages to recapitulate an entire relationship almost completely by way of facial expressions, in less than ten minutes.

When I interviewed Robert De Niro, he was generous and voluble but—not surprisingly—he was not terribly forthcoming when it came to explaining how he does what he does. ("Don't talk it away" is one of his favorite aphorisms, and he doesn't.) But when I spoke with other filmmakers about De Niro, "restraint" was the word that came up most often. No matter how outrageous or physically expressive the role, they agreed, he always seemed to be holding back something essential from the audience. "I think a lot of times great actors . . . always seem to have a secret," Barry Levinson said. "[It's] that extra thing you can't quite find out about. I think what makes Bob great as an actor and fascinating as an individual is that you can never figure the man out completely." We often hear about the camera "loving" certain actors, but curiosity comes into play as well: great screen actors compel us always to want to know more, and to be satisfied with never knowing enough.

CASTING FATES

Was it a bad performance, or bad casting?

Did the actor seem to be fusing with the role or fighting it?

"Cast a movie well and your troubles are over."

That's the writer-director John Sayles, affirming what so many filmmakers have told me over the years: casting the right actors is easily 90 percent of the job.

The annals of Hollywood are full of delicious, some-
times mortifying, what-ifs in movie casting: at one point,
George Raft, Ann Sheridan, and Hedy Lamarr were
considered for the lead roles in *Casablanca*, which would
have been a dramatically different movie from the one
it became—and maybe not a classic. Similarly, imagine
Miriam Hopkins or Tallulah Bankhead instead of Vivien
Leigh as Scarlett O'Hara in *Gone with the Wind*, or Doris
Day and Robert Redford in *The Graduate* instead of Anne
Bancroft and Dustin Hoffman. (All were early choices for
those roles.)

If acting is the primal tool of cinema, casting is the
opposable thumb. The art of choosing actors for specific
roles is a combination of experience, taste, instinct, risk,
horse-trading, and pure dumb luck. First and foremost,
the filmmaker must acknowledge past work and whatever screen identity the actor has built up with the audience over his or her career. There was only one actor
Roger Michell wanted for *Hyde Park on Hudson*, his movie
about Franklin Delano Roosevelt's extramarital affair
with a family friend: because of the delicacy of the subject
matter, it had to be Bill Murray, Michell said, "because
there's something forgivable about Bill. There's something
which is mischievous about Bill. There's something in-
effably charming about Bill. And he's not saturnine. If it
was going to turn into a kind of Dominique Strauss-Kahn
story, the game would be up ten minutes into the film. . . .
It would be a kind of ghastly graybeard story about an
abusive seducer. And I was absolutely convinced that Bill
could carry it off without it being totally offensive."

The problem, of course, comes when a role demands
Bill Murray but Ed Harris is cast instead: When calam-
ity inevitably ensues, is that because the actor delivered a
bad performance, or because he was fatally miscast? There

are certainly instances of good actors failing to live up to their roles—delivering performances that are mannered, histrionic, obvious, and trite. But more often, what we perceive as a poor performance is actually a case of a fine actor stranded in the wrong part. After she delivered impressive dramatic turns in such indie movies as *Being John Malkovich* and *Things You Can Tell Just by Looking at Her*, viewers knew better than to dismiss Cameron Diaz as just another pretty blonde ditz. But she was still fatally miscast in Martin Scorsese's *Gangs of New York*, in which her modern-day persona never convincingly meshed with the nineteenth-century character she was supposed to be playing. Every time she appeared on-screen, it was like a tear in the film's fabric, through which the twenty-first century visibly peeked through.

Because director Lee Daniels made *The Butler* as an independent production, to attract financing he needed to cast actors with strong name recognition. Forest Whitaker, who played the title character, didn't have enough "pull" on his own to guarantee the film's production budget; therefore, Daniels had to walk the tricky line of casting stars in supporting roles—especially as the US presidents that Whitaker's character served over several decades in the White House—without turning the production into a cheesy pageant of cameos à la *The Poseidon Adventure*. That's why Jane Fonda pops up as Nancy Reagan, Robin Williams plays Dwight D. Eisenhower, and John Cusack plays Richard Nixon, even though unknowns or "character actors"—whose unusual features and demeanors make them readily believable as eccentric, real-looking people—would most likely have disappeared into those roles more unobtrusively.

On the flip side, casting unknowns can help set a film's tone more effectively than casting famous stars for the same roles. When Kathryn Bigelow cast *The Hurt Locker*, she knew that her best-known actor, Guy Pearce, would be killed off in the movie's first scene, completely upending viewers' expectations; when Jeremy Renner arrived as a replacement for Pearce's character as staff sergeant, the audience's lack of familiarity with him took away the sense of reassurance that a star's presence usually brings. With Pearce dispatched so suddenly and violently, aesthetic distance is banished. The audience is plunged into the action alongside a group of young men we've never met before—much as if we'd been drafted into service ourselves. One need only conduct a thought experiment reversing Pearce and Renner in their respective roles to realize how crucial casting was in making *The Hurt Locker* the unpredictable, ultimately potent experience that it was.

STARS, THEY'RE *SO* NOT LIKE US

Did even the biggest movie star manage to disappear and a character emerge?

If the star didn't disappear, did the character coexist easily with the star's persona?

What is a movie star? Most simply, a star is an actor who, thanks to his or her physical beauty, charisma, or unique relationship to the camera, has connected with the zeitgeist, developing an on-screen persona and a public version of their off-screen self that transcends any individual role.

In the 1930s and 1940s, actors were expected not to veer too far from the identities they'd built for themselves;

viewers going to a "William Holden picture" knew what they were in for. Today, stars are damned if they do, damned if they don't, navigating a narrow channel in which they can explore their technical and emotional range without alienating the fans who expect them to behave like the stars they've come to love. Actors like George Clooney, Angelina Jolie, and Denzel Washington have become so well-known that it's almost impossible for them to disappear entirely into a role. They must choose their projects all the more carefully, to make sure the characters they play can integrate seamlessly with the myriad associations their fans bring with them to the movie theater.

Stars have historically had a contradictory relationship with the movies they're in. As with Daniels and *The Butler* and Scorsese with *Gangs of New York*, producers often need big-name actors in order to get financing for films that aren't special-effects extravaganzas or superhero spectacles. But as often as not, those films would be better served by character actors who, while not as sexy or well-known, would bring more nuance and perhaps even technical craft to the project. Managing a star's presence in a small project relies on both the actor—his willingness to subsume his own ego to the larger whole—and the director, who needs to be able to help that process along without destroying the magnetism that inspired hiring the big star in the first place.

Robert Redford was an enormous star when he produced *All the President's Men*, about Bob Woodward and Carl Bernstein, the *Washington Post* reporters who broke the Watergate story. Redford never intended to play Woodward, and director Alan J. Pakula concurred, wondering if he would be able to "sublimate himself" to the story, and concerned that his "indelible sense of competence" would contradict a character who was finding his way almost blindly through confounding leads and dead ends. Although he preferred the idea of unknown actors playing Woodward and Bernstein ("because the story was so much about unknowns"), Redford reluctantly agreed to star in order to placate Warner Bros., the studio cofinancing the picture. "My whole focus was on being totally accurate, trying to downplay whatever personality I had to fit Woodward," Redford told me when I interviewed him thirty years later, adding that he never saw it as a star vehicle for him and Dustin Hoffman. "I wasn't prepared for the glamorization of just Dustin and I being in it. I just wasn't thinking."

Although *All the President's Men* wound up anchored by not one but two of the era's biggest stars, it succeeded brilliantly—not as a Hollywood novelty act or winking "buddy" picture where the stars' fame and sex appeal became the main event, but as a taut, superbly calibrated thriller in which Hoffman and Redford allowed themselves to disappear into the larger story. This is what happens when huge stars also happen to be superb actors. And it's exponentially more difficult to achieve today, when fans feel even more intimately connected to stars through social media and 24–7 gossip sites like TMZ. In light of this new, voraciously intrusive media landscape, it's no wonder that actors become obsessed with their public image and seek to protect it—and it's all the more impressive when they can put in the time and hard work it takes to let go of those habits, and drill down into their characters' behaviors and thought processes until they're automatic and not "put on." (Jennifer Lawrence, who became famous virtually overnight after being nominated for an Oscar for her work in the tiny indie film *Winter's Bone*, has done a particularly adroit job of cultivating a likable, fan-friendly off-screen persona.)

The most canny stars know their range and limitations, as well as what their audience will not accept. Marilyn Monroe was a superb example, delivering comic performances in *Some Like It Hot, How to Marry a Millionaire*, and *Gentlemen Prefer Blondes* that might have been dumb-bunny on the page, but were utterly brilliant in timing and delivery. Jack Lemmon chalked her success up to instinct rather than acting talent, saying she "often acted at you rather than with you." Whether Monroe was a creature of reflex or well-disguised technical prowess, she had an innate sense of when a scene was working, and she heeded that impulse to create some of the most indelible screen performances of the mid-twentieth century.

When I asked George Clooney about whether he's ever considered headlining an action franchise à la Liam Neeson in *Taken*, he said he's "past that" age-wise, and added, "I don't think it's my world." His world, not surprisingly, is the modern-day Rat Pack of the rebooted *Ocean's Eleven* franchise, which has been Clooney's most lucrative project; if the box office is to be believed, Clooney's fans like him staying in Vegas, preferably with a heist up his sleeve. Where they don't like him is in quirky, one-off projects by the likes of Steven Soderbergh (*Solaris, The Good German*) or the Coen brothers (*O Brother, Where Art Thou?, Hail, Caesar!*), which didn't do particularly well financially, despite Clooney's alternately moving and amusing performances. Interestingly, Denzel Washington almost never puts a foot wrong in terms of giving fans what they want, whether he's starring in an action film (*Unstoppable, The Taking of Pelham 1–2–3*), a tough contemporary thriller (*American Gangster, The Equalizer*), or a Western (*The Magnificent Seven*). Whatever role he's playing, Washington makes sure it fits with his persona of reliable integrity and steady-eyed command, even if he's the villain of the piece.

There's a fine line between Washington addressing his persona in order to subvert it, as he does playing a charismatic alcoholic pilot in the airborne thriller *Flight*, and someone who falls back on expected expressions and gestures simply to pander to audience expectations. In recent years, Al Pacino's histrionic delivery and overemphatic gestures have begun to look more like someone delivering an Al Pacino impersonation than a fully inhabited character being brought to life, whereas Tom Cruise has done fascinating work deploying his public personality in transgressive ways, especially beginning with his startlingly edgy performance in *Magnolia*, then hiding himself under a fat suit in the Hollywood satire *Tropic Thunder*. In the time-travel sci-fi movie *Edge of Tomorrow*, he runs through almost all of his beloved personae—affable nice guy, tough action hero, bemused everyman—in a movie that gave him a chance to prove just how versatile and self-aware an actor he really is underneath the jut-jawed bravado.

Angelina Jolie is another huge star who possesses a shrewd sense of how she's been perceived, first as a predatory bad girl, more recently as a humanitarian, activist, and mother. In the action thriller *Salt*, she played a classic antihero—a Russian spy—that didn't demand much in the way of audience sympathy. The film's director, Phillip Noyce, noted that "very few performers could maintain the connection to the audience, given the contradictory nature of [her character's] actions and the total bad-ass attitude with which she does things in the movie. But she was willing to go there and more so. . . . In many ways, the extremes of the character are her work. And I think as much as we were pushing her, she was pulling us."

"The instinct would be, if it's a woman, to kind of make it softer," Jolie explained to me when I interviewed her about the movie, "and instead we decided [she] had to be meaner. She had to make harder choices and she had to fight dirty and darker, because that's what you'd have to do to win against a man who's much bigger than you."

Interestingly enough, two films in which Jolie took on "softer," traditionally feminine roles, *A Mighty Heart* and *Changeling*, fared poorly with audiences, even though she did convincing work in both films. (Not surprisingly, her biggest hit to date is the live-action wicked-witch tale *Maleficent*, which perfectly dovetailed with Jolie's many personae, and made the most of her ice-sculpture cheekbones.) While many actors dream of Jolie's super-stardom, few would envy the shackles it entails when it comes to filmgoers' willingness and ability to separate well-known actors from their most famous roles, or their off-screen lives. The best actors will know how to play into this difficulty—or will dexterously work around it, so that we'll be thinking, "Hey, that's Angelina Jolie!" only when she deigns to allow us to.

DOWN TO THE BONE

Was the performance from the feet up?

Were the actors in the now of the now?

Did the actor act, or indicate?

"From the feet up."

That's how David O. Russell described his approach—and his advice to the actors—in the 1970s-era caper film *American Hustle*, as well as *The Fighter* and *Silver Linings Playbook*, which preceded it. "I don't believe any story is a cliché if you do it from the feet up," he told me. "If you've lived it, it's not a cliché."

"From the feet up" was also how the wonderful actress Beulah Bondi described playing a character: "from the foundation—in voice, body, imagination, interest in humanity." In practice, playing a character from the feet up means literally walking, talking, thinking, and living life in his or her shoes. It's more than just saying the lines—it's creating a life for the character above and beyond what's in the screenplay, developing as detailed a backstory as possible so that every word and action will be grounded in a unique personal history and an interior and exterior world that the actor will inhabit—and draw us into—for the duration of the movie.

Unlike surface impersonations or playing pretend, the feet-up approach exposes layers of unspoken urges and motivations both in the character and in the larger story. It's that quiet, single-minded focus that often results in performances that viewers find themselves instinctively believing, without knowing precisely why. This is how an actor can be riveting, whether he's tying a shoe or heading a battalion that's storming Omaha Beach.

It sounds glib to describe acting as "disappearing into the character." But it's true that the best actors utterly transform themselves—physically, vocally, and psychologically—to become the person they're playing. Actors achieve this kind of merging through any number of techniques—sense memories (using sights, sounds, smells, tastes, and touches from the past to help evoke an appropriate emotional response in a scene), "private moments" (wherein the actor replays an otherwise private act in front of an audience to unlock inhibitions), animal exercises (using an animal as a cue for physical posture and movement)—but the result is always highly personal and specific.

Example: On the set of *It Should Happen to You*, Jack Lemmon was having trouble giving an argument with Judy Holliday the kind of life the scene needed, until the director, George Cukor, asked him how he usually reacted to conflict. Lemmon said he'd get terrible chills and stomach cramps—which he promptly incorporated into his performance, giving the entire scene new credibility.

Film is dominated by great faces—it's a medium ruled by the close-up, after all—but the best performances don't just happen from the neck up. Although we remember Anthony Hopkins in *The Silence of the Lambs* as cold eyes behind a frightening mask, he brought his entire physicality to the role, imagining his character, Hannibal Lecter, as a cross between a cat and a lizard: "Somebody who doesn't blink, who is absolutely still for hours at a time. Like a praying mantis, or a spider on the wall. . . . For Lecter, he just stares, and watches, and then he moves." And when he does, watch out.

In the era of silent film, when sets didn't have to be noise-free, directors would often coach their actors throughout important scenes, making screen performance a truly collaborative art. Today, acting is all about the specific choices made by each individual actor, with the director usually using a light hand in suggesting how an actor might best inhabit the role. If an actor has survived acting classes, auditions, callbacks, rehearsals, and production, we can be reasonably safe in assuming he or she has mastered such basic skills as memorizing lines and hitting marks. Choices about how to embody and interpret the role are where originality and artistry come in.

When Heath Ledger starred as the repressed gay cowboy in *Brokeback Mountain*, he reportedly decided to play him as if he had a clenched fist in his mouth, meaning that every word he uttered would be the result of a struggle for expression. That single choice informed the entirety of Ledger's performance: the character was defined by what he held back, rather than what he said. In filming a scene with Eva Marie Saint in *On the Waterfront*, Marlon Brando impulsively picked up a glove she had dropped and idly tried it on his own longshoreman's hand. The gesture was spontaneous and touching, relaying his character's tenderness without obviousness or even dialogue.

These small touches speak volumes on-screen. Because film is such an intimate medium, it doesn't call for the kind of vocal projection or broad gestures that are necessary onstage. In fact, when we say someone delivered a "bad" performance, we often mean that he or she overacted—delivered a stiff, artificial, over-the-top rendition that wasn't believable or even moderately convincing.

In acting parlance, this kind of obviousness is called "indicating" or "mugging," whereby a performer uses mannerisms and vocal inflections to convey emotions rather than to simply live them. They "play" what they think the character would act like, rather than letting the character emerge from their own personality. (Some of the most memorably wince-inducing examples of indicating can be found in *Showgirls*, now considered a camp classic for the way Elizabeth Berkley overplayed her character's aggressive, impulsive sexuality.) While bug-eyed stares and O-shaped moues of surprise may be necessary to project feeling in a stage performance, within the intimate world of the camera they're gratuitous and insulting to the viewer.

Perhaps no modern performer has come in for more polarizing criticism than Nicolas Cage. Despite winning an Academy Award for his uncompromising portrayal of a suicidal alcoholic in *Leaving Las Vegas*, he is routinely ridiculed for bizarre choices, ostentatious mannerisms, and just plain hammy overacting.

In many ways, Cage is a one-man tutorial in how aesthetics and audience expectations have changed along with film itself. At the medium's inception, when movies were still silent, broad theatrical gestures were not just familiar to viewers, from their experience of theater and vaudeville, but necessary to convey information without spoken words. Even with the onset of sound and throughout the "Golden Age" of the 1930s and 1940s, a certain amount of high style and theatrical refinement reigned, although broad, easily "readable" gestures became more invisible.

A new canon of acting behaviors and speech patterns emerged in the 1940s, when Spencer Tracy and Henry Fonda brought new naturalism to the screen, which opened the door for Marlon Brando to revolutionize screen acting with the idiosyncratic, spontaneous, psychological style associated with the Method. By the 1950s, the carefully enunciated, highly stylized performances of such Golden Age icons as Katharine Hepburn and Cary Grant had given way to the mumbling, deeply interior broodings of Brando, James Dean, and Montgomery Clift.

Cage has swung dramatically between those styles, ultimately revealing both as archaic to twenty-first-century

eyes. In a way, he's the closest thing we have to a Brecht-
ian performer, in that he embraces the artifice of acting
and seeks to underline it rather than erase it with practiced naturalism or understatement. (One could argue that
he's following in the footsteps of Jack Nicholson, whose
choice to broadly overplay his bad-boy persona in *The
Shining* is still controversial.) As often as Cage can seem
wildly outsized compared to the movies he's in, there are
times—such as in his committed performance in *Leaving
Las Vegas*, or, more recently, in the hugely entertaining
Bad Lieutenant: Port of Call New Orleans—when he's enormous fun to behold precisely because he's willing to go
big or go home.

What Cage brings to his movies is akin to the self-
conscious sensibility of such filmmakers as Wes Anderson
and the Coen brothers, whose scripts often demand actors
to be similarly declamatory and practiced in their delivery.
Although one would think that the self-consciously artificial settings of Anderson's films would constrict actors and
limit their expressive choices, the opposite is true, according to those who have worked with him.

"Sometimes there's freedom in bondage," Edward
Norton explained while doing press for Anderson's *Moonrise Kingdom*, which, like all of Anderson's films, was designed, planned, and choreographed down to the last
micrometer. "What might look like a very managed environment is actually providing an actor with a lot of rich
fodder to interact with. When certain things are prede-
termined, then other things that are improvisational can
bloom out of it." Norton pointed to a scene where his
character, a scout leader, moves through a boys' camp
and stops to speak to a kid making fireworks. Because
the scoutmaster is a smoker, he has to hold his cigarette at

arm's length, away from the fireworks, lest they ignite—a piece of amusing physical business that Norton relished. "Those are the fun kind of things that emerge because of the constriction in the way the shot is set up."

After decades wherein loose, seemingly improvisational delivery has been the standard, such carefully managed deviations feel like arch throwbacks to a more precise, polished, and "stagey" era. But whether it's quietly understated or wildly excessive and theatrical, a performance should always be judged in terms of the viewer's emotional engagement: Did the performance help us enter the world on-screen, or did it distract us to the point where we "dropped out" of it? Wes Anderson's perfectly groomed worlds require perfectly groomed performances— anything else would pull us out of the scene.

When an actor isn't dealing with something so defined, much of what we see on-screen comes down to individual choices about a character and how to portray a role. Such choices often require research, and research has always been part of a great screen performance. In fact, long before Daniel Day-Lewis became known for staying in character every minute of a film's shoot, Joan Crawford was known for the prodigious homework she did before playing her roles. The moment an actor receives a script, his or her first job is to analyze it, taking apart each character's dialogue and behavior to get to the meaningful core of every word the character utters and everything he or she does (or doesn't do).

But does the audience need to know about that preparatory work? Does knowing improve our moviegoing experience? I think not. It has become convenient marketing to sell a movie for its perceived authenticity. At Oscar time, research hype goes into overdrive, such as Leonardo

DiCaprio regaling eager celebrity reporters with tales of eating a real bison's liver for *The Revenant* or Julianne Moore talking about spending time with Alzheimer's patients for *Still Alice*.

Like research, extreme physical transformation has become a recurring trope in the making and marketing of films, from De Niro gaining weight for *Raging Bull* and Christian Bale losing weight for *The Machinist* to William Hurt, Hilary Swank, and Eddie Redmayne playing characters of different sexual and gender orientations in *Kiss of the Spider Woman*, *Boys Don't Cry*, and *The Danish Girl*, respectively. There's no doubt that actors going to self-sacrificing lengths to submerge their identities is impressive, exemplifying single-minded commitment to their craft. But they're also part of an economy that feeds off the cult of transformation in the interest of artistic seriousness and old-fashioned PR ballyhoo. Stories about the lengths to which an actor went to get into character make easy grist for the interview mill, giving reporters and actors something to talk about other than verboten personal lives or arcane matters of technique. What's more, during awards season, the game of one-upmanship in sacrifice to craft becomes a "narrative" with which actors can distinguish themselves from their fellow nominees.

Dramatic physical changes like weight gain and adopting foreign accents will always get press, especially during awards season. If they're not rooted in an actor's own thoughtful choices, however, they can veer dangerously close to gimmickry. Knowing too much about the process can often prevent viewers from embracing the reality the actors labor so mightily to create. Just as viewers don't need to know what kind of personal introspection, improvisations, or warm-up exercises an actor did to prepare

for a role, we don't need to know about how much research actors have done to create the worlds they inhabit
on-screen. We just need to enter it with them.

THE ROLE OF A LIFETIME

Was it a performance or an impersonation?

Did the actor create a "third character" who personi-
fied the qualities and symbolic values we associate with
the person he or she was playing?

Actors have been playing real-life people since the inception of the movies.

Audiences have an insatiable appetite, it seems, for
watching actors take on the fact-based stories that, re-
constituted as drama, come to occupy a third dimension
between myth and reality. That can be tricky for actors,
who must avoid mere "imitation" and instead create an
impression through a delicate balance between familiar
physical gestures and expressions and their own gifts for
interpretation.

For viewers to believe the dramatized reality on-
screen, the actor must deliver a carefully calibrated collection of externals—how the character looks, walks, and
talks—and psychological internals, a subtle mix of play-
acting and psychic osmosis. When it works, the movie not
only depicts someone whom audience members can instantly recognize and accept as the person they know from
history or current events, but also brings forth a new creation, a third character born of the actor's own emotional
truth and transparency.

When a performance is constructed merely of mimicry, however accomplished, it becomes an exercise in camp: rather than gaining new or meaningful insight into the person being portrayed, the audience gets the diverting but relatively transient pleasure of novelty and technical achievement (for example, watch Kevin Spacey play the singer Bobby Darin in *Beyond the Sea*). When the actor and character mesh in more complex, unexpected ways, the resulting creation becomes both an entertaining cultural artifact and an edifying work of art.

It would have been easy for Frank Langella to play the familiar version of Richard Nixon in *Frost/Nixon*. If he had, his performance as the disgraced former president would have had little more artistic heft than an old Rich Little bit on *The Tonight Show*. Don't get me wrong: a good impression can be entertaining and hilariously funny, as Jimmy Fallon, Jamie Foxx, and Bradley Cooper often prove on the late-night talk-show circuit. But they're not characterizations, in terms of developing a psychology and fully realized interior life for the person they're lampooning.

By contrast, Langella developed an outsized, almost Shakespearean physical and vocal persona, giving Nixon a brooding, bearlike physicality and a growling baritone completely at odds with Nixon's actual cadences. The reason the performance succeeded is that it wasn't superficially "right," but grounded in Langella's own imagination and physical choices, which were further grounded in his research and preparation. The result was a character who may not have looked or acted precisely like the Richard Nixon many viewers remembered, but whose piercing intelligence and doleful temperament they recognized as just Nixonesque enough to accept.

It was relatively easy for Philip Seymour Hoffman to capture the physical externals of Truman Capote for the eponymous 2005 film; in fact, he started his creative process by working on Capote's outward characteristics: his distinctive baby-talk voice, his walk, and his mincing demeanor. But it wasn't until he began to understand and internalize Capote's ambition, fragility, and loneliness—and align them with his own ambition, fragility, and loneliness—that Hoffman's portrayal of Capote went from impersonation to performance.

As the acting coach Larry Moss observed at the time, it was a matter of matching the right externals to the right internals. "If he didn't find the internal life [of Capote], it would be like a cartoon," he said. "It's easy to do the lisping, limp-wristed oddness and eccentricities of Capote, but [he showed us] the hunger inside the man, and that's where the real action lies."

David Oyelowo undertook a similar process to play Martin Luther King Jr. in *Selma*. His first job, he said, was to dismantle the icon that had become sanctified and, in a sense, denatured since King's assassination. "It's not about puffing out my chest, saying, 'I'm a strong black man,'" Oyelowo told me. "I'm a conflicted, flawed, insecure, at times brilliant, at times nonplussed human being who is facing obstacles and trying to overcome them."

Two of the most fascinating exercises in biopic acting in recent memory came by way of screenwriter Oren Moverman, whose scripts for *I'm Not There* and *Love & Mercy* chronicled the lives of musicians Bob Dylan and Brian Wilson, respectively. But Moverman made the canny decision to have them played by multiple actors, in Dylan's case by six actors who portrayed the singer-songwriter at various stages of his personal and professional life. The most abstract performance by far was delivered by Marcus Carl Franklin, a young African American actor who channeled Dylan's influences and infatuation with black musicians, as well as his willingness to take on dramatically different personae in the name of his art; at the other end of the spectrum, Cate Blanchett turned in an uncannily on-point impression—not an impersonation—of Dylan at his most fan-besieged and embittered. In *Love & Mercy*, Wilson was played as a young man by Paul Dano in an astonishingly resonant, physically authentic turn; in the second half of the movie, John Cusack, who by contrast bore no resemblance to Wilson in middle age, nonetheless brought pained honesty to his portrait of an artist suffering from mental illness and creative block.

Dano and Cusack's twinned portrayal of Wilson provides a perfect opportunity to consider the difference between caricature and characterization, and why, although literal resemblances in facial, physical, and vocal features can be helpful, they're far from the point in creating a fully realized person who can reach through the screen and connect with the viewer. That's when acting goes from mere parlor stunt to something more like spiritual communion. And a third person is created, a liminal figure between actuality and impersonation, who allows the audience to conjure some essence of the real person in question, and reflect on what his or her life means to us today.

THE "PROBLEM WITH" PROBLEM

If you dislike particular actors, is that because of characteristics they can't help, or because of choices they make as performers?

> Was the performance strong enough to allow you to let
> go of even your most negative preconceptions?

We all have problems with certain actors—performers who, through no fault of their own, simply turn us off, leave us cold, fail to connect.

This isn't a matter of virtuosity, or finding fault in past performances. This is what happens when, despite legions of fans thinking so-and-so is a genius, you just don't get it. Maybe you don't find him physically appealing. Maybe she reminds you of your middle school Queen Bee. The point is, you're not buyin' 'em, and there's nothing any critic, Oscar, or Twitter horde can tell you that will convince you otherwise.

Most viewers have the luxury of avoiding movies starring actors they're not crazy about; critics, on the other hand, are paid to put our biases to the side and give everyone the benefit of the doubt. This isn't always easy— despite a couple of appealing performances in *Punch-Drunk Love* and *Spanglish*, I'm almost at the point of giving up on Adam Sandler's lazy, narcissistic comic persona, and I've yet to be entirely convinced that Rose Byrne is as comically gifted as her frequent casting in contemporary raunch-coms suggests.

At this juncture, it's important to note that none of this is personal. No one, least of all a professional critic, should bear hardworking creative artists ill will. When the lights go down, only the most uncharitable among us would be rooting for them to fail. Indeed, the sheer courage it takes to put one's inner and outer lives on display for our derision or delectation can only be admired.

And yet, evaluating actors and their performances is by necessity deeply personal, because their person is the only thing they bring to their work. Understanding what we irrationally like and dislike about certain actors actually helps get to the essence of what they do, which is to be an interpretive instrument through which the audience can understand a story's meaning and emotion. The only tools actors have for this job are their physical beings—their faces, bodies, and voices—and their psychic beings, in the form of the reflection, analysis, and imagination it takes to bring their characters to credible life.

When assessing the performance of an actor you don't particularly "like," it's incumbent on the viewer to separate what actors can control from what they can't. Actors aren't able to make themselves physically taller, shorter, fatter, or thinner on command. But they are able to carry themselves in ways that are more or less graceful, dignified, coarse, or self-effacing, as the occasion requires. It's natural for viewers to have a reaction to actors' faces, whether they're presenting the ones they were born with or a version that's been altered through plastic surgery or cosmetic procedures. But after accounting for that first impression, the question for viewers to ask themselves isn't whether they find an actor attractive or desirable, but whether they believe him or her in the role at hand.

Every choice an actor makes—from his or her gait and facial expression to line readings and spontaneous gestures—allows the audience to become either more immersed in the reality on the screen or alienated from it. This is why actors like Adam Sandler can be so polarizing with viewers: they tend to bring the same mannerisms, tics, and tricks to every role they play, forgoing the subtleties of characterization in favor of pandering to audience expectations. (Before dismissing them as hacks, it bears noting that Jack Nicholson, Bill Murray, and Kristen Wiig can be accused of doing the same thing, but haven't faced nearly as much hostility.)

There's no right or wrong answer when it comes to the actors we instinctively dislike: whether you're looking at someone from across a table or on a thirty-foot screen, it all comes down to chemistry. Love can't be forced. But it can grow, and I'm living proof. After years of finding Kevin Costner bland and one-note, I've come to admire his performances, which have become exponentially more layered and expressive as he's aged. I used to consider Sam Rockwell snarky and self-impressed, but he did a magnificent job projecting both pathos and swagger as an astronaut falling apart and finding himself in *Moon*, and made for a downright sexy leading man in the little rom-com *Laggies*. I shortsightedly dismissed Elizabeth Banks as a "generic blonde" until she costarred opposite Cusack in the aforementioned *Love & Mercy*, in which she delivered a breathtakingly sensitive, nuanced, and moving performance as Melinda, Brian Wilson's future wife.

Banks's performance in *Love & Mercy* was all the more remarkable for the fact that she spent most of the movie simply listening. Which, of course, is precisely what acting is, at its best. And when actors manage to tune us in completely to what they're hearing, everything else falls away, including our own pet peeves and preconceptions. They're no longer who we thought they were. And, for a few hours, they invite us to become someone else, right along with them.

EVALUATING AN ACTOR'S PERFORMANCE IS one of the most difficult tasks of a critic. Because a good performance looks so natural—because it conforms so believably with our ideas of how people live and talk and behave—it almost literally defies description. And because the best performances are usually the product of often invisible preparation, analysis, and reflection on the part of the actor, it's nearly impossible to identify what that actor is "doing" when he or she is finally in front of a camera. Good acting is simply telling the truth, without the benefit of clumsy "indicating" or mugging, through the control of voice, body, facial expressions, emotion, and some deep-seated, inexplicable intuition.

After all the training and exercises and script analysis and research, after an inner life has been invented and a physical life settled upon, after the sense memories have been plumbed and the lines memorized, when the lights are hot and the camera is on—that's when the actor ceases to act and simply is. He's not just in the now. He's in the *now* of the now.

It's at this point that the audience completes the circuit, imparting meaning to a role that once existed only on the page and cowriting the character along with the actor. When Gary Oldman played the MI-5 agent George Smiley in the 2011 thriller *Tinker Tailor Soldier Spy*, the final shot of the film was him simply sitting at a conference table, turning to look at the audience. "Someone asked me . . . what I was thinking in the last scene," Oldman recalled when I interviewed him. "And I said, 'Well, I come in, I sit down, I have to look and glance at imaginary people who are not there. Then at a certain point I know that I have to turn my head and look toward the camera, and the camera has to get a certain way over the table before I turn. So I sit, I look, and then turn my head.' I said, 'That's what I was thinking about. But you've just seen the movie, so you're putting [thoughts] in my head. You're doing the work for me.'"

Oldman was echoing his fellow Smiley, Alec Guinness, who recalled when he received an honorary Oscar in 1980 that as an acting student, "it dawned on me that if I was seriously going to have a career in movies, the wisest thing was to do absolutely nothing at all. And that is more or less what I've done since then." And that, more or less, may be what all great actors have in common: they do nothing, and make it something.

RECOMMENDED VIEWING ···

Maria Falconetti, *The Passion of Joan of Arc (1928)*
Marlon Brando, *On the Waterfront (1954)*
Robert De Niro, *Taxi Driver (1976)*
Meryl Streep, *Sophie's Choice (1982)*
Chiwetel Ejiofor, *12 Years a Slave (2013)*
Viola Davis, *Fences (2016)*

CHAPTER THREE

PRODUCTION DESIGN

F ilm critics often use the phrase "production value" when assessing a movie. But what, exactly, does that mean?

Generally, the term refers to the overall look of a film, the sense of richness, texture, and detail that goes into establishing a world on-screen that looks real and lived-in—even if it's set long ago or in a galaxy far, far away. Production value is a function of several disciplines, including cinematography and sound. But it's most readily apparent in the form of visual design, a craft area that spans the entire physical realm of a film, from backdrops, locations, sets, and props to costumes, hair, and makeup. (Generally, the director hires the production designer at the very beginning of the production; the production designer then oversees a department comprising set decorators, artists, and craftspeople. The production designer works in close collaboration with hair and makeup stylists and costume designers, and all of them report to the director.)

Put most simply, the production designer is responsible for everything we see on the screen—every environment the characters inhabit and pass through, every item they use or look at, every piece of décor, no matter how tiny. Even the most naturalistic, "un-dressed" locations have been changed in some way by the production designer to fit the needs of the story being filmed.

Some people use the French phrase *mise-en-scène* (literally translated as "putting onstage") to refer to the appearance and arrangement of a film's visual elements within each frame. I also call it the material culture of a movie: the tactile, palpable "stuff" that establishes a sense of place and encourages the audience to invest in the reality of what they're being asked to believe. Design elements project information—not only about the world and characters on-screen, but also about the taste, perspective, and aesthetic judgment of the person behind the camera.

In fact, the director works so closely with the production designer—and they both work so closely with the cinematographer—that frequently it can be hard to tell where one person's contribution ends and another's begins.

The title "production designer" originated with William Cameron Menzies; although he had already done pioneering work in art direction for such silent films as *The Thief of Bagdad*, and later *The Adventures of Tom Sawyer*, the producer David O. Selznick gave him the title of production designer for *Gone with the Wind*, for which Menzies created the elaborate burning-of-Atlanta sequence, as well as the film's opulent, exquisitely detailed interiors. Crediting Menzies as production designer reflected his authority on the film, on which Selznick gave him final say on all visual elements, including the film's richly vibrant Technicolor palette.

Sometimes credited as art directors and set decorators as well as production designers, Menzies and such contemporaries as Cedric Gibbons (*The Wizard of Oz, Singin' in the Rain, The Philadelphia Story*), Albert S. D'Agostino (*The Magnificent Ambersons, Notorious*), and Van Nest Polglase and Perry Ferguson (*Citizen Kane, Suspicion, The Best Years of Our Lives*) created some of the lushest, most imaginative sets in cinematic history, spanning storybook fantasy, idealized glamour, everyday realism, and surreal abstraction.

Today, we tend to associate production design with directors of strong, singular visual style: the Wes Andersons, Guillermo del Toros, and George Millers of the world. And, as we'll see with editing, Oscars for production design typically reward the most obvious and ostentatious examples of the craft—extravagant historical costume dramas or visually inventive extravaganzas, such as the 2016 winner *Mad Max: Fury Road*. This tendency is understandable because design is most readily apparent in period and fantasy movies. But it also suggests to viewers the mistaken notion that ostentation is the point—that good production design always means the busiest, most over-the-top settings. In fact, production design is just as crucial to the dressed-down, realistic movies as it is to the lavish ones.

The best production design is so seamless and understated that it might barely register at all with a viewer—an ethos embodied by the small black stones designer John Box added to the desert scenes of *Lawrence of Arabia* to give the audience a visual point of reference in the vast, dun-colored expanse, or the ingenious staging tricks Joe Alves employed to transform a malfunctioning mechanical shark into a realistic, menacing monster in *Jaws*. When production design falters, it can be painfully obvious, as when Bradley Cooper cradles a clearly fake baby in *American Sniper*, eliciting a momentary eye-roll within an otherwise convincing movie.

At its most sumptuous and imaginative, production design incalculably magnifies audience pleasure. For decades, the gadgets, cars, and villains' lairs created by Ken Adam defined the playful-sexy fantasy world of James Bond, just as the costumes, creatures, and physical environments of Ridley Scott's movies give them their distinctively stylized looks and dark emotional resonance. By contrast, the loose, seemingly improvised contemporary dramas of such filmmakers as Mike Leigh (*Secrets & Lies*) and Noah Baumbach (*While We're Young, Mistress America*) often look as if they are capturing moments on the fly, even though their productions may have been carefully curated and constructed over months. The effect of the final movies is one of loose, unstudied spontaneity. The best designs are animated by inherent tensions—between invisibility and obtrusiveness, verisimilitude and self-conscious style—that result in pleasing, textured visual experiences for viewers, and highly detailed settings in which performers can deliver their most grounded performances.

BACKGROUND AS FOREGROUND

What's going on in the background, and what does it tell us?

Is it helping to tell the story, or is it distracting from it?

The first question a well-written movie poses is "Where are we?" The production design provides the most obvious and immediate answer.

In most contemporary dramas—or historical narratives that aspire to accuracy—the goal is realism, so that the audience will believe the story is taking place in New York or Boston, even if it's being filmed in Toronto.

For *All the President's Men*, production designer George Jenkins didn't just reproduce the *Washington Post*'s 15th Street newsroom to scale in Los Angeles; he flew in the actual garbage from reporters' wastebaskets (they were given cardboard boxes for tossing in the junk mail and detritus they would otherwise throw away). Jenkins's obsession with detail reflected the sensibilities of both the film's director, Alan J. Pakula, and its producer-star, Robert Redford, both of whom insisted on punctilious accuracy in re-creating the real-life Washington locations of the film, especially the newsroom. "Beyond focusing on the foreground, we were constantly focusing on the background," Redford told Pakula biographer Jared Brown. "Alan and I shared a feeling about how important background detail was, because it filled in and made it a deeper piece." (Reportedly, the walkie-talkies used in the opening scene were the exact same model that the real Watergate burglars employed, and the $100 bills they were paid were in the same sequential order.)

Such obsessive attention to verisimilitude might strike viewers as excessive, even wasteful—but if a director and production designer decide to take shortcuts, or are forced to because of budget or time constraints, the result will be a physical environment that never quite rings true, regardless of how authentic the action, dialogue, and behavior are within it. Elia Kazan, working with art director Richard Day, insisted on the use of real-life locations in Hoboken for the 1954 drama *On the Waterfront*, about workers on the New Jersey docks, in part because he had been dissatisfied by the production design of his directorial debut,

A Tree Grows in Brooklyn, ten years earlier. Although it was a period piece, he later admitted that its look was "essentially false. . . . [T]he rooms were too clean, too nice, too much the work of the property man."

Jeannine Oppewall, who worked as a production designer on *L.A. Confidential, Catch Me If You Can, Pleasantville*, and Warren Beatty's 2016 film *Rules Don't Apply*, defends obsessive attention to detail as a means for the designer to set the work ethic for the entire rest of the crew. "We come first," she said, noting that the design and art department are often the first ones hired on a shoot. "It's our job, in the best of all possible worlds, to set the tone, the bar and the mood. . . . I have to set the bar as high as I possibly can for everyone coming behind me, so that no one slips into a lazy mode, so that everybody's feet are held to the fire, so that everybody realizes that there's a level of work that they have to live up to. So that's why we save people's trash, and that's why we photograph everybody's desk and that's why we spend so much time chasing materials."

When Oppewall was designing sets for Steven Spielberg's 1960s-era caper film *Catch Me If You Can* (2002), in which Leonardo DiCaprio plays a young man impersonating a pilot, she sent an assistant to the Pan Am archive for materials she used to create backdrop for a brief scene set in a corridor. As DiCaprio and another character walk and talk, the entire history of aviation can be seen behind them in a series of photographs and stewardess mannequins in exhibit windows. The vintage imagery and outfits certainly add visual interest to an otherwise boring hallway, as Oppewall intended. But they also convey DiCaprio's character's own idealized relationship with flying, and allow the audience to experience it, too. "It was a moment in American history when flying was wonderful, it was freeing, you could go places you'd never been before," Oppewall explained. "So I was thinking, what could we put there to give something of that feeling of how fun it was, how interesting it was, and how much this kid has to learn? Even if you don't focus on the photographs, you know that there's information there that he could get."

Similarly, in *The Social Network*, director David Fincher and designer Donald Graham Burt dispensed with the image of Harvard as a posh ivory tower; instead, they played up the threadbare, scruffy reality behind the façade, with "bad pre-fab furniture and scratchy sheets and fire alarms in the middle of the wall," as Fincher put it. (They found what they needed, by the way, at Johns Hopkins University in Baltimore.) Those choices not only reflected *The Social Network*'s pronounced lack of romance but helped establish a particular idea from the outset: that protagonist Mark Zuckerberg and his peers started out on the same "level playing field" despite their differing social classes.

In some cases, though, movies call for design that acknowledges, even embraces, the fact that it's all make-believe. In *Dick Tracy*, for example, production designer Richard Sylbert and director Warren Beatty chose matte paintings for their set backdrops instead of more state-of-the-art computer imagery, to stay consistent with the stylized aesthetic of the comic strip they were bringing to three-dimensional life. (Sylbert, whose career spanned *A Face in the Crowd*, *The Manchurian Candidate*, *Chinatown*, and *Mulholland Drive*, won his second Oscar for his work on *Dick Tracy*.) In their use of such immediately identifiable Los Angeles locations as palm tree–lined streets and landmarks like the Pantages Theatre and the Formosa

Café, *Chinatown* and *L.A. Confidential* announced their literal physical setting; with their Venetian blinds, fedoras, jungle-red lipstick, and smoldering cigarettes, they located themselves within a tradition of movies-about-other-movies, in this case the 1940s noir thrillers that served as their inspirations.

A somewhat similar style informed the look of Ridley Scott's science fiction thriller *Blade Runner*, in which familiar noir elements of neon, smoke, and shiny streets were layered with obviously speculative cars and architecture to create a "used future"—the same fusion of old and new that gave *Star Wars* the sense of a world that had always existed, even if we were only now just discovering it.

Alfonso Cuarón wanted a similar densely layered quality of past and future for his science fiction thriller *Children of Men*, which was set in a dystopian England of 2027. In all of his films, starting with *Y Tu Mamá También*, Cuarón told me, "background is as important as character." Nowhere is that truer than in *Children of Men*, which is a veritable feast of visual information as Theo, the protagonist played by Clive Owen, makes a desperate journey through homes, abandoned spaces, and a seaside refugee camp. Cuarón directed his designers Jim Clay and Geoffrey Kirkland to make sure every visual element referenced the present day, with subtle futuristic touches, right down to the carefully selected postcards that decorate the wall of a character played by Michael Caine. Every single frame is packed with evidence of what the time and place are like for the people living there—in fact, because the material environment was so important to Cuarón, *Children of Men* includes barely any close-ups.

For *Dick Tracy*, Sylbert embraced artificiality—we are not meant to feel at home in his world, even though the story itself is a familiar one. By contrast, the filmmakers behind *Blade Runner*, *Star Wars*, and *Children of Men* made their obviously fantastical stories more credible by making them look run-down, distressed, and real. Then there are movies whose theatricality exists in an unsettled no-man's-land between credibility and sometimes bizarre stylization. Stanley Kubrick's *Eyes Wide Shut* made no effort to hide the fact that it was filmed on a London soundstage, although it purportedly took place in New York.

Although production designers Les Tomkins and Roy Walker obsessively re-created the dimensions of Greenwich Village for Kubrick's film—even measuring street widths and noting the locations of newspaper boxes—the set comes across as arch and theatrical, a stylistic choice that reverberates through Tom Cruise's curiously distant, impassive performance. Between the recurring shop fronts and moments of stagy-looking rear projection (an archaic technique whereby actors are filmed in front of a previously filmed footage to suggest scenery in the background), nothing looks or feels remotely genuine in the film—but, as Kubrick's defenders are swift to observe, that might be the point of a film that is meant to occupy a space between dream and reality.

The danger, especially with a period film, is that a director and designer might take details into the fetishistic territory of pastiche, throwing in every period-specific visual signifier they can. As David Fincher said of his 1970s crime drama *Zodiac*, "we didn't want to make a movie about fat ties and sideburns." David O. Russell's *American Hustle*, another movie set in the 1970s, tiptoes right up to the edge of pastiche with its foiled wallpaper, Lucite accessories, and ficus trees; *The Man from U.N.C.L.E.*, on the other hand, tips right over, its mod-1960s aesthetic

feeling imitative—and, admittedly, poppy and playful—
rather than authentic. Both seamless verisimilitude and
obvious stylization are valid aesthetic approaches, as long
as they're intentional and of a piece with the story being
told.

Sometimes, the delicate balance between realism and
stylization can be helped by witty, well-placed creative
anachronisms—little winks or ruptures in the visual narrative intended to connect an era long past to our own.
Directors Derek Jarman (*Caravaggio*), Alan Rudolph (*The
Moderns*), and Baz Luhrmann (*Moulin Rouge!*) have all playfully injected modern-day visual cues into period pieces in
order to imbue their stories with fresh relevance. Perhaps
the boldest—and most effective—example could be found
in Sofia Coppola's 2006 *Marie Antoinette*, in which the director snuck a pair of pastel Converse sneakers into the
teen queen's period-correct closet.

Whereas purposeful "mistakes" worked for a film
that sought to humanize Marie Antoinette as a vulnerable young girl who would ultimately be destroyed by her
heedless materialism, cinema history is littered with examples where the overall look was fatally at odds with the
time periods—the kitschy stylings of 1950s Bible epics, or
the artfully distempered walls in Tom Hooper's *The King's
Speech*. Designer Eve Stewart defended these as accurate to
real-life therapist Lionel Logue's theatrical taste, but in the
movie they looked oddly out of place, a pretty attempt to
gin up visual interest in an essentially static tableau. Put
another way, the design of *The King's Speech*—and that of
The Danish Girl, another Hooper-Stewart collaboration—
too often behaves like a backdrop *against* which the performances are taking place, rather than an internal world
within which people are speaking, breathing and living

fully realized lives. Background or foreground, a movie's design should be as alive as the people within it.

PSYCHOLOGICAL DESIGNS ON THE AUDIENCE

What feelings do the physical spaces in the film evoke?

What feelings do they reflect?

Production design doesn't just establish a physical setting. It conveys crucial psychological and emotional information as well.

Although the self-consciously artificial production design of *Eyes Wide Shut* was distractingly ersatz, the films of Stanley Kubrick provide a master class in the use of exaggerated design to stir strong feelings in the audience, from the imposing war rooms of *Paths of Glory* and *Dr. Strangelove or: How I Learned to Stop Worrying and Love the Bomb* to the echoing emptiness of the Overlook Hotel in *The Shining*.

Built on a London soundstage by Roy Walker, the Overlook set serves as a towering example of how a movie's setting can emphasize and echo the psychology of its characters. As Jack Nicholson's blocked writer goes insane, the hotel's bizarre combination of period details, exaggeratedly high ceilings, garish color schemes, and repeating motif of maze-like designs accentuate the mood of dislocation and encourage the sense of humans being dwarfed by overwhelming, sinister forces. (Walker was surely inspired by Perry Ferguson's monumental designs for *Citizen Kane*, which reinterpreted William Randolph Hearst's San Simeon estate as a mansion called Xanadu, an imposing,

sparsely furnished fortress that Ferguson conceived specifically to make the most of *Citizen Kane*'s dramatic deep-
focus photography.)

Even when designers are striving for maximum realism and accuracy, they're aware of the psychological
symbolism of their work. In the case of *All the President's
Men*, the goal was realism, but Pakula, Jenkins, and cinematographer Gordon Willis also chose their Washington
locations with an eye toward playing up the monumentality of the institutions Bob Woodward and Carl Bernstein
were challenging, photographing their edifices so that
they took on fascist overtones. In *The Graduate*, director
Mike Nichols and designer Richard Sylbert agreed that
the two families in the film, the Braddocks and the Robinsons, should embody two sides of the California dream
of prosperity and leisure—one wholesome and defanged,
the other more sinister and predatory. The Braddocks'
home would signal middle-class values with its straight
lines and turquoise swimming pool, while the Robinsons'
environment should be more inaccessible, jungle-like, and
implicitly threatening.

Kristi Zea, the production designer on *The Silence
of the Lambs*, created two distinct spaces for the heroine,
Clarice Starling, to move through: the cold, neutral, and
bureaucratic environs of the FBI facility where she's been
training, and the dank, labyrinthine Gothic prison that
holds her foil, Hannibal Lecter. Each symbolizes part of
her journey in the film: one political, as she seeks ad-
vancement in a male-dominated career, the other deeply
emotional and psychological, as she overcomes her most
primal, self-defeating fears. *The Silence of the Lambs* might
be responsible for what has become a recurrent piece of
production design, whereby a police thriller must include

at least one shot of a bulletin board crammed with photographs, maps, names, and random documents, all connected by pieces of red string. It's such a frequently used
idea that it borders on the cliché, but it admittedly serves
a useful purpose in avoiding windy expository sequences
and helping the audience keep track of multiple characters and their relationships. We may not be aware of it at
the time, but a movie's production design is constantly
helping to anchor our perception and comprehension, and
allowing the film to work on us visually, mentally, even
subconsciously.

COLORING OUR WORLD

Are the colors intrusive, garish, obvious? Or understated and barely there?

Are the colors helping to tell the story, or are they providing quote marks around emotions and information
that are already perfectly clear?

Color can define a movie, creating its symbolic and
emotional universe and triggering unconscious reactions
in the audience.

Color is such a powerful tool, in fact, that establishing a film's palette is often the first thing a designer does
after reading the script. Think of how the drained, almost
colorless atmosphere of David O. Russell's *The Fighter* captured the downtrodden environment of Lowell, Massachusetts, and compare that to the pops of yellow and gold
that enlivened the far less naturalistic, more fable-like
American Hustle a few years later. The color scheme of each

movie sent vital signals to the audience about its tone, perspective, and emotional intent.

Production designer Sarah Greenwood was scouting locations for *Atonement* at stately homes in Britain when she came across a particularly arresting shade of "incredible arsenic green" in a kitchen. She decided to make it a visual leitmotiv for the prewar period she associated with the verdant sensuality of late summer and reproduced the tone throughout the film. Similarly, Sylbert's color scheme for *Dick Tracy* allowed only the seven colors originally utilized by the comic's creator, cartoonist Chester Gould. The result was a playful embrace of the movie's populist roots in newspaper comics, rather than the self-serious, contemporized adaptations that are so prevalent today. Interestingly, Lee Daniels and his designer Roshelle Berliner also concentrated on bright reds, blues, and yellows for the backdrops of the searing drama *Precious*, about a girl's troubled coming-of-age amid poverty and abuse in modern-day New York. Although it would have been easy, maybe expected, to present her world as a dreary environment devoid of color or joy, Daniels wanted to capture the vibrancy and optimism of her indefatigable struggle to thrive. "We had to show the beauty as well as the pain," he said.

Most filmmakers strive for understated colors that accurately reflect their times and settings. But there are those who aren't afraid of lurid, even vulgar color to give their films unapologetically heightened emotionalism. A masterpiece of this approach is Jacques Demy's 1964 musical *The Umbrellas of Cherbourg*, a doomed-romance fable brought forth in the bold, candy-colored pinks of a confectionary, an extravagantly bright palette echoed in the 2016 doomed-love musical *La La Land*. The directors Spike Lee, Pedro Almodóvar, and Todd Haynes have used color with similar boldness, evoking the striking style of the 1950s melodramas they adore. An entire thesis could be written on the use of red in *Do the Right Thing*, *All About My Mother*, and *Carol*, in which the color denotes feminine artifice, desire, and impending violence, respectively.

From the strategically placed red coat (there's that color again!) of the little girl in Steven Spielberg's black-and-white Holocaust drama *Schindler's List* to the saturated hues of Michael Mann's thrillers *Heat* and *Collateral*, color is essential to a movie's visual and psychological makeup. Unfortunately, it can also fall prey to cliché, such as the sulfuric yellow-green fog that seems to have taken over military dramas since *Black Hawk Down*, or the blue-gray mists of time that have enveloped Spielberg's most recent period films, including *Lincoln* and *Bridge of Spies*. If and when you notice color, ask yourself: What is its function in the scene or overall movie (this can be as basic as helping keep track of a protagonist in a crowd, or to highlight the most important part of the action)? If it's attractive and useful, either symbolically, narratively, or in physically directing the eye, then it's working.

A VIEW OF ONE'S OWN

Whose world are we in?

The best production designs make it possible for viewers to not only understand a protagonist's point of view, but share it.

For the centerpiece hypnosis scene of John Frankenheimer's Cold War–era thriller *The Manchurian Candidate*, Richard Sylbert constructed three different sets, one for a group of US soldiers being brainwashed, one for a meeting of a ladies' garden club, and one for the hypnosis session seen entirely from the perspective of African American soldiers. Working with cinematographer Lionel Lindon, Frankenheimer filmed the scene in its entirety three times, circling each set completely. He then worked with editor Ferris Webster to cut the pieces together so that they dovetailed into one smoothly unfolding dream.

Similarly, the often nightmarish visual elements of Alfred Hitchcock's *Vertigo* and Darren Aronofsky's *Requiem for a Dream* pull viewers into the feverish, distorted worldviews of their protagonists, who suffer from crippling anxiety and addiction, respectively. (Production designer Thérèse DePrez executed a similarly subjective production design for *Black Swan*, which traced a ballerina's emotional breakdown through the use of ingenious doubling motifs involving mirrors, windows, and other reflective surfaces.) Part of what made *Trainspotting* such a breakthrough for director Danny Boyle when it came out in 1996 was how it captured the physical and psychological experience of its protagonist's heroin addiction with such bold and queasily arresting detail. The film's most notorious scene, when the audience goes with Ewan McGregor's character into a toilet as he tries to retrieve his lost drugs, was a masterstroke of visual imagination and execution, all the more impressive for being relatively primitive: production designer Kave Quinn simply cut a toilet in half and had McGregor slide down a chute that had been strategically placed behind it (McGregor added the witty touch of twisting his legs so that it looked like he was literally going down the drain). In capturing the squalor and desperation of drug addiction with such witty, wince-inducing subjectivity, Quinn and Boyle created one of the most memorable set pieces of that era.

Production design not only helps define character for viewers, but it can often communicate values, longings, and desires that the main characters can't—such as in *Carol*, about two women falling in love in 1950s New York, in which director Todd Haynes and production designer Judy Becker went just to the edge of kitsch in evoking the tailored, everything-in-its-place-ness of the era, inviting viewers both to admire the surface sheen and contemplate what the characters were using it to hide or communicate about themselves.

Especially in period pieces, production design does the heavy lifting in conveying the changing fortunes of the characters, whether it's the skeletal Pacific Northwest settlement in *McCabe & Mrs. Miller*, whose buildings become gradually more solid and ornate over time, or the domestic interiors designed by Patrizia von Brandenstein for *Amadeus*, which become gradually barer of furniture and accessories as Mozart's expenses rise and his commissions dry up. At Martin Scorsese's direction, designer Kristi Zea packed every scene of *GoodFellas* with as much information as possible to telegraph Henry and Karen Hill's relative prosperity and sense of security at any given time. As Scorsese noted later, "there had to be . . . a frenetic quality of getting as much over to the audience as possible, almost overwhelming them with images and information, so that you could see the film a couple of times and still get more out of it."

For his semiautobiographical 2010 film *Beginners*, Mike Mills shot in a historic Richard Neutra house in Los Angeles, which served as the fictional residence of a man loosely based on his father, the late museum director Paul Mills. "The Topper family [had] lived there for, like, forty years, and it has all the patina and clutter of a family," Mills said at the time. "So . . . in the kitchen and some of the little bedrooms, it's just all their stuff. I barely touched it, because it's impossible to re-create that accumulation. . . . We used barely any lights, and the paint's all the same, and the dining room table and chairs are theirs, and I just brought some of my parents' chairs and different old folk-art stuff and some of their fabrics on the couch and bedspreads. So it was a sort of documentary handling of space."

As a result, the house in *Beginners* looks exactly like the fashionably crowded home of a former curator. Then Mills—a former graphic designer—put his own drawings and designs into the film as the work of the character based on himself, played by Ewan McGregor. "He's quite a reflective character. He doesn't express a lot," Mills said of McGregor's Oliver. "So the drawings, the graphic sections . . . all became ways [to] help the audience see what he was going through." Mills took a similar approach in designing his 2016 film *20th Century Women*, in which he paid homage to his late mother; he provided actress Annette Bening with some of his mother's silver bracelets to wear and decorated the set with the same textiles from his parents' Montecito home. It's just in this accumulation of thoughtful, character-motivated detail that a movie can come to life, immersing the audience in environments that reveal as much about their inhabitants as our real-life homes do about us.

I'M READY FOR MY CLOSE-UP

How did the actors look?

Did their hair and makeup serve their characters?

We want our stars to look good. The problems start when *they* want to look good.

Hair and makeup represent relatively minor, but nonetheless significant, sacrifices actors make to their craft, especially when they're forced to present themselves in less than flattering ways. The good ones cast vanity to the wind and allow their characters to dictate their look, whether it's Charlize Theron becoming unrecognizable as the doughy, strung-out protagonist of *Monster*, or Javier Bardem allowing the Coen brothers to give him an absurd bowl-cut for his role as a psychotic killer in *No Country for Old Men*. Although such uncanny transformations are often rewarded in the press and at awards time (both Theron and Bardem received Oscars for their trouble), stars just as often either refuse or aren't allowed to dramatically alter their looks for a role, lest they alienate their fans.

An actor's appearance is a delicate balance between authenticity and audience expectations, and usually the expectations win, a fact attested to by Julie Christie's, Faye Dunaway's, and Barbra Streisand's mid-twentieth-century hair and makeup in the period films *Dr. Zhivago, Bonnie and Clyde*, and *Funny Girl*, respectively; Patrick Swayze's '80s-tastic mullet in the '60s-era musical *Dirty Dancing*; or the picture-perfect hair and makeup in *Pearl Harbor*, in which Ben Affleck and his costars look like they're playing a particularly expensive game of vintage dress-up.

Commentaries of Talmudic complexity are still being written both for and against Nicole Kidman's prosthetic nose in the high-toned 2002 literary adaptation *The Hours*. For some, Kidman's willingness to forgo vanity in order to portray Virginia Woolf was an admirable gesture of artistic seriousness; for others, the nose was a needless distraction.

I happen to think the nose worked. But there are
plenty of instances when prosthetics have gotten in the
way of an otherwise fine performance: There was no
need to make Emma Thompson so cartoonishly hideous
in the family comedy *Nanny McPhee*. Nor did Leonardo
DiCaprio need to look quite so rubbery in order to star in
J. Edgar, the biopic about the longtime FBI director
Hoover. More recently, the decision to resurrect Julia
Roberts's red wig from *Notting Hill* for the misbegotten
comedy *Mother's Day* might have seemed like a droll in-
joke, but it looked fake and unforgivably unattractive,
as did Angelina Jolie in a climactic scene in *The Tourist*,
when her look went from glamorous international spy to
dowager-in-training simply by virtue of a dowdy-looking
black ball gown and an equally fusty updo.

Whereas complicated makeup jobs were once a matter
of an actor sitting in a chair for hours having makeup and
prosthetics (called "appliances") put on, these days they're
often a combination of old-fashioned greasepaint and
state-of-the-art technology. That was the case with Brad
Pitt, who submitted to hours in a chair in order to have
life casts made of his face for *The Curious Case of Benjamin
Button*, during which he reverse-aged more than seventy
years, an illusion achieved through a flawless combination
of makeup and digital effects. Although both processes
were painstaking and time-consuming, involving translu-
cent, micro-thin patches of forehead wrinkles of varying
depths, sophisticated motion-capture technology, and meticulous matching of Pitt's face to the bodies of the actors
who "played" him at different ages, none of that was at
the forefront of viewers' minds while they were watching
the film, so caught up were they in the unusual love story
unfolding between Button and his childhood sweetheart.

Rather than asking ourselves, "How'd they do that?", we only cared about what happened next—the litmus test for hair and makeup that service the story rather than calling attention to their own spectacle, however impressive.

CLOTHES MAKE THE MOVIE

Did the actors wear the clothes or did the clothes wear the actors?

Just as clothes make the man, they can make—or break—a movie.

As a budding film writer, one of my first movie-star interviews was with Michael Douglas, who graciously agreed to provide quotes for a story about the costume designer for *Wall Street*, Ellen Mirojnick. Mirojnick had meticulously planned and assembled the $28,000 wardrobe for Douglas's character, Gordon Gekko, creating a look that would become a sartorial signifier of the go-go 1980s—impeccably tailored Alan Flusser suits, bespoke shirts, playful suspenders. But, for Douglas, the wardrobe served a different role: it helped him find his character. "When I put on those suits and those cuff links in the morning, and had that first cigarette, it all came together," he told me. Mirojnick had the added challenge of having dressed Douglas in *Basic Instinct*, which had come out the same year. "I wanted to make Gekko bigger than life," she explained. "It's the cut of the suit, how it's put together, that basically says, 'Fuck you.'"

Just as the actors use psychology, facial cues, and physicality to convey the people they're playing, the costume designer works with silhouette, draping, color, and texture to reinforce and express those characters, whether they're unrefined and animalistic (Marlon Brando's stained, chest-hugging T-shirt in *A Streetcar Named Desire*), changing in important but unspoken ways (Greta Garbo's severe Russian suits in *Ninotchka* giving way to frillier, more feminine chiffon), or living minute-to-minute on borrowed time (Matt Damon wearing just one thin jacket and a coat in *The Bourne Supremacy*).

Just as costumes convey a character's class, background, regional roots, even religion and sexual habits, they can express unspoken desires and unrealized self-images. Costumes, to quote Elia Kazan, should "appear to be an expression of the character's soul." But costumes also present the stars at their most glamorous and seductive, giving the audience a frisson of aspirational escapism and sensuous pleasure. Fashion and cinema have symbiotically intertwined since the latter's inception: starting with couture-themed newsreels and continuing through de-rigueur fashion show sequences and makeover montages, seeing our favorite actors in exquisite clothing has been an enormous part of the aesthetic experience of going to the movies. Costuming also provides subtextual meanings: think of the unspoken division of enslaved labor that goes into Hattie McDaniel's house servant lacing up Vivien Leigh's flouncy dresses in *Gone With the Wind*, or Marilyn Monroe's innocent (or is it?) white halter dress in *The Seven Year Itch*, or the robe that Katharine Hepburn puts on after swimming in *The Philadelphia Story*, her character's emotionally distant persona indelibly inscribed in the garment's severe, statuesque draping. That silhouette would be elaborated to even more iconic effect thirty years later in *Star Wars*, in which Darth Vader's black cape and helmet give him the heft and monumentality of an imposing god.

But clothes operate on a subtler level, too, creating fashion trends that emerge in our own tastes and choices. Flusser's designs for *Wall Street*—and the Armani suits in *American Gigolo* before it—strongly impacted men's fashion during the 1980s, just as Faye Dunaway's sleek midi-skirts and rakish berets in *Bonnie and Clyde* and Diane Keaton's khakis and skinny ties in *Annie Hall* led women to embrace those looks in the 1960s and 1970s. Like most other elements of a film's design, costumes usually succeed or fail depending on their authenticity, but they exert an equally powerful force as a means of audience identification, inviting viewers to imagine themselves, literally, in the shoes of the people they're watching on-screen. When a movie's costumes manage to cross over into mass-market fashion, that means it has connected on a level beyond story and character to the spectator's most aspirational self.

Whether they're being meticulously designed and sewn by hand or bought off the rack, the best movie costumes work in tandem with the larger production design to define setting, period, character, and emotion—and they do so right down to the last extra, who should be as carefully conceived and dressed as the leading players. (Interestingly, the director Ang Lee told me that, when he was casting extras to wear the cutoff shorts and tie-dyed T-shirts that dominated the wardrobe of his set-in-the-1960s movie *Taking Woodstock*, he had trouble finding young bodies that weren't too Pilates-cized to be believable as more soft-edged baby-boomer teens.)

This is why films like *Mad Max: Fury Road* and *Star Wars* won Oscars for costume design, rather than the usual period costume dramas: each evinced an extraordinary level of detail suggesting a ragged, worn-in world that existed outside of the soundstage. Far less lionized but just as spot-on were the pleated khakis and bland, ill-fitting button-down shirts that the reporters wore in *Spotlight*, in which the workaday duds didn't lend much glamour or style to their wearers, but disappeared—just as they should have.

SPECIAL EFFECTS

They might have made you look, but did you notice?

Unlike most production design, visual effects are usually added at the end of the production. Yet their contribution to the overall look of a movie can be just as essential as set construction and decoration, costumes, hair, and makeup, and those elements are often knitted together to create a unified, smooth-looking whole.

Special effects have become such a staple of the film-going experience that audiences are forgiven for feeling a little jaded. Are special effects really all that special anymore?

To wit: When was the last time a movie's special effects blew you away? Now compare that to the last movie you watched that created a world so richly imaginative, so thoroughly fleshed-out and inhabited and so utterly out of your everyday experience that you *forgot* you were watching special effects. (One of the most recent instances for me was watching 2016's completely transporting *The Jungle Book*, which was almost entirely composed of computer-generated imagery, save for live-action footage of the film's only human star, Neel Sethi, who played little Mowgli.)

In considering special effects, a few landmark titles are always mentioned: Georges Méliès's crude—and still captivating—1902 experiment with nascent visual trickery in *A Trip to the Moon*; the miniatures, matte paintings, and composite editing of Fritz Lang's *Metropolis*; the detailed sets and innovative photography techniques of Kubrick's *2001: A Space Odyssey*. In more recent years, such films as *The Matrix*, *Titanic*, *Avatar*, and *Life of Pi* have taken effects to new levels, as digital technology has made it possible for filmmakers to realize even their most outlandish visions.

Too often, however, the means by which a film achieves its most impressive physical feats—re-creating the sinking of a legendary ship, for example, or making viewers believe that a young boy shared a small boat with a live Bengal tiger—become a marketing hook and little else. Although director James Cameron's dedication to researching the Titanic and re-creating it down to the last detail resulted in a technically impressive spectacle, that didn't help the screenplay overcome the weaknesses discussed earlier; those limitations were even more painfully clear in Cameron's *Avatar*, which solved the challenge of melding live-action performances with motion-captured and digitally enhanced performances, but all in the service of a clichéd story and forgettable characters.

Avatar might have been state-of-the-art in 2009, but I far preferred Guillermo del Toro's less technologically advanced *Pan's Labyrinth* a few years earlier, for which del Toro and his design team constructed elaborate latex-and-fiberglass puppets to populate a young girl's frightening dreamworld during Franco-era Spain. Part of the appeal of *Forrest Gump* for audiences was observing how director Robert Zemeckis used new editing techniques to insert the guileless title character, played by Tom Hanks, into real footage of famous world events; but within a ham-handedly simplistic story, it quickly began to feel like a too-clever-by-half gimmick. Years later, the actor Armie Hammer played twin brothers in *The Social Network* with similar visual sleight-of-hand, but with far more subtlety and finesse (especially in his vocal performance, which he slightly adjusted depending on which brother he was playing). All that is to say, usually the best special effects are the ones you don't notice at all.

With the current onslaught of comic-book movies and effects-driven spectacles, Hollywood seems intent on discovering how many fireballs a group of macho heroes can walk nonchalantly away from before the audience will stop being impressed. For my part, that threshold was reached several years ago. Thanks to "pre-visualization" software, whereby effects technicians can insert the booms, collisions, and explosions into computerized sketches of the film, we now have films that use the same rote version of those effects every time they need an adrenaline shot (there are actual digital libraries that exist for this purpose—the savviest insiders can spot explosions and generic action stunts that have been reused for different movies). Far more impressive than merely blowing stuff up for the thousandth time is when technology and practical, real-life sets are used to create a convincing world on-screen—which can then be destroyed to great effect.

I'm convinced that the reason I enjoyed Christopher Nolan's *Inception* as much as I did was that he and his design team achieved as many of the film's preposterous dreamscape effects without computers as they could. The result was a world that crumbled, spun, tilted, and rotated with stomach-turning verisimilitude. Another fine example is Steven Spielberg's *Minority Report*, for which the director set out to create a "grounded future" set in

Washington, DC. Working with designer Alex McDowell and a team of advisers from the worlds of medicine, criminal justice, transportation, and computer science, Spielberg created a "technology bible" containing all the gadgets and appliances that Tom Cruise's character would use in his daily life. But after meticulously creating the futuristic visuals, Spielberg continually "threw them away," downplaying their importance within the frame. From the outset, Spielberg insisted, he wanted *Minority Report* to be a "psychic chase" film, not a special-effects movie. "I paid a lot of money to have a cereal box talk," Spielberg told me when the movie came out in 2002. "But rather than have a close-up of it, I put it in the background." (Spielberg's offhanded approach to technology turned out to be amazingly predictive, especially in the holographic images and personal computing that twenty-first-century consumers now take for granted.)

It's the nature of cinema—which is just as much a technology as an art form and industrial practice—to continually seek out new frontiers in the means of production. Pioneers like James Cameron, *Mad Max*'s George Miller, and Peter Jackson will no doubt see to that. Within a few years, we're likely to see the first feature film exploiting the immersive capabilities of virtual reality. But what's next and newest isn't necessarily what's better. As Jackson's own *Hobbit* movies so dismally proved, hyped-up special-effects extravaganzas can be just as dreary, repetitive, and workmanlike as the most low-tech dud.

Although great special effects are the result of intensive planning, imagination, and meticulous, time-consuming execution, when they're presented to the audience, they should be nearly invisible: rather than asking ourselves how they made it look like Sandra Bullock was floating through an abandoned spacecraft, or Tom Cruise was hanging on to an ascending airplane, or Sigourney Weaver was being threatened by a slobbery extraterrestrial monster, we should be in those realities—each of which, in varying degrees, has been grounded in some part of our own. One of the finest uses of visual effects recently was in the film *Ex Machina*, in which Alicia Vikander played a robot who longs to be human; although her physical "shell" was created by way of complicated computer wizardry, it was her facial and physical performance—delicate, expressive, balletic—that literally brought her character to life. *Mad Max: Fury Road*, which came out the same year, was also set within a dystopian future, but with a far more outrageous, uninhibited visual style that helped set the tone; visual effects were used almost invisibly in one, more graphically in the other. And they were flawless in both.

THE PLEASURE PRINCIPLE

Was it beautiful, and should that matter?

Some fans of Nancy Meyers, who wrote and directed the romantic comedies *Something's Gotta Give*, *The Holiday*, and *It's Complicated*, among others, love her movies for their banter, or their keen-eyed observations of middle-aged life.

I just lust after the copper pots in their kitchens.

At its most primal, production design contributes enormously to the audience's pleasure, creating an opportunity either to luxuriate in what's being shown on-screen or to take it in obliquely, as an almost subconscious but no less satisfying part of the visual experience. Cinema has always been vicarious, a voyeuristic and escapist medium, whether viewers are putting themselves in the art deco opulence of a Fred Astaire musical, the enviable interior designs of those Nancy Meyers rom-coms, or Wes Anderson's timeless, meticulously appointed jewel boxes. Part of the fun of watching such classics as *Rear Window* and *Gone with the Wind*—as well as such recent films as *Her*, Joe Wright's *Anna Karenina*, and *A Bigger Splash*—is the sheer beauty of their material environments and costumes.

But can a movie be too pretty? In the 1980s and 1990s, the work of Ismail Merchant and James Ivory—best known for such British "heritage" pictures as *A Room with a View, Maurice*, and *Howard's End*—became shorthand for the kind of overdressed costume drama that was submerged within a froth of crinolines, crunchy gravel, and crumpets, a cosmeticized history that film historian Jane Barnwell has called "the comfort blanket of the past." As ambivalent as historians are about Merchant-Ivory's version of Britain, those productions at least had the benefit of Ruth Prawer Jhabvala's scripts and outstanding actors to keep them from slipping into pure frippery and what Oppewall mordantly calls "decorator porn."

Perhaps the most visually strong—and narratively weak—costume drama of this sort was Stanley Kubrick's *Barry Lyndon*, a punctiliously staged comedy of eighteenth-century manners and maquillage in which the director's pictorial sensibility far outpaced his sense of meaning, momentum, or metaphor. Less a movie than a series of elaborate, static tableaux, *Barry Lyndon* exemplifies production design at its most fetishistic: clothing is never tattered or worn, furnishings are never scuffed or tackily mismatched. It's perfectly false, continually favoring spectacle over the title character, portrayed by Ryan O'Neal.

Kubrick and designer Ken Adam were influenced and inspired by such eighteenth-century painters as William Hogarth and Thomas Gainsborough, whose works they often directly quoted in their staging and set design. Forty years later, British filmmaker Mike Leigh created his own homage to an artist—in this case J. M. W. Turner—that evinced a painterly look in terms of light and color, but with a far less distancing sense of artifice.

Working with designer Suzie Davies, Leigh banished any hint of comfort for his characters or his viewers: instead he plunged the audience into an austere but captivating approximation of the studios, houses, and coastal communities that Turner worked in and captured on his canvases. A sometimes dour, downbeat study of an artist at the end of his life, *Mr. Turner* never privileges visual allure over psychological authenticity: Although the backdrops are often attractive (the artist's walks in Flanders and Margate are particularly evocative in their painterly light and composition), beauty is offered not for its own sake but as a counterpoint to Turner's eccentricity and isolation. The characters don't indulge in lots of eye-catching costume changes, but allow their clothing to wear and fade. The result is a textured, lived-in world on-screen that reflects J. M. W. Turner's world as it might have been, and as he perceived it through his own rigorously discerning eye. It's never pretty; instead, it's quietly, transportingly beautiful.

Credibility, attractiveness, novelty, and originality all come into play when evaluating a film's production design. But, like every other aspect of watching a movie, these qualities are ultimately subjective. I once interviewed a director who felt great about every scene in the movie except for one, which took place in an apartment that, she felt, just didn't "fit" the character who was supposed to live there. I remembered very briefly thinking the same thing when watching the movie, but it wasn't enough of a disconnect to take me out of the film, which I adored.

What does take me out, however, are those generic, "middle-class" houses that are supposed to pass for midwestern suburbia when the palm trees of the Hancock Park neighborhood in Los Angeles are clearly in the background. Or those instantly forgettable films where houses are interchangeable white-picket-fence affairs, their inhabitants outfitted in equally undistinguished ensembles from Dockers and J. Jill. Rather than provide an extra layer of characterization or symbolism, the production designer has gone shopping, providing little more than an attractive backdrop to people talking.

Polished, inoffensive, and impersonal, these movies feature décor, not design; commodities, not carefully curated signifiers. Some filmmakers rely so heavily on product placement to boost a film's budget that there's a distracting parade of Bud Light labels and Doritos packages. (That said, some product placements—like the Reese's Pieces in *E.T. the Extra-Terrestrial* and FedEx in *Cast Away*—are integrated smoothly enough into their characters' lives and environments that they feel authentic rather than ad-like.) Production design should be invisible, in the sense that it should never intrude into or contradict with what the filmmaker is trying to convince us is true or possible. But it should never entirely disappear; it's much too important for that in conveying information and emotion. To paraphrase Elia Kazan, the difference between mere background and great production design is the difference between watching a story play out against a static backdrop and living inside a dynamic, palpable world. The question isn't whether that world is always pretty, but whether it rings true enough to believe and enter completely.

RECOMMENDED VIEWING ···

The Magnificent Ambersons (1942)
Blade Runner (1982)
L.A. Confidential (1997)
The Royal Tenenbaums (2001)
Marie Antoinette (2006)
Pan's Labyrinth (2006)

CHAPTER FOUR

········· CINEMATOGRAPHY ·········

Movies are a collection of images—each frame a discrete aesthetic object, connected to other frames by physical means and the remarkable ability of the human eye to create the illusion of continuity in time and space.

Cinematography is the art of capturing those images, determining their lighting, look, and mood—and, by extension, what the audience sees and feels. How a film is photographed encompasses choices as varied as which film stocks, lenses, filters, and lights to use; whether the camera should move or not; whether its color palette should be bright and saturated or pastel and subdued—or, indeed, whether it should be in color at all. When a great director and an equally gifted cinematographer work together, those decisions are made as a team, almost instinctively; sometimes, especially in the case of new directors with little or no experience using a camera, it's left to the cinematographer (sometimes also called the director of photography) to make important aesthetic choices on

his or her own. Regardless of how collaborative the process is, when cinematography is used with thoughtfulness
and creativity, it can make the most carefully constructed
movie look as if it were filmed almost accidentally on
the fly—or, conversely, it can make a low-budget indie
glow with the rich, velvety textures of an Old Masters
painting.

Lighting, color, composition, temperature, and the
texture of the image all come under the purview of cinematography. And the parameters of how we perceive each
of those elements have changed dramatically over the decades, as filmmakers have continually pushed the boundaries of what constitutes pictorial beauty and naturalistic
realism. Inevitably, as the meaning and relative value of
those terms have changed, audience expectations have
shifted as well. Part of what makes vintage films from the
1930s, 1940s, and 1950s so distinctive is their polished,
perfected look, which was achieved through meticulous
production design and equally careful lighting schemes; to
audiences of that era, the blurry, jagged images of today's
"found footage" horror films (inspired by the phenomenal
success of 1999's *The Blair Witch Project*) would not only
be jarringly unattractive, but virtually illegible: they most
likely would not even recognize them as a movie.

Just as film fans can readily quote the best lines of their
favorite movies, they can also easily conjure what they
looked like: Compare the sharp angles and dramatic shadows that cinematographer Gregg Toland created for *Citizen Kane* to the honey-lit wheat fields captured by Nestor
Almendros in Terrence Malick's *Days of Heaven*. Or the
luridly hot color scheme that Ernest Dickerson cooked
up for Spike Lee's *Do the Right Thing* to the alternately
washed-out and intensely hued suburban dreamscape

Edward Lachman helped create for Sofia Coppola's *The Virgin Suicides*. Think of the jittery, jumpy camera of *The Bourne Supremacy* or *The Hurt Locker*, and contrast that with how it glided in *Birdman or (the Unexpected Virtue of Ignorance)*, or kept a discreet distance from the dramatic action in *Spotlight*. Each of those films exemplifies how atmosphere, period, setting, and state of mind are established simply through where the camera is placed and how it is deployed.

During Hollywood's "Golden Age," which roughly spanned the 1930s to the 1950s, cinematographers aspired to invisibility, emphasizing clarity and simplicity for the story and glamorous lighting for the stars who were the studios' most valuable commodities. In the 1940s, as filmmakers came under the influence of German expressionism and wartime photography, lighting became more moody and self-consciously expressive. In the 1960s and 1970s, when the French New Wave and American street photography and documentary filmmaking came to the fore, camerawork became more gestural and choppy, with unapologetically grainy and imperfect film stocks.

Today, we're surrounded by cinematography—from the homemade videos and visual snippets we share on social media to gargantuan IMAX spectacles in state-of-the-art theaters. Modern movies represent every point along that wide spectrum, embodying the kind of unobtrusive classical values of the 1930s and 1940s, the restless, keyed-up *cinema verité* of the 1960s, and the edgy "found footage" aesthetic of the 1990s, brought into the twenty-first century by films containing footage captured on iPhones, surveillance cameras, and drones. Cinematography has become so ubiquitous that it's easy to forget every shot can be its own work of art.

PAINTING WITH LIGHT

How much could you see, and was it enough?

Was the lighting obvious or unobtrusive, natural or theatrical?

Was the lighting harsh or gentle? Kind to the actors or revealing every wrinkle and scar?

For a movie to work, we need to be able to see it.

At its most elemental, cinematography is "good" when the actors are lit well enough to be visible to the audience, with their best features enhanced and accentuated. In addition to the performers, all important aspects of the production should be discernible to the eye without too much strain, allowing viewers to get the visual information they need: natural background, built environment, props, costumes, and the myriad details that can convey so much about a story's setting and subtext. As we've already discussed, sometimes production details aren't necessarily meant to be noticed—but what's the point of equipping a room with carefully selected accoutrements only to submerge them with dreary, dingy lighting?

Cameras, lenses, and lighting have become so sophisticated that it's rare these days to see a really poorly shot film—a newcomer with a good eye and the right lighting can make a decent-looking movie on a smartphone. But it's possible to see films that are shot lazily, and without much distinction. The multiplexes are full of uniformly flat, brightly lit comedies that could easily be mistaken for sloppily shot network sitcoms, whether it's the latest Farrelly brothers comedy or a digitally captured action scene that has the "smooth-motion" look of a Monday Night Football game, in which everything is super-sharp, cold-looking, and free of naturally occurring blur. (The cinematographer Reed Morano is so put off by the smooth-motion aesthetic that she started a Change.org petition asking high-definition television manufacturers to stop making it the default image setting on their TVs. Reader, I signed.)

Studies have shown that movies have become increasingly darker since the 1930s, a trend that took hold as American films started to reflect the influence of German expressionist films—which used minimal, tightly focused lighting and deep shadows—and of wartime newsreels and Depression-era photography. In 1941, *Citizen Kane* reflected a breakthrough in movie grammar as director Orson Welles, designer Perry Ferguson, and Toland broke with the Golden Age tradition of glamour and realism and used deep shadows and shafts of light to illustrate the story's Shakespearean themes of hubris, isolation, and unresolved loss. The crime thrillers of the film noir period explored similarly theatrical lighting to reflect their own psychological landscape of paranoia and postwar ennui.

In expert hands, the manipulation of darkness becomes a shrewd, even painterly use of negative space. Gordon Willis, who shot the *Godfather* trilogy, became known as the "Prince of Darkness" for his willingness to photograph actors in shadow. In the famous opening sequence of *The Godfather*, for instance, Don Corleone holds court in a dimly lit study while his daughter's wedding reception transpires in a sunny garden outside, conveying his own morally bifurcated world of criminal depravity and familial devotion. Interestingly, Willis also shot *All the President's Men*, in which the almost punishingly bright

newsroom of the *Washington Post* juxtaposes with the dark
parking garage where reporter Bob Woodward receives
tips from the shadowy figure Deep Throat. Willis and director Alan J. Pakula shared a preference for shadows, and
it was the perfect aesthetic metaphor for an era steeped in
mistrust and paranoia.

Today, with precious few Gordon Willises gracing the
profession, low-light photography has become a lamen-
table cliché. Big-budget movies use it to impart sophistication and moral seriousness; independent films do so to
save on expensive lighting setups. In both cases, the same
standards apply: withholding visual information should be
done in a way that draws viewers further into the narrative, rather than forcing them to fight their way in. The
darkness, however overwhelming, needs to be balanced
and softened by moments of light, so that watching the
film never feels like swimming through a murky, incomprehensible soup.

One of the finest uses of darkness in recent years was
in the horror film *The Witch*, director Robert Eggers's tale
of English settlers in seventeenth-century America. Cinematographer Jarin Blaschke filmed every interior scene
but one in candlelight, framing the characters' faces in an
amber glow and leaving the background inky black, much
like a Rembrandt painting. Not only are the images in *The
Witch* mesmerizing to look at, but their inviting formal
beauty becomes a visual and psychological counterpoint to
the terror that grips the characters—and the audience—as
the film's story pursues an increasingly disturbing course.

Eggers and Blaschke were following in the footsteps
of filmmakers from the 1970s: armed with newly advanced camera equipment and lenses, they resolved to use
only "available light"—naturally occurring illumination

without benefit of electric bulbs—to give their work more directness, honesty, and unadorned authenticity.

Some directors, such as Terrence Malick, were just as committed to beauty as they were to the principles of available light. They and their cinematographers shoot primarily during "magic hour," the time of day just after sunrise or just before sunset when light is at its warmest and most flatteringly diffused. Magic-hour shooting accounted for the burnished look of Malick's rapturously poetic *Days of Heaven*; it's also when recent Oscar winner *The Revenant* was shot, resulting in a film that seems lit from within as it captures the harsh beauty of a western winter landscape.

It's no coincidence that *The Revenant*'s cinematographer, Emmanuel Lubezki, was also Malick's chief collaborator on such films as *The Tree of Life*, *To the Wonder*, and *Knight of Cups*. All were photographed primarily using available light. There's no denying Lubezki's artistry in working at the magic hour, but it's in danger of becoming an over-aestheticized end in itself, used more to impress an audience with the filmmaker's virtuosity and to provide some impressive stories for publicity tours than in service of the story.

One area where lighting comes most expressively into play is depictions of the past: Along with *Days of Heaven*, Robert Altman's *McCabe & Mrs. Miller* and Stanley Kubrick's eighteenth-century rogue's tale *Barry Lyndon* were hugely influential films of the 1970s. *McCabe* because of the smoky, hazy look Altman and cinematographer Vilmos Zsigmond created for a Western taking place in the Pacific Northwest; *Lyndon* because Kubrick and cinematographer John Alcott shot much of the movie in candlelight (with help from reflectors). Whereas *Lyndon*'s

carefully composed, painterly look set the gold standard
for subsequent period pictures—evoked in the productions
of Ismail Merchant and James Ivory, for example, and
countless Jane Austen adaptations—*McCabe*'s dreamy aesthetic became a visual touchstone for the entire 1970s era,
to the point where such filmmakers as Steven Soderbergh,
Paul Thomas Anderson, and Sofia Coppola went for the
same smeary looks when setting movies in that period.

Soft edges and filmy, gentle light have become so syn-
onymous with historical pictures that when a filmmaker
breaks with that tradition, it represents an unusually audacious move: it's a sign of artistic vision when directors like
John Sayles (*Matewan*) or Kelly Reichardt (*Meek's Cutoff*)
eschew softness and instead deliver historical dramas that
are startlingly sharp and realistic in their tone and visual
values. When he made the Edwardian-era parlor drama
Gosford Park, Altman consciously sought to break out of
the neat, precise visual formula of most period pictures and
make something looser and more spontaneous—putting
the audience on notice that they would have to pay attention or risk missing something. For his part, when Steven
Spielberg made the World War II drama *War Horse*, he and
cinematographer Janusz Kamiński purposefully gave the
movie the polished, patently theatrical look of a Golden
Age epic à la *Gone with the Wind*—a refreshing choice that
was also motivated by the source material's fable-like romanticism and mythic symbolism. (One effect Spielberg
and Kamiński reproduced was key lighting, a classical
technique that used particular, tightly focused lights for
a film's stars, illuminating them in a glamorous, almost
beatific glow.)

Similarly, Soderbergh has embraced a mercurial approach to lighting his movies, hewing to conservative,

classical values in mainstream blockbusters such as *Erin Brockovich* and the *Ocean's Eleven* franchise but pursuing a looser, less exacting aesthetic approach in his lower-budget films. Even when working on a slightly bigger canvas—as with *The Informant!* or *Contagion*, for example—he's been willing to break the rules of classical lighting, allowing his stars to disappear into backlit shadow, or "blowing out" the image with bursts of light coming through windows or other sources. In the hands of an assured filmmaker, even lighting "mistakes" can enhance a film's mood, sense of physical atmosphere, and overarching story.

THE CURSE OF THE MEDIUM CLOSE-UP

Where was the camera and why was it there?

How did the camera's position affect the emotional impact of certain scenes?

If the camera moved, why did it move?

Once the lights are set, the cinematographer's most crucial decisions—always reached in close collaboration with or at the instruction of the director—involve where to place the camera and whether and when to move it. A telltale sign of a student filmmaker is a camera that can't sit still: either it's roving and wandering around the frame like an errant garden hose, or it's capturing the action from some "interesting," often distractingly arty, narratively nonsensical angle.

Camera placement is a subtle art, but one that has an enormous psychological influence on individual scenes and the movie as a whole. Some of the most exhilarating films I've seen are ones in which the camera barely budged—the documentaries *Visitors*, Godfrey Reggio's enigmatic portrait of humanity and its relationship to the environment, and *Maidan*, about the 2013 demonstrations in Ukraine, are two recent and awe-inspiring examples, as is the audacious feature-length video portrait of David Beckham that Sam Taylor-Wood created for London's National Portrait Gallery, for which she trained a camera on the soccer star as he took a nap after an exhausting training session. Inspired by such experimental films as *Empire* and *Sleep*, by Andy Warhol, these films are simultaneously painterly, sculptural, and anything but inert, creating an impressive amount of dynamism and tension simply by what they capture in their implacably unmoving frames.

Nowadays, we rarely see the kind of ambition with which directors used to approach camera placement. Consider the sad fate of the "establishing shot." In the era of big-screen epics, directors such as David Lean turned occasionally to these breathtakingly expansive shots of landscapes to tell the audience where the story was taking place and prepare them for the aesthetic and psychological experience to come (think *Lawrence of Arabia* or *Dr. Zhivago*). "Sit back," they seemed to say. "You're in for a thrilling, larger-than-life journey to a time and place completely beyond your puny daily lives."

Today, aware that their movie will as likely be seen on an iPhone as on a big screen, filmmakers are content with shooting "coverage," which usually consists of a perfunctory establishing shot of each scene's physical setting, and a series of medium close-ups (showing the actors from the chest up) and close-ups, toggling between those two shots with workmanlike regularity. Efficient, utilitarian, and supremely unimaginative, this is the kind of filmmaking that Alfred Hitchcock famously dismissed as "pictures of people talking," and it's become the plague of mainstream filmmaking at its most generic, bland, and dumbed-down. What's more, it has locked movies into a kind of artificial pictorial and editing structure that feels boring and synthetic, keeping viewers from entering a scene rather than simply watching it ping-pong along. The scourge of the medium close-up—also known as MCU—has resulted in a film rhetoric that's as emotionally unsatisfying as it is visually inert. Recounting an ongoing argument she has with cinematographers, the production designer Jeannine Oppewall told me, "I'll say, 'If you tell me one more time that it's only two actors and their heads sitting against one wall, I will meet you in the parking lot with two grip stands and a roll of black Duvetyne [matte fabric used in photographic backgrounds], and you can have good hair and makeup, good costumes, good dialogue and see how many people go to that movie.' We don't shoot theater in the round. People go to films at least partially for the pleasure of seeing other people in environments. They don't go to see them talking against walls."

Throughout *Citizen Kane*, Toland's camera seems to be crouching, looking up at the title character Charles Foster Kane and giving him an imposing monumentality. This technique is called a "Dutch angle," and Toland used it to convey not only Kane's growing power, but his increasingly distorted view of himself. By contrast, the director Yasujirō Ozu used low angles contemplatively, capturing Japanese daily life in the 1940s and 1950s at eye-level with his characters as they moved through low, horizontal planes. In *Do the Right Thing*, Spike Lee and cinematographer Ernest Dickerson combined low angles with dramatic camera movement to capture the simmering tensions of a torrid summer day in 1980s Brooklyn. In contrast to these films, the self-consciously dramatic camera angles used in the films *Catwoman*, *Battlefield Earth*, and *Batman & Robin* existed simply to distract viewers from their dreary stories, bad dialogue, and misbegotten special effects.

In addition to stylized camera angles, Spike Lee almost always includes a "double-dolly" camera movement that has become his signature, wherein an actor stands on one dolly, the camera on another, and one moves toward the other in a strange, dreamlike movement wherein the actor seems to float. Lee used the technique in *25th Hour* to capture Anna Paquin's character's distorted perception as she walks through a throbbing nightclub; in *Malcolm X*, he used it when the title character, portrayed by Denzel Washington, is on his way to meet his fate at the Audubon Ballroom, where he will be shot and killed. Although critics and viewers disagree about the effectiveness of these flourishes—for some, it's a gratuitously showy gesture, whereas for others it's a bravura artistic touch—the double-dolly shot is a matter of principle for a director who constantly seeks to infuse expressiveness and cinematic value into every one of his scenes. "I want vibrant energy, movement, and life in my films," Lee has explained. "Shooting any other way, for me, is too much like television."

Like Lee, many filmmakers liken a static camera to a death knell: they want their camera to *move*, whether on top of a dolly, attached to a human operator, or on a swooping crane.

The effect can be useful for an audience: in large crowds Altman frequently instructed his camera operators to pan—move the camera laterally across the scene—and zoom—quickly coming in for a close-up—to help the audience impose order on what would otherwise be an arbitrary collection of faces and voices. David O. Russell habitually works with a Steadicam, a portable camera the operator wears on a harness, so that the camera can weave within and around his shots, giving his scenes a gliding, improvisatory feel. The camera style is in keeping with his practice of filming very few takes, and standing close to the actors to give them cues as opportunities arise. "I'm always next to the camera," he told me, adding that he tends to favor "a big foreground [and a] deep background." More important, he said, "I'm not going to stop the camera. We're going to keep swimming in the take, and maybe halfway through when we're all swimming in this take, it's no longer 'bedroom perfect,' as De Niro calls it."

And, let's face it, a moving camera can also be flat-out thrilling: the scene following Ray Liotta and Lorraine Bracco through the back hallways and kitchen of the Copacabana in *GoodFellas* to the accompaniment of the Crystals' "Then He Kissed Me" is exhilarating to watch. It is also a textbook example of the tracking shot, whereby the camera travels alongside or behind the characters—in this case by way of a Steadicam, although tracking shots are sometimes accomplished by mounting a camera on a dolly and pushing it along a set of tracks.

But the *GoodFellas* tracking shot isn't just showing off: it viscerally captures the sense of discovery, seduction, and vicarious power felt by Bracco's character. In *The Wrestler* and *Black Swan*, director Darren Aronofsky had his cinematographers closely follow the films' protagonists from behind, the "subjective camera" inviting the audience to occupy, as much as possible, each actor's intimate physical and psychological space.

Some of the most intoxicating moments at the movies come by way of these bravura moments: the camera swooping down to land on a key in Ingrid Bergman's hand in *Notorious*; the opening image of Welles's *Touch of Evil*, moving up and out over a teeming Tijuana street; the pendular panorama view of the evacuation of Dunkirk in the middle of *Atonement*; Alexander Sokurov's *Russian Ark*, shot in one long, magnificent take in St. Petersburg's Hermitage Museum; the complicated forward zoom, combined with a reversing dolly shot, that so vividly captured James Stewart's character's fear of falling in Hitchcock's *Vertigo*. In *The Shining*, John Alcott's restlessly moving camera drifted through the Overlook Hotel's padded corridors and gigantic rooms in long, unbroken takes that enhanced the psychological power of the production design—a feeling that would have been destroyed by conventionally shorter, choppier shots.

Each of these examples points to camera movement that imparts a sense of energy, dramatic scope, historical sweep, and taut, fatalistic urgency. They are also admired by critics and among filmmakers for their go-for-broke ambition and because the degree of difficulty is so high—not only for the actors getting all their dialogue and movement right on one take, but also for the expertise involved in hiding shadows, reflections, microphones, and other technical appurtenances required for the shot.

Yet there's a crucial difference between a genuinely bold choice and a stunt. Whatever visual flourishes a movie possesses should never distract or detract from the story and characters at hand. The next time you're watching two people converse as the camera circles them in a wild tarantella of movement, ask yourself what it's accomplishing, other than distracting you from the fact that you're watching two people talking.

After tracking shots, the most common way filmmakers move the camera is by shaking it (or allowing it to shake), a gesture that harks back to the *cinema verité* documentary movement in America in the 1960s. Also known as "observational" or "direct" cinema, *verité* filmmaking did away with such conventions as staged interviews and voiceover narration, instead capturing—or seeming to capture—events as they happened, like a proverbial fly on the wall. At that time, lighter, more portable sound and photographic equipment meant operators could take their camera off the tripod and walk alongside their subjects; the result was footage that was anything but smooth, symbolizing the era's desire for authenticity and spontaneity, and its mistrust of artifice. The camerawork in the brilliant 1966 drama *The Battle of Algiers*, about the Algerian revolution, was so convincing that director Gillo Pontecorvo added a disclaimer at the beginning of the movie assuring audiences it was a staged drama, not a documentary.

An early masterpiece of the *verité* aesthetic was *Medium Cool*, a drama set amid the 1968 Democratic National Convention in Chicago, directed by cinematographer Haskell Wexler. Interweaving a fictional story with the actual violent events that unfolded during the convention, Wexler took his camera into the streets, picking up shots of real-life people and seamlessly integrating them into a story that felt urgently of its time. John Cassavetes and, later, the Danish filmmaking group known as Dogme 95 used handheld cameras in domestic contexts, conveying anxieties and pent-up passions through jarring movements and extremely tight, agonizingly intimate close-ups.

More recently, such directors as Paul Greengrass and Kathryn Bigelow, as well as the makers of *The Blair Witch Project* and its "found footage" horror-film successors, have used the jittery grammar of *verité* in their films: the cinematographer best known for handheld style is Barry Ackroyd, who shot Greengrass's masterful 9/11 drama *United 93* and *Jason Bourne*, as well as Bigelow's *The Hurt Locker*. Janusz Kamiński utilized the technique in Steven Spielberg's *Saving Private Ryan*—the opening sequence of the invasion of Normandy resembles raw, chaotic newsreel footage, as Kamiński noted—and in *Schindler's List*, where the filmmakers sought a feeling of stealing shots rather than staging dramatic action.

Not surprisingly, jittery, unstable camerawork has invaded the action-film space, creating a new visual vernacular that connects with even a viewer watching on a laptop. One can argue that the technique makes sense for the *Bourne* movies and *The Hurt Locker*, which sought to capture the disorientation of amnesia and the chaos of war, respectively. In the hands of more generic practitioners, though, the herky-jerky camera has become a cliché, a shorthand for "edginess" and authenticity that is otherwise lacking in trite, predictable scripts. When Michael Bay shakes the camera in *The Rock*, the effect is style for its own sake, resulting in a visual experience that is incoherent, meaningless, and, frankly, incredibly dull. The camera is our way into the world being depicted on-screen. The question is whether the filmmakers are using it to bring us closer in, to keep us at arm's length, or to keep us out entirely.

THE GOLDEN RATIO

What shape was the frame? How did it affect what I did and didn't see?

What was in the frame? Was it crowded or sparse, ar-
tificially composed or offhandedly jumbled together?
Where were the characters in relation to one another?

Was everything in the frame in focus, from foreground
to background? Or were foreground figures in sharp
relief, with the background blurrier?

Painters work with the concept of the Golden Ratio,
whereby the objects represented on a canvas adhere to a
mathematically precise formula; movies have similar rules,
even if they're obeyed purely by instinct on the part of
directors and cinematographers. The best filmmakers
know exactly where to put the actors in relation to the
background to achieve the most pleasing and meaningful
image.

At its most basic, cinematic grammar is built around
three shots: the long shot, the medium shot, and the
close-up. Long shots, also known as wide shots, encom-
pass a great deal of physical space: if people are featured
in them, they are often subservient to their physical sur-
roundings, whether natural or man-made. Because they
convey so much information about time and place, long
shots are most often used as establishing shots, as discussed
above. But they can be used to great counterintuitive effect, such as in the Hitchcock thriller *Torn Curtain*, when
a crucial scene of Paul Newman revealing a secret (that
the audience already knows) to Julie Andrews is filmed
entirely in a silent long shot rather than the expected series
of talky close-ups.

Medium shots approximate how most people move
through the world and encounter and converse with others:

the camera captures people from a few feet away, so that they're visible from the waist up (medium shots are not to be confused with the aforementioned medium close-ups, which capture their subjects from the chest up). In the hands of sensitive artists like Yasujirō Ozu and François Truffaut, the medium shot can be a mode of compassionate tact or ironic detachment; more often, unfortunately, it's simply the easiest and laziest way to film performances at their most banal, bland, and TV-ready.

Close-ups bring the camera in so that it's just inches away from the subject's face. An entire book could be written on the changing significance of the close-up in film rhetoric: when deployed on behalf of Golden Age stars like Greta Garbo, Marlene Dietrich, Clark Gable, and Bette Davis, it served as a conduit for Hollywood glamour and audience desire. In films like 1928's *The Passion of Joan of Arc*, starring Maria Falconetti, and forty years later in the works of Ingmar Bergman, John Cassavetes, and their successors, the close-up was a deeply psychological cinematic gesture, often starkly, even uncomfortably, revealing of characters' vulnerabilities and flaws.

Today, the close-up has become the go-to shot in films that their makers know will have only a short life on the big screen before ending up on someone's phone. Although filmmakers must adapt to emerging technologies, the all-close-up-all-the-time formula has, in my opinion, stripped one of film's most potent elements of its aesthetic and emotional power. Happily, there are some filmmakers left who understand the aesthetic and emotional power of the close-up, whether it's David Lynch's unsettling use of tight shots to get inside his characters' heads, or Martin Scorsese zooming frantically into a close-up of Henry Hill in *GoodFellas* precisely at the moment that his life spirals out of control (it's one of the very rare close-ups in the entire film, which was an almost anthropological survey of a familial, tightly knit community).

Far rarer are movies that dare to pull the camera back and allow actors to work together in a scene, using their entire bodies to express physical and emotional relationships. The 2016 drama *Spotlight*, about a group of journalists investigating sexual abuse within the Catholic Church, pulled the camera back to a daring degree, conveying volumes of information to the audience about the reporters' environment and how they relate to one another within it. "I respect the spaces these people were playing in," director Tom McCarthy explained when *Spotlight* came out, "and I let that guide us."

Both McCarthy and cinematographer Masanobu Takayanagi felt that the scheme of close-up/close-up/medium shot would dilute the verisimilitude of the professional world on-screen and fail to capture the ensemble chemistry of the actors that provided much of the film's narrative tension and drive. "After a while, our shorthand became really clear," McCarthy said of his collaboration with Takayanagi. "We realized, these [actors] were so dialed in, we could just place the camera and let them talk, and then we would just punch in [for a close-up] when we needed it."

Giving the actors enough space is hugely important in dance musicals, where part of the pleasure lies in watching two people move together in perfect synch: compare such Astaire-and-Rogers classics as *Top Hat* and *The Gay Divorcee* to contemporary, close-up-dominated fare like *Chicago* and *Dreamgirls*, and consider how far the musical has fallen in terms of stately visual language. As well as being shot too tightly, modern-day musicals are overedited, too often chopping up dance numbers into incomprehensible, unattractive pieces.

Physical movement can be just as expressive and enjoyable in narrative films with no music. The arrangement of actors within the theatrical space of a film—also called staging—is on the verge of being a lost art, but when it's done well, it's a thing of rare beauty: witness the nearly silent scene at the end of *Big Night*, wherein Stanley Tucci and Tony Shalhoub quietly fix breakfast together, their bodies circling one another in the cramped space with balletic grace and anticipation of each other's moves, clearly demonstrating their easy familiarity and brotherly intimacy.

In addition to using staging to frame the action, filmmakers can adjust the aspect ratio, which describes the relative relationship of width-to-height of the image. Most American films today are filmed with the widescreen aspect ratio of 1.85-to-1, which means that they're almost twice as wide as they are high. A number of filmmakers recently have used widescreen formats of 2.35-to-1 and wider for their films, including Christopher Nolan (*Inception, Interstellar,* and the *Dark Knight* films), Quentin Tarantino (*The Hateful Eight*), Paul Thomas Anderson (*The Master*), Alejandro González Iñárritu (*The Revenant*), and Barry Jenkins (*Moonlight*).

The visually rich settings of Nolan's films and the panoramic vistas of epics like *The Revenant* make widescreen the natural choice for those films, but widescreen isn't just for scenery. Indeed, it's far more interesting as a way to explore tension and movement within the frame, and to establish a detailed sense of the film's environment. *The Master* might have been "a little chamber drama," as Anderson called it when I interviewed him about the film.

But his decision to shoot it on 65 mm film—a large format reminiscent of lush 1950s movies like *North by Northwest* and *Vertigo*—lent it period-specific tones and textures (the movies we think of as conventional, mainstream films were mostly shot on 35 mm stock).

A wide frame has vastly different impact, depending on how the director stages the action within it. Lynne Ramsay made the counterintuitive choice to film the domestic psychological thriller *We Need to Talk About Kevin* in extra-wide-screen, a format that the film's star, Tilda Swinton, observed is "a battle frame, a Western frame, face-off, *epic*." The choice turned out to be appropriate, not only for the subject matter—which was a war raging within a family—but because it gave the actors time to do long takes: rather than a rote collection of shots/reverse shots, the film wound up being a far more effective assembly of wide shots that gathered momentum and tension as the movie went on.

For his 2016 film *Moonlight*, director Barry Jenkins and cinematographer James Laxton chose the same widescreen format. "We wanted to shoot 2.35, but not like a Western," Jenkins explained. Instead he chose to film *Moonlight*'s protagonist—a young man grappling with his sexual identity amid poverty, crime, and narrow codes of masculinity—as almost lost within the engulfing tropical atmosphere of Miami, where the story was set and where the filmmaker himself grew up.

"My memory of Miami is of this very wide, open, spacious place with really deep greens and really big, bright light and blue skies," Jenkins said. "And yet I also felt kind of isolated and hemmed in." To capture that sense of isolation within the wide frame, Jenkins noted, he "wanted him to have a lot of space that he chooses not to use. . . .

He can go wherever he wants, and yet he chooses to stay hemmed in to himself."

Kelly Reichardt filmed her 2010 Western *Meek's Cut-off* using the nearly square 1.33-to-1 aspect ratio, reminiscent of the boxy look of early Westerns by Anthony Mann and Howard Hawks, partly as an homage to her forebears, partly to capture the perspective of her protagonists, settlers who couldn't see more than a few hundred feet ahead of them at any one time. ("In widescreen, there's tomorrow and there's yesterday," Reichardt explained after the film's premiere at Sundance. "The square really just [helps keep us] in the moment with them.")

The Hungarian filmmaker László Nemes used a similarly tight frame, 1.37-to-1, for *Son of Saul*, a harrowing first-person drama set in Auschwitz that also benefited from Mátyás Erdély's urgent handheld camera work. For Nemes, the framing was not just an aesthetic choice but a moral one: in keeping the horrors of the concentration camp just out of view, Nemes demanded that viewers use their own imaginations to conjure unspeakable violence, rather than reenact "images that can't be reconstructed and shouldn't be touched or manipulated." The most playful use of aspect ratio in recent years was in Xavier Dolan's domestic drama *Mommy*, which was mostly filmed in a claustrophobically tight 1-to-1 aspect ratio—until the main character literally reached out and seemed to push the sides of the image apart to widen the film's frame and his own blinkered horizons.

One of the most important decisions directors and cinematographers make together is which lenses to use. Wide lenses create a shallow depth of field, meaning the actors in the foreground are the only elements in focus, with the background fading into varying degrees of blurriness;

narrow or "long" lenses create a far deeper depth of field, rendering everything in the image sharp and clearly defined. The most famous use of long lenses was Gregg Toland's magnificent deep-focus shots in *Citizen Kane*, in which the rise and fall of Charles Foster Kane are communicated not only by his behavior but also by the sharply defined physical world over which he seeks more and more control. (Although *Citizen Kane* is the Welles movie most associated with the expressive use of deep focus, I also admire cinematographer Stanley Cortez's masterful work in *The Magnificent Ambersons*, in which a mansion in turn-of-the-century America becomes a constantly evolving character in itself.) Similarly, Alan J. Pakula and Gordon Willis used deep focus to stunning effect in *All the President's Men*. Using an enhancement called a split diopter, which can split the frame through the middle either horizontally or vertically, Pakula and Willis kept everything in focus during particular shots, showing Woodward and Bernstein working the phones in the foreground of the scene, while the *Post* newsroom bustled and moved with sharply delineated detail in the background, rather than fading into visually mushy nothingness.

For *The Social Network*, David Fincher and his longtime cinematographer, Jeff Cronenweth, used a shallow depth of field, keeping the main characters and their rapid-fire repartee front and center in the shot and within the viewer's attention span. In *12 Angry Men*, Sidney Lumet and cinematographer Boris Kaufman used progressively longer lenses to create a deeper and deeper depth of field, which, together with moving the camera from a height above the characters' eye-level to below it, created a sense of compression and mounting tension. For the final shot of the film, when the jurors finally leave the courthouse, the filmmakers chose a wide-angle lens, Lumet later explained, "to give us all air, to let us finally breathe, after two increasingly confined hours."

It's almost impossible for lay viewers to be able to identify whether a filmmaker used a 40 mm lens on a movie or a 17 mm lens, but we can notice when different lenses have been used for expressive, rather than realistic, ends: The Coen brothers have often used wide, "fish-eye" lenses for absurdist effect (see *Raising Arizona*), as has Terry Gilliam, most notably in the surrealistic futuristic satire *Brazil*. Wes Anderson's signature is using widescreen lenses in a conventional aspect ratio, resulting in frames with slightly rounded, curved edges—a pictorial technique that lends an extra air of dollhouse-like artifice to his carefully composed, almost neurotically symmetrical set designs. Lenses also allow cinematographers to expand the range and palette of otherwise sterile digital cameras, which have historically tended to produce slick, cold, un-textured images—from the late Harris Savides's work with Sofia Coppola on *Somewhere* and *The Bling Ring* to the vintage lenses that gave *The Witch* its lambent, antique quality. Like the most philosophical questions in life, often how we perceive a film depends on how it is framed.

FILM AS MATERIAL OBJECT

Were the colors deep, bright, washed-out, barely there?

If the film was in black and white, were the tones starkly contrasting, or monochromatic?

Did the images look slick or handmade? Grainy or smooth?

The best movies have their own temperature and texture; they feel almost palpable.

Is the film you're watching in black and white, or color? If it's in black and white, is it a velvety chiaroscuro or a harsher, edgier contrast? If it's in color, are its tones supersaturated, rich and dense, or washed-out, pastel and monochrome? Are the images pretty or unpleasant? Realistic or dreamlike? Similar to paintings or a rough, shot-from-the-hip documentary? None of these options is definitively better than another; it all depends on the demands of the movie's setting and story. A contemporary portrait of a New York City heroin addict may seek to eschew pretty colors and flattering lighting to convey immediacy and authenticity; another filmmaker might choose to tell the story of transgender sex workers in Los Angeles with bright, sunny hues to impart a sense of optimism and unbridled brio. Both are entirely legitimate, although my personal preference is for filmmakers to approach color counterintuitively—introducing vibrancy and cheerfulness to an otherwise hopeless scenario, for example, or approaching a historical drama not with the usual burnished-gold palette but a tougher sense of realism.

The first time I became aware of cinematography as a discipline—with its own material and aesthetic values—was in the 1980s, when I was living in New York and the city was still blessed with theaters that specialized in playing classic repertory films. It was at just such a retrospective that I first saw *Sweet Smell of Success*, Alexander Mackendrick's 1957 poisonous portrait of sleazy tabloid ethics.

As a writer, I was naturally drawn to the film's fast, elaborately quippy dialogue (cowritten by Clifford Odets), given musical emphasis by Elmer Bernstein's jazz-infused score. But I was just as entranced by the look of the film, which took place completely at night in Manhattan clubs and rainy streets: filmed in black and white, it was both shimmeringly glamorous and seedy, resembling a Weegee photograph come to life, its interiors glowing with swank allure and a sickening sense of corruption. A few years later, when I rewatched Scorsese's boxing drama *Raging Bull*, I immediately recognized *Sweet Smell*'s influence on Michael Chapman's gleaming, operatically scaled black-and-white photography.

Sweet Smell of Success was filmed by one of the great cinematographers, James Wong Howe (nicknamed "Low-Key Howe" for his talent with shadow-heavy lighting), who literally painted the film's nightclub sets with oil to get that shiny effect that was so sleazy and seductive. Around the same time I saw this film, Spike Lee released *She's Gotta Have It* and Jim Jarmusch released *Stranger Than Paradise*. Both were filmed in black and white, but they had dramatically divergent goals and effects. Lee and his cinematographer, Ernest Dickerson, used the limited palette to imitate documentary work, with his actors directly addressing the camera. Jarmusch and cinematographer Tom DiCillo, meanwhile, created a series of static, stylized shots in three different locations, playing up their vignette-like, absurdist humor by fading to black after each "chapter" to create what Jarmusch described as a cinematic photo album "about America, as seen through the eyes of 'strangers.'"

Filmmakers often use black and white to evoke the era of their films—witness *The Last Picture Show* (1971), *Schindler's List* (1993), Soderbergh's 2006 drama *The Good German* (filmed in period-accurate 1.66-to-1 aspect ratio for good measure), and *The Artist* (2011). They can also achieve this same effect by dramatically desaturating a full-color movie: the Coen brothers, working with cinematographer

Roger Deakins, digitally manipulated the palettes of *O Brother, Where Art Thou?* and *Inside Llewyn Davis* to evoke sepia-toned Depression-era photographs and wintry, 1960s-era drabness, respectively. One of the finest uses of black-and-white photography recently was Phedon Papamichael's work on *Nebraska*, a seriocomic father-son road trip that could easily have slipped into caricature of its exurban midwestern characters. Instead, Papamichael and director Alexander Payne imbued the people and land-scapes of *Nebraska* with dignity, poignancy, and monumentality worthy of an Ansel Adams photograph (an effect heightened, by the way, by the film's widescreen aspect ratio). Whether in the name of nostalgia or stylized realism, black-and-white cinematography harks back to cinema's past and, in a subtle way, evokes a kind of heightened state in the viewer, who instinctively understands we're being invited into a space that's a few steps removed from life as we know it.

Just as *Sweet Smell of Success* awakened my interest in black-and-white cinematography, the work of the codirectors Michael Powell and Emeric Pressburger (known collectively as The Archers) showed me how bright, vibrant color can be so important to a film that it takes on the dimension of another character. Powell and Pressburger shot 1948's *The Red Shoes* in Technicolor, a then-novel film stock that emphasized jewel-like reds and greens. The team's cinematographer, Jack Cardiff, was a master at using Technicolor's brightness to create images of striking beauty that bordered on the lurid. Rather than detract from the film's fable-like story, the palette harmonized and enhanced the exaggerated production design and melodramatic acting techniques that were key elements of Powell and Pressburger's "house style," and it all worked together to create an almost hallucinatory experience for the viewer.

Following in Powell and Pressburger's footsteps, such directors as Spike Lee, Oliver Stone, Pedro Almodóvar, Wes Anderson, and Todd Haynes have all used color to dramatic aesthetic and psychological effect. Although they've since embraced digital photography, Lee and Stone have often used a type of film—called reversal stock—whose chemical properties result in a supersaturated, almost surreal look. (A breakthrough use of reversal stock can be seen in the 1998 dramas *Belly* and *He Got Game*, both of which cinematographer Malik Sayeed filmed using reversal film with visually stunning results.) In Lee's earlier film, *Do the Right Thing*, cinematographer Ernest Dickerson (working closely with production designer Wynn Thomas) drenched the Brooklyn location in hot yellows and reds to reflect the sweltering summer day over which the movie takes place; for *Malcolm X*, he created a three-part color scheme to capture the distinct chapters of the title character's life: bright, theatrical colors for the exuberant early years; a crisp, classical palette for his coming-of-age as a political figure; and more impressionistic tones for his spiritual awakening.

Sayeed and Dickerson are part of a vanguard that has its roots at Howard University, where such groundbreaking cinematographers as Arthur Jafa (*Daughters of the Dust*, *Crooklyn*) and, more recently, Bradford Young studied photography and film. Since 2011 when I saw Young's work for the first time—on Andrew Dosunmu's urban drama *Restless City*—he has become my favorite cinematographer working today, mostly because of his sensitivity to color and texture, whether in Dosunmu's vibrantly saturated portraits of the African diaspora in New York, the poetic realism of Ava DuVernay's *Middle of Nowhere* and *Selma*, or the woody, archaic look of David Lowery's *Ain't Them Bodies Saints*.

Along with color, film images also have texture—or what is commonly called "grain." Photochemical film stock, the photographic medium all movies were shot on before the advent of digital photography, possessed natural grain, which cinematographers could enhance or hide through different processing techniques. For example, when Altman told Vilmos Zsigmond that he wanted *McCabe & Mrs. Miller* to resemble a faded antique photograph, Zsigmond offered to "flash" or "fog" the negative, exposing it to tiny amounts of light before developing it, to reach the desired effect. The result was the grainy, hazy look that is still a visual touchstone for 1970s moviemaking, copied by such present-day directors as Sofia Coppola and Paul Thomas Anderson to evoke the era.

A great tutorial in grain—and in cinematography in general—is Stone's *JFK*, shot by Robert Richardson in a multitude of film stocks, including the 8 mm home-movie stock used by Dallas businessman Abraham Zapruder to accidentally film John F. Kennedy's assassination. The result resembles a dizzyingly dynamic collage of periods, colors, period looks, and textures, appropriately reflecting the kaleidoscopic point of view of what Stone intended to be a "countermyth" to the official story of the assassination. Although critics came out in force to excoriate the director for trafficking in unhinged—and harmful—conspiracy theories, I've always contended that Richardson's cinematography emphasized that *JFK* was not a documentary-like representation of reality, but an explicitly constructed, albeit wildly expressionistic, artifact of one man's febrile imagination.

To my eye, grain has always provided an extra richness and dimension to film, emphasizing its qualities as a
material medium that, in the hands of gifted directors and
cinematographers, can be every bit as expressive as paint,
stone, or fabric in the hands of artists and designers.

That depth—that *stuff*ness—went missing as photochemical processes became more sophisticated, and
looked like it might disappear entirely with the onset
of digital photography, which initially produced images
with the pixelated and "wavy" look many people compared to cheap video and daytime soap operas. Although
Seabiscuit was photographed on 35 mm film, it was con-
verted to a digital file—called a "digital intermediate"—
for the purposes of cleaning up the image before it was
turned back into a film print for theatrical exhibition; to
many viewers, the final product still looked more like
a DVD than a rich, textured film. The limits of digital were particularly evident in Michael Mann's 2009
gangster picture *Public Enemies*, which was filmed with
high-definition digital cameras in order, Mann said at the
time, to make the story feel new and immediate. Video
"looks like reality," he told the *Guardian*'s John Patterson.
"It has a verité surface to it. Film has this liquid kind of
surface, feels like something made up." Instead, it looked
cheap and almost amateurish, with nighttime action
scenes evincing the "hyper-real" look of videotaped rehearsals, and the rest of the movie resembling a daytime
soap opera. I had a similar problem with Peter Jackson's
Hobbit movies, which were shot using a high frame rate—
meaning the images were captured twice as fast as they
would be on traditional film. It was supposed to result in
heightened vividness and realism, but wound up looking
cheap and unforgivably dull. (The audience's tolerance

for high-frame-rate photography was tested in 2016 by *Billy Lynn's Long Halftime Walk*, which Ang Lee filmed at a rate of 120 frames per second; viewers soundly rejected the movie.)

Although initially digital cinematography had a limited dynamic range in color, saturation, brightness, and contrast, the format has made enormous advances in recent years with the advent of cameras and lenses that do away with distracting "video-y" artifacts and with the help of careful and creative postproduction work, especially in color timing, which adjusts the colors throughout a film and makes them consistent. I learned of the new importance of color timers from director Nicolas Winding Refn, whose moody thriller *Drive* looked so sophisticated and supersaturated that I assumed it was photographed on some hyper-vivid film stock. The entire movie was shot digitally, he told me, adding that the fact that it looked like a "movie-movie" was attributable to postproduction tweaking that made otherwise flat colors lusher, more concentrated and consistent. "The color timer is the new gaffer," he said with a laugh, referring to the head electrician on traditional movie productions.

Directors such as Refn, David Fincher, Coppola, and Iñárritu—working with such cinematographers as the late Harris Savides and Oscar winner Emmanuel Lubezki—have managed to produce a remarkably subtle range, translucence, and grain structure in the digital medium. For Coppola's *Somewhere*, Savides found 1970s-era camera lenses and used them with digital cameras to create the film's soft, hazy LA look. The filmmaker J. J. Abrams often adds a digital "lens flare"—a filmmaking artifact of light bouncing off the camera's glass surface—to give his digitally captured movies a reassuringly "classic" vibe.

When Barry Jenkins and James Laxton filmed *Moonlight*, they used a processing tool called a lookup table, or LUT, to give the digitally captured drama the look and feel of 35 mm film. Each section of the three-part film has its own distinctive look, although the differences might be indistinguishable to the untrained eye. "You can usually tell in the whites and the blacks," Jenkins told me. "The way a white cloud looks in Story Two is very different from the way a cloud looks in Story One."

For all the progress in technology, however, alert viewers will still notice aesthetic lapses in digital photography, especially in low-light situations with lots of movement, like nighttime action scenes. If they look "video-y," it's usually because the director and cinematographer chose the wrong equipment and shutter speeds, or didn't light the sequence carefully enough. In recent years, I've been distracted by this effect in everything from *Date Night* to *Gangster Squad*—movies that looked fine until those smooth-motion nighttime scenes. I've learned to blame not digital cinematography for this hiccup, but filmmakers who don't have the time or patience to light their scenes correctly.

There are still directors who have stated their refusal to work in digital, including Nolan, Abrams, and Tarantino. As much as I admire their advocacy of a medium that's still superior from an archival standpoint (whereas digital images are subject to the obsolescence of constantly "upgrading" computer playback technology, all you need to show an old-fashioned film is a reel, a light source, and a bedsheet), there have been enough advances in lenses and postproduction processing that the film-versus-digital argument is, by now, almost entirely moot. The goal, for filmmakers and filmgoers alike, is to preserve what's most tactile, expressive, and enveloping in a medium that, at its best, is felt as much as it's seen.

DIGITAL HYPE

Did I just take a trip to Uncanny Valley?

Some of the greatest strides in digital photography have been in action-adventures that combine computer-generated animation and live action. The trend took hold with the final two movies of the *Matrix* trilogy, made enormous leaps in films like *Avatar* and the *Lord of the Rings* series, and reached new artistic heights in *Life of Pi* and *The Jungle Book*. Although publicity for these films often revolved around their technical sophistication and state-of-the-art computer graphics, viewers should judge them by the same criteria as any movie: in terms of story, character, visual dynamism, and overall coherence. As technologically groundbreaking as *Avatar* was, no one thought its storyline was particularly engrossing and, as is the case with many of James Cameron's scripts, the dialogue was often painfully on-the-nose; similarly, I found the *Lord of the Rings* films, for all their visual spectacle, to be movies that were ultimately just characters walking and talking.

By the time *Life of Pi* won four Oscars in 2013—including for best cinematography—virtual filmmaking had become so sophisticated that audiences could truly believe a boy spent two hours on a tiny boat with a tiger, with no one catching on to the fact that the tiger was almost entirely animated. It was a far cry from such films as *The Polar Express*, 2009's *A Christmas Carol*, and *The Last Airbender*, all of which plunged their characters into an uncomfortable netherworld between animation and live action, resulting in an eerie, not-quite-human look that industry professionals call the "uncanny valley."

The advent of virtual cinematography has had enormous impact on camera movement as well. With its potential to send the viewer down any number of visual rabbit holes, with a similarly unlimited number of points of view, virtual cinematography naturally borrowed ideas from another computerized world: video games. Increasingly, action–adventure movies are borrowing the perspective of first-person shooter games, putting viewers "behind the wheel" as the camera moves through a series of episodic vignettes and bombastic set pieces. An early—and distressing—example of the influence of video games on films was the Wachowski siblings' adaptation of the vintage cartoon *Speed Racer*, a chaotic, hyperkinetic mishmash that created a world of punishing sound, color, and light but very little depth or dimension. More recently—and far more interestingly—such dystopian thrillers as *District 9*, *Attack the Block*, and *High-Rise* have borrowed video-game perspectives to maneuver viewers through their single self-contained locations, much the way gamers navigate the "unified spaces" of their virtual worlds. Since the days of *Speed Racer*, the video-game aesthetic has taken firm hold as a visual standard that, to the eyes of young people and succeeding generations, will surely look progressively less strange, or even not be noticeable at all.

3-D: IS IT WORTH IT?

Was 3-D used as a stunt? Or to increase visual depth and dimension?

Could depth and dimension have been created by wise production design and adroit camerawork instead?

Was the extra dimension worth the trade-off in reduced visual brightness, detail, and color?

There are few things I truly despise in life—other than bullies, white chocolate, and the designated hitter rule—but 3-D has earned a spot at the very top of that list.

Over the past twenty years, the film business has inexorably changed, as the smart, mid-budget drama aimed at grown-ups has been squeezed out by enormous action-adventure flicks whose violence and cartoonish drama are easily exportable to new markets in China, South America, and beyond. With home entertainment centers growing in sophistication (and more and more talkers, texters, and other miscreants inevitably invading the theatergoing experience), it's becoming harder to woo viewers out of their living rooms and into the multiplexes. Studios and theater owners alike have decided that spectacle is the answer, meaning they've become dedicated to making movies that are so big, so loud, and so in-your-face that you won't want to see them anywhere but on a massive screen.

In addition to spectacularizing action thrillers by filming them in super-widescreen or IMAX, studios have re-embraced the 1950s gimmick of 3-D, a format that is generally not replicable at home and that, not coincidentally, adds three or four dollars to the average ticket price. With very few exceptions—Martin Scorsese's *Hugo*, the science fiction adventure *Gravity*, and Werner Herzog's documentary *Cave of Forgotten Dreams* are a few—I've found 3-D to be little more than a marketing ploy and cash grab rather than an aesthetic advance—it sacrifices pictorial detail and color saturation while providing very little in return. (I'm still bothered by how figures and objects in the foreground become blurry blobs during close-ups.) In an effort to get away from using 3-D for "gotcha" effects, filmmakers now use it simply to create enhanced depth of field—sixty years after Gregg Toland ingeniously did the same through simple 2-D photography in *Citizen Kane*. Still, I once adamantly preferred film to digital photography, and now I barely notice the difference. In the hands of artists like Scorsese, Cuarón, and Herzog, and with ever-progressing technological advances, 3-D may well win me over someday. I might even learn to love white chocolate.

JUST AS VIEWERS SHOULD ASK themselves whether a movie really needed to be told in three dimensions, whether it was worth the trade-off in color, brightness, detail, and tonal range, they should ask themselves the same questions about every cinematographic choice made in a movie. Put most simply: every single thing we see—and don't see—in a movie is on purpose. Or at least it should be.

At its most artful, cinematography is far more than simply the mechanism for recording performances. Every lighting element, every shadow, every camera move or lack thereof, every shot that seems either drenched in or drained of color informs our understanding of what's happening on-screen and our feelings about it. Watching can be a plunge into pure visual pleasure, or it can give you a whopping case of eyestrain. The camera can make you feel as if you're gliding, soaring, and spinning, or it can make you want to reach for the motion-sickness bag. It can starve the eye with murk and darkness, or assault it with garish over-lighting.

Each of these strategies is legitimate as long as it serves the subject at hand, whether it's a gritty, naturalistic urban drama or a lush, escapist romance. It can be incredibly exhilarating to appreciate great cinematography, because it makes viewers feel like we're in cahoots with the filmmaker, reveling in the sheer artistry of the camerawork. But if you're noticing the photography and fancy moves during a movie, ask yourself whether they're being used organically, or simply as an impressive way to cover for a clichéd story and unimaginatively staged scenes. Cinematography can be used with utilitarian straightforwardness or with wild, expressive flair; it can be used carefully— almost philosophically—or simply as spectacle for spectacle's sake. At its best, it draws the audience further into the world on-screen. How we look at movies nearly always comes down to how the movies look themselves.

RECOMMENDED VIEWING ···

Citizen Kane (1941)
The Red Shoes (1948)
McCabe & Mrs. Miller (1971)
Do the Right Thing (1989)
JFK (1991)
Selma (2014)

CHAPTER FIVE

EDITING

I f the screenplay is the blueprint of a movie, and the performances, settings, and images are its bricks, then editing is the mortar.

It's been argued, persuasively, that editing defines cinema as an art form: without the ability to connect individual scenes and shots through editing, movies wouldn't move at all. They would be a series of static, separate photographs. Many filmmakers consider editing the "third rewrite" of the movie, when the original intent of the screenwriter and the unifying vision of the director are given their final chance to become fully realized.

Good editing involves far more subtlety than the slashing, smash-cut aesthetic that dominates so many of today's films (think of the incomprehensible chase scene that opens the 2008 James Bond film *Quantum of Solace*). A good editor possesses an intuitive understanding of how images work together to tell a story and evoke powerful, sometimes unconscious emotions in the audience. It's a matter of clarity, structure, rhythm, momentum, and emotion.

Editing is painstaking work, and yet it defines both the narrative spine and deep core of feeling that should anchor every film, allowing viewers to sink into its imaginary world effortlessly, almost instinctively. If the screenplay lays out the rules of how to watch the film, the editor enforces those rules like a tyrant, reading the script, organizing the footage as it's shot each day, and, finally, working with the director to assemble the best version of the movie possible with the material they have to work with.

The best editing doesn't draw attention to itself. Instead it disappears. When it works, the audience comes away with the satisfied feeling that what they just saw was the movie as it was always supposed to be, from beginning to end—no hiccups, awkward transitions, unexplained non sequiturs, or moments of boredom or confusion. In my interviews with editors over the years, they have often used phrases like "seamless" and "swept away" to describe well-edited movies. Rather than notice each and every cut within a film, they want viewers to feel caught up in the journey, unaware of the false starts, dead ends, and stops for gas that went into putting the trip together.

It's the editor who catalogs every single take of every single scene, and, thanks to computer technology—and ideally under the assured guidance of the director—puts them in and takes them out and recombines them until every scene works on its own terms and serves the unified whole. Depending on how much footage the director has shot, this task can be arduous or relatively economical and straightforward: for *Mad Max: Fury Road*, for example, editor Margaret Sixel had the daunting task of cutting down nearly five hundred hours of filmed material into a two-hour movie, whereas Quentin Tarantino shot a lean thirty hours of film for *The Hateful Eight* (which, ironically, clocked in at forty minutes longer than *Fury Road*).

As the chief surrogate for the audience, the editor anticipates what viewers will need from one moment to the next in order to stay oriented and emotionally engaged. Most big-studio movies are shown to test audiences long before they open, to make sure viewers aren't needlessly confused or alienated; after receiving feedback, the editor and director will (sometimes begrudgingly) dive back into the footage to address viewers' concerns, adding or subtracting dialogue, snipping or elongating sequences, or rearranging scenes until nagging questions are answered and the movie moves according to its own rhythm and rhyme and internal logic.

There are legendary examples of movies that were butchered as a result of test screenings: to this day, Orson Welles's *The Magnificent Ambersons* bears the battle scar of an obviously tacked-on happy ending dictated by Welles's parent studio. Then again, test screenings can provide filmmakers with invaluable guidance. Consider how different *E.T. the Extra-Terrestrial* would have been had the little alien died at the end, or if Richard Gere had kicked Julia Roberts out of his car at the end of *Pretty Woman*. Those were both original endings, and both were fixed at the editing stage.

FADE IN . . .

Was I with the movie from the start?

Did it take me where it promised me it would go?

Seasoned filmgoers can tell, almost within the first moments, whether a film has grabbed them.

It's the editor's job to ensure that buy-in, firmly establishing the film's setting, main characters, emotional pitch, and sense of coherent forward movement from the get-go. With the pacing, tone, and coherence clearly and firmly established at the outset, the editor then makes sure they're followed throughout the film's running time.

This is one of the most crucial challenges for an editor, who needs to establish so much within such a compressed amount of time. If viewers can't figure out right away exactly where they are and what story they are being asked to believe, the movie won't work.

I'll never forget watching the astonishing, virtually wordless opening sequence of British director Steve McQueen's *Hunger*. Set in Northern Ireland's brutal Maze Prison in the early 1980s, it consists of searing images of violence and dehumanization within the facility. Brilliantly realizing Enda Walsh's script—which sought to convey the realities of the Maze not through expository dialogue but through action and environment in long, unbroken pictorial shots—editor Joe Walker cut together the sequence, which performs two primary functions at once: introducing viewers to the world they'll be inhabiting for the next hour and a half, and setting up expectations for a film that will eschew traditional episodic storytelling as well as the manipulations typical of most films dealing with such a highly charged subject. I knew within the first *seconds* of *Love & Mercy* that Paul Dano's portrayal of musician Brian Wilson would be uncanny and that the tender, meditative tone director Bill Pohlad was establishing would be far more compelling than that of the typical biopic.

All of these openings were conceived by the films' screenwriters, of course, and all benefited from superb direction and galvanizing performances from the actors who appeared in them. But they lived or died in the editing, whether that meant choosing Dano's best take, or timing and juxtaposing the images of prison life in *Hunger* to establish with superb economy the effect that the environment was having both on prisoners and their guards.

Alternatively, I also remember one of the worst opening sequences I've ever witnessed: the aforementioned *Quantum of Solace*, which began with the usual 007 set piece of improbable physical derring-do. In this case, though, the scene was edited as if thrown into a blender and set to Puree, reducing what should have been a taut, cleanly legible establishing passage into a haphazard, incoherent stunt salad of shiny cars, screeching wheels, and blazing guns.

Contrast that ignominious sequence with the opening sequence of *GoodFellas*, which, from its first shot, plunges viewers into a series of flashbacks narrated by the film's protagonist, Henry Hill. "As far back as I can remember, I always wanted to be a gangster," Hill (Ray Liotta) proudly declares as we watch him and his partners-in-crime kill a badly wounded man. The scene ends on an attention-grabbing freeze frame; a few moments later, we're taken back twenty years to when Henry started working as an errand boy for his Brooklyn neighborhood's crime boss.

Edited by Scorsese's longtime collaborator Thelma Schoonmaker, *GoodFellas* establishes its social environment and the characters within it immediately, giving the audience utter confidence in a story that will transpire over Henry's decades-long rise and fall within the mob. Within minutes—seconds, even—we're inside the story, content to tag along with our Dante-like guide to whatever depths of hell he's inclined to take us. (Schoonmaker continued to use those freeze frames, not only to give *GoodFellas* its expressive energy and verve, but to underline the most pivotal, unwittingly consequential moments in Henry Hill's life of crime.) The producer Albert Berger, who with his partner Ron Yerxa produced *Little Miss Sunshine* and most of Alexander Payne's movies, recalled how Payne recut *Nebraska* after the film made its world premiere at the 2013 Cannes Film Festival. "We restructured the beginning of the movie so there was a scene with Will Forte's girlfriend that was in a different place. And we moved some other things around and tightened it up. It was just little tweaks here and there that [created] a better way into the movie. It was just tighter and better, and it flowed." It's instructive, somehow, that Berger couldn't remember precisely what they moved and cut. That's what the art of editing entails: moving the pieces around until the movie's metabolism is balanced and fits with our own.

WHAT'S GOING ON?

Did I know where the characters were, what they were doing, why they were doing it?

Were the physical settings clearly delineated?

Did the movie make sense?

When a movie is clear—the plot is understandable, the characters are well-defined and follow their own internal logic—it's reassuring and confidence-building. We can relax until instructed otherwise. When a movie isn't clear, however, it creates feelings of anxiety and dissatisfaction that are almost impossible to diagnose. After seamlessness, clarity is the chief aim of the film editor, whose task it is to ensure that the audience stays oriented, tuned-in, and invested at every juncture.

Clarity is such a simple concept. But when you consider the material editors are asked to work with—and the often tight schedules and stressful working conditions under which they do their jobs—what seems simple is anything but. Quite often, editors are working with material that the director has been living with for at least a year or two, sometimes much longer than that. In the course of long, difficult productions, perspective tends to get lost, certain shots or scenes become so beloved that the director can't imagine cutting them, certain sequences so difficult or expensive to film that it's inconceivable they won't end up in the finished movie.

It falls upon the editor to be the objective party in these instances, advocating for one person and one person only: the viewer. If that super-expensive scene doesn't move the story forward or, worse, confuses or disorients the audience? Cut it. The scene where the actress cries perfectly on cue, but delivers her lines too quickly to be understood? Choose the take that best serves the viewer's comprehension, and ditch the one that favors emotion over audibility. Does the big revelation in the third act feel like it's coming out of nowhere? Go back to your first or second act and plant a little hint that won't be obvious, but will make the later moment completely logical and coherent. (If the editor doesn't have enough material to work with and the budget allows, the director will occasionally reconvene the actors and creative team to fill in the blanks.)

In *Michael Clayton*, every beat of the title character's journey had to be supported by information conveyed early in the film, so that his actions at the tautly constructed climax would be comprehensible and utterly believable. For example, Clayton, played by George Clooney, throws all of his belongings into a burning car and yet, in the next scene, has clearly purchased a brand-new parka. So it had to be established early on that he had cash in his pocket; the filmmakers—editor John Gilroy and his brother Tony, the writer and director—made sure the audience sees him empty his pockets for a security guard at a poker game during the film's early scenes. After test audiences expressed confusion about Clayton getting out of his car to stand by some horses, the Gilroys inserted shots of his son's fantasy-adventure book, in which a similar grouping of horses figured prominently.

Perhaps the most challenging—and successful— example of how editing can clarify a movie can be found in the Vietnam War drama *Apocalypse Now*, directed by Francis Ford Coppola in a notoriously difficult production that involved last-minute cast changes, natural disasters, lengthy halts in shooting, and elaborate scenes that never made it into the final version of the film. Put together by a team headed by picture editor and sound designer Walter Murch, the final cut of *Apocalypse Now* so easily could have been reduced to an incomprehensible rubble. Instead, Murch and his coeditors wove together disparate scenes and a hurriedly improvised ending to create a movie that worked both as a linear story—about an American soldier in Vietnam who is ordered to travel upriver from Saigon to assassinate a rogue army colonel—and as a wildly expressionistic, almost abstract evocation of the chaos and sensory overload of the war itself.

What makes *Apocalypse Now* a masterpiece of editing is how, even at its most irrational and dreamlike moments, it obeys narrative logic while simultaneously feeling utterly illogical and instinctive. By contrast, the director Howard Hawks (working with editor Christian Nyby) couldn't have cared less about logic and the audience's sense of orientation when he was making the noir suspense drama *The Big Sleep*—instead, he just wanted every scene to look great. The result is a movie that is full of style and attitude, but one that to this day I find frustrating and profoundly unrewarding to watch.

Editing for clarity is most important for fractured, nonlinear narratives like *Pulp Fiction* and *Memento*, as well as for ambitious, intellectually gnarly movies like *Being John Malkovich*, *Eternal Sunshine of the Spotless Mind*, and *Inception*, where the plots are knotty, the dialogue is thick with complex arcana, and the world on-screen is so deeply personal to the director that the viewer needs constant help in discerning what the hell is going on—without feeling pushed or led by the nose.

All of the movies mentioned above were edited with outstanding attention to keeping the audience oriented and informed, even at their most idiosyncratic and opaque. A film equally ambitious in tone, but less well-crafted in editing, was Terrence Malick's *The Tree of Life*, a film about three brothers coming of age in 1950s Texas. Structured symphonically, in three distinct "movements," it was often moving and extraordinarily beautiful to watch, especially an ambitious opening sequence depicting the creation of the universe, and the film's impressionistic portrait of the boys' coming of age.

But *The Tree of Life* was also unnecessarily confusing, especially when it came to the brother played as an adult by Sean Penn. So much about Penn's character went un-explained or felt insufficiently motivated that the movie became hermetic and self-indulgent, needlessly alienating viewers when it should have drawn them in; indeed, several viewers left the film not knowing precisely which brother Penn was supposed to be playing. (Penn himself expressed befuddlement with the film, telling a reporter for the French newspaper *Le Figaro*, "Frankly, I'm still trying to figure out what I'm doing there and what I was supposed to add in that context! What's more, Terry himself never managed to explain it to me clearly.")

Editing is also particularly crucial to ensemble movies, where—as with the nonlinear movie—the audience must keep track of multiple storylines and characters that collide and overlap. No one was more accomplished at this form than Robert Altman and his editors, whose movies *Nashville* (edited by Dennis Hill and Sidney Levin), *Short Cuts* (Suzy Elmiger and Geraldine Peroni), and *Gosford Park* (Tim Squyres) exemplify how editing can turn an otherwise disorganized collection of vignettes into a coherent experience worth investing in. Altman's most able successor in the genre might be Paul Thomas Anderson, whose *Boogie Nights* and *Magnolia* (both edited by Dylan Tichenor) evince a similar sensitivity to bringing characters to vivid life in the course of highly charged parallel encounters.

Working with their editors, both Altman and Anderson knew precisely how long each scene needed to be for a viewer to understand their characters' essential conflicts and their emotional stakes, just as they knew when to "check in" with a character who hadn't been seen in a while. The term of art for this is keeping characters "alive" throughout a movie, as opposed to introducing them in the first act and then forgetting them until they're needed in the third; it makes a movie feel less like a one-dimensional story than a glimpse at a world in microcosm, teeming with confounding but always recognizable life. Another wonderful example of editing groups is the movie *Milk*, about political leader Harvey Milk, in which director Gus Van Sant and editor Elliot Graham did a superbly graceful job of delineating Milk's irrepressible character, but also then pulled the focus of the film back to capture the collective effort of the grassroots activists he led, at one point effectively using the archaic visual trope of a split-screen with multiplying images of people organizing a political action.

In addition to clarity of story and character, there's clarity of symbolic meaning. When Stanley Kubrick and his editor, Ray Lovejoy, cut from a shot of a prehistoric bone being tossed in the air to a rotating space station at the beginning of *2001: A Space Odyssey*, entire worlds and epochs were not only traversed in one significant cut, but Kubrick metaphorically—and purely visually—posited the film's philosophical core of ideas regarding evolution, human nature, and the ambiguity of technological "progress." This kind of intuitive, associative editing is the backbone of the experimental films of Chris Marker, Bruce Conner, and Stan Brakhage, and it has increasingly defined the work of Terrence Malick, whose most recent films aren't edited into narratives as much as they are assembled into amorphous collections of images, meant to evoke timeless questions within the viewer akin to the filmmaker's own spiritual quest. It's up to the editing team to make sure the resulting film has a chance of connecting with even a rarefied audience, rather than remaining solipsistic and impenetrable.

TICK-TOCK, TICK-TOCK

Was I swept along, or swamped?

Did the movie move like the wind, or just sit there like sludge?

Every movie has its correct tempo.
Some are meant to move at a comfortable trot. Others gallop, bringing viewers along on a breakneck ride for dear life. Still others seek to slow us down from our habitually overstimulated metabolisms, examining the minutiae of daily life, relationships, and our own mortality. If the film does its job at the outset—signaling what kind of pace viewers can expect, and why—then even the most chaotic action-adventure flick will feel comfortable, the editor having astutely judged when viewers need a break or might welcome being pushed just a bit further over the edge.

Similarly, each individual scene has its own internal tempo, a proper start and end point so that its function in the film—to convey important information, a crucial emotional breakthrough, or change in tone—is fulfilled with the most impact. The rule of thumb in most movies is to get in late and get out early, eliminating needless physical business and dialogue. The director David Lean—who began his career as an editor—was so obsessed with flawless transitions that he made sure to include the final image of one scene and the opening image of the next in all the screenplays he worked on—hence the famous image of a striking match becoming a rising sun over the desert in *Lawrence of Arabia*. (Interestingly, that transition was written as a dissolve in the original script; editor Anne V. Coates is credited with making it a far more dramatic "straight cut.")

Editor and sound designer Walter Murch, whose book *In the Blink of an Eye* has become an essential primer in the art and science of film editing, along with Michael Ondaatje's collection of interviews with him, *The Conversations*—and who also has collaborated frequently with Francis Ford Coppola and George Lucas—put it this way: "Where do you end the shot? You end it at the exact moment in which it has revealed everything that it's going to reveal, in its fullness, without being overripe. If you end the shot too soon, you have the equivalent of youth cut off in its bloom. Its potential is unrealized. If you hold a shot too long, things tend to putrefy."

When *Bonnie and Clyde* came out in 1967, it was seen as revolutionary, imbuing a Depression-era crime legend with the visual values of the "living-room war" taking place in Vietnam. Today its pacing hardly seems radical, but a closer look reveals just how groundbreaking it was. Working with director Arthur Penn, editor Dede Allen started as many scenes as she could *in medias res*, or in the middle of things, avoiding entrances and exits to get right into the action, even if it was a quiet domestic scene. The resulting film possesses a subtle but fateful sense of heedless forward movement: by the time the title characters are killed in a hail of police bullets, the editing has become much faster and more violent than it was at the beginning of the film. Similarly, in his book *Making Movies*, the director Sidney Lumet described how he and editor Carl Lerner sped up the jury-room drama *12 Angry Men* in its last thirty minutes, bringing what had been a prolonged argument to a dramatic conclusion by cutting more frequently, a strategy that added excitement and also signaled—along with the staging and cinematography—that the situation the jurors were facing was becoming more claustrophobic and volatile.

The edgy, handheld camera work and dizzyingly fast editing style of *Slumdog Millionaire* imparted an enormous amount of information, in very brief bursts, about the poverty and vibrant street culture of modern Mumbai and the lives of its characters. But the frantic movement and constant toggling back and forth through time would have been overwhelming without occasional rests, such as when the protagonist, Jamal, sits quietly in his game-show chair, or bathes his wounded face in a moonlit stream. These moments are crucial in giving viewers a respite from what would otherwise be sensory overload.

Pacing also comes into play when the editing is largely "straight," moving from scene to scene with no visible breaks. Even an otherwise smooth series of episodic encounters will every once in a while be broken by a visible cut that is followed by a black screen, like a punctuation mark, as if the filmmaker wants viewers to feel like something is coming to an end or another chapter is beginning. Although they're being guided by both the screenplay and the director, astute editors can predict when a scene is best served by a gradual fade to black, to allow the audience to let a moment sink in, or when a scene should be gradually faded in, to indicate to the audience that time has passed. (Dissolves—wherein one image gradually gives way to another that has been superimposed on top of it—are rarely used today, their gauzy, impressionistic romanticism feeling out of step with our less sentimental times.)

Of course, "episodic" is a double-edged sword: there's a thin line between a smooth, easily flowing narrative and a dreary this-happened-then-that-happened trudge. Although the latter should be avoided at the screenplay stage, it's also a function of perceptive editing, which can give grace and propulsive interest to otherwise mundane

material. In his 1996 drama *Lone Star*, about history, identity, and memory on the Texas border, John Sayles edited
every scene but one by simply panning the camera, erasing
the visual border between "then" and "now," "here" and
"there," and creating a flawlessly paced journey beyond
the conventional confines of time and space. The conceit
worked beautifully in allowing viewers to feel caught up
with what was unfolding on-screen and erasing their own
interior boundaries between past and present. Sayles edited in the camera—a lost art today—in a way that used
movement itself to convey *Lone Star*'s oblique structure
and steady, loping heartbeat.

DOES THIS EDITING MAKE MY MOVIE LOOK FAT?

Did the movie fit the dimensions of the story?

Were there pieces left out, odd bits stuck in, a bulge
here, a sag there?

Some films are sleek and streamlined, lean and mean;
others are a little paunchier, not so uptight about keeping their tummies in. They're a little digressive, distracted,
maybe a bit overstuffed.

Both types can be rewarding in their own way: the art
lies in knowing what shape a movie wants to be.

When a movie isn't the correct shape, we register that
distortion, even if it's unconsciously. We may end up lik-
ing the movie, but we don't *love* it, although we can't put
our finger on why. It's not a matter of being too long or
too short; rather, it's a matter of proportion. It just didn't
feel right. The editor's job is to pick up on those vibes and

anticipate those cul-de-sacs, and either to snip away the bits that slow a particular scene down, or adjust the ones immediately before and after it so that they feel more of a piece.

Most conventional mainstream movies don't have a discernible shape: they simply flow, obeying life's rhythms as a continuous, sequential series of events. But there are some movies whose shapes and proportions are meant to be obvious, even startling.

[handwritten margin note: could use this point in presentation]

Once again, *Hunger* provides a memorable example. I first saw the movie at the 2008 Toronto International Film Festival with my dear friend Paul Schwartzman. The first half-hour or so is unrelentingly brutal, prison guards and prisoners treating each other with inhuman cruelty from opposite sides of the cell bars. Having reached his limit for violence, Paul turned to me and asked why on earth he should sit for such abuse one moment longer.

At that precise moment, director Steve McQueen and his editor, Joe Walker, shifted the film's focus from the cacophonous cell block to a hushed visiting room, where Bobby Sands—contemplating the political action that would end his life—is meeting with a priest. For the next twenty minutes, Sands (Michael Fassbender) and Father Moran (Liam Cunningham) debate the political and moral implications of Sands's plan in an unbroken scene in which the camera moves only slightly as the men's initial banter turns to matters of life and death. Having barely taken a breath while this quietly urgent tour de force played out, Paul turned to me and whispered, "I take back my question."

The midpoint verbal duet in *Hunger* is the movie's linchpin. Not only does it offer stark relief from the noise, chaos, and misery that have come before, but it also sets up the film's final section, an agonizing re-creation of Sands's hunger strike and death, punctuated by flashbacks to his early life. Its placement within the film and its un-interrupted intensity offer viewers not just aesthetic beauty but also crucial insights into Sands's self-sacrificing (some would say pointlessly self-destructive) behavior. Rather than delivering a conventional, chronological portrait of his subject from his childhood to his death, McQueen approached Sands's life as a visual artist would, creating a cinematic triptych that was as powerful visually as it was emotionally.

Other movies that used sudden changes of pace to great effect were Romanian director Cristian Mungiu's *4 Months, 3 Weeks, 2 Days*—a tense, moment-by-moment drama about a young Bucharest woman trying to obtain an abortion, punctuated by a long, relaxed dinner party at her family home—and *The Hurt Locker*, in which frenetic, dizzyingly dynamic action is brought to a temporary halt during a long, quiet sequence involving a sniper played by Ralph Fiennes.

As much as I admire taut, economically constructed narratives, I have a soft spot for movies that refuse to fit into neat boxes. Indeed, some of my favorite movies are films that, strictly speaking, are unwieldy and misshapen, but make up for it with moments that, even though they sag and bag, ring with emotional truth. By most lights, Judd Apatow's *Funny People*, in which Adam Sandler stars as a comedian reassessing his life, takes a radical, jarring turn in the third act, when the comedian sets out to ruin the mar-riage of a former flame. Like most of Apatow's films, *Funny People* isn't tightly edited—in fact, it can fairly be accused of being long-winded and undisciplined. But in this case, I warmed to its loose unpredictability, its examination of male friendship and self-deception, its affection for even the most flawed characters. (*Funny People* also happens to contain one of my all-time favorite transitions, an emotional, funny, gracefully edited montage in which Sandler's and Seth Rogen's characters fly to a MySpace corporate event where Sandler is set to perform; the sequence is accompanied by James Taylor singing "Carolina in My Mind," which we see in the final reveal is being performed live by Taylor himself at the MySpace gig.)

Another one of my favorite un-sleek movies is Kenneth Lonergan's *Margaret*, in which Anna Paquin portrays a headstrong teenage girl at large in Manhattan. It meanders and digresses through the heroine's peregrinations and ethical quandaries—an approach altogether appropriate to her own searching naïveté and burgeoning awareness of the world. In their messiness and refusal to stay in the lines, *Funny People* and *Margaret* mirror life with compassion and deeply personal candor, taking account of its most misshapen, ungovernable moments that don't fit into tidy, metronomic "beats."

This brings us to the inevitable "too long" problem: it's a truism that movies today are far too long, especially comic-book spectacles and comedies that have no business clocking in at anything over 110 minutes. Whether movies are actually longer than they've ever been is subject to debate: some studies suggest that running times have indeed ticked up by a few percentage points over the past twenty years, whereas others insist that it's the three-hour outliers (such as *The Lord of the Rings*) that have pushed current averages up disproportionately.

The point, though, isn't whether films *are* longer, but whether they *feel* longer. When we say a movie is too long, it means that it's repetitive, boring, or padded out with yet one more scene of mayhem and destruction to qualify as a big-screen spectacle (I call this one-more-thingism, a syndrome that crops up most often in the third act, in the form of multiple endings). When a movie works—when it's been well-edited—we don't care how long it is: it has earned every minute of its running time.

AND . . . *SCENE*

Did the movie make me laugh, cry, despair, have hope?

Did the characters' emotions make sense based on their experience, behavior, and motivations?

Every emotional moment in a film must be earned.
"Earned," in fact, is a favorite rhetorical arrow in the critic's quiver. Put simply, it means that if we cry at the end of a movie, we'll question whether the filmmakers "earned" our tears: Did they bring us to that emotional point after carefully developing their characters and story, or were we manipulated and cheated into the emotional catharsis? If a character has a bracing change of heart—if he sees the light and proposes to the girl, or if she over-comes her defenses to reconcile with her estranged sister—were the seeds planted early to make those transformations possible, or were they convenient Damascene conversions?
Emotional through-lines are essential in films, but they must be unobtrusive and natural. When Martin Scorsese and his longtime editor, Thelma Schoonmaker, were editing *The Departed*, they realized that, when the relationship between Leonardo DiCaprio's Billy Costigan and Vera Farmiga's Madolyn Madden deepened, it wasn't

entirely believable given what viewers knew of Billy so far. So they decided to move a scene of Billy making love to Madolyn earlier than was originally intended, mostly so that his vulnerability would be more clearly established.

Emotion might be trickiest when it comes to a film's ending. Albert Berger recalled that *Little Miss Sunshine*—about a dysfunctional family's attempt to fulfill a little girl's dreams of competing in a children's beauty pageant—originally had a dramatically different ending, in which, after dancing to Rick James's "Super Freak" on the pageant stage, the family gathered in the parking lot and left to get ice cream—the emotional equivalent of a "that was fun" shrug.

"It was just very flat and anticlimactic," Berger recalled. When the filmmakers did test screenings with friends and family, they realized that a moment midway through the movie, when the family pushes the VW bus they're driving and hops on, was "a huge crowd pleaser." The directors Valerie Faris and Jonathan Dayton decided to reconceive the ending so that the family would be in the bus again, crash triumphantly through a gate, and barrel down the highway heading toward home. "So you get the emotional uplift and the comedic hook of everybody pushing together one last time," Berger noted.

As the editor Billy Weber told me, it's far easier to edit action than human drama: "When's the last time you mowed people down with an AK-47?" he asked me, adding that if you're staging an argument between a married couple over breakfast, the audience will know within seconds whether it rings true. When editing for emotional truth, Anne McCabe—who edited the wry serio-comedies *The Daytrippers*, *Adventureland*, and *You Can*

Count on Me—told me that it's more often "about a look
rather than a line." For example, when a character says, "I
love you," the editor can decide whether it's more important to have the camera on the person saying the line or
hearing it, depending on the emotional values of the scene.

One of the finest examples of editing for emotion—for
getting the audience inside a character's head—is the montage set to Simon and Garfunkel's "Sounds of Silence" in
The Graduate. In an ingeniously choreographed series of
shots that blend into each other by way of matching black
backgrounds, we see Benjamin Braddock (Dustin Hoffman) move impassively from the swimming pool through
his upper-class Los Angeles home to the hotel bed where
he's sleeping with his middle-aged lover, Mrs. Robinson
(Anne Bancroft), and back again, in what looks like an unfeeling daze. When director Mike Nichols later explained
what he and editor Sam O'Steen were going for, he described an "anesthetized state" that he needed to establish
for Benjamin, setting up his later "awakening" when he
falls in love with Mrs. Robinson's daughter.

Editing for emotion is particularly tricky—and crucial—in scenes with no dialogue, when editing can create
a power of association that helps the audience intuitively
understand what the character is thinking, simply through
the actor's facial and physical performance. A superb example of this is actor Clive Owen's often wordless sequences in *Children of Men,* which director and coeditor
Alfonso Cuarón pared down more and more to create a
movie that was as nonverbal and purely visual as possible;
he obviously brought the same values to bear on *Gravity,*
in which Sandra Bullock portrayed a stranded astronaut
whose fear and desperation were palpable even through
the layers of her spacesuit and helmet. Audiences could

have left *Gravity* feeling like they'd been on a vertiginous thrill ride through outer space; instead they felt con-
templative, chastened. Had *Little Miss Sunshine* ended as
originally planned, viewers would have left the theater
shrugging instead of cheering. These are the subtle edits
that make a movie not just a visual experience, but an
emotional one.

DEATH BY 1,000 CUTS

Was the movie seamless?

Did it move easily, gracefully, without stops and starts?

Was it too "cutty?"

The first time I noticed film editing was in the 1980s,
when I saw the 1967 romantic drama *Two for the Road*, in
which Audrey Hepburn and Albert Finney portray a jaded
couple revisiting their courtship and marriage through
various trips they've taken. (The *Two for the Road* screening was something of a seasonal ritual in New York, drawing crowds of devotees to the old Regency Theatre on the
Upper West Side, where it played every year.)

Visually echoing Henry Mancini's lilting, sophisticated
score, *Two for the Road* bounces between different eras in
the couple's relationship, signaled by their wardrobes and
the cars Finney drives; working with editors Madeleine
Gug and Richard Marden, director Stanley Donen cleverly intercut between past and present to create a visually
dynamic mosaic of how time and memory continually
erode and rebuild our experience of love and marriage.

In 1967, *Two for the Road* was considered revolutionary for what was then considered rapid-fire editing. Seen
today, the movie seems less radical and avant-garde than
witty and graceful. The film's time-shifting style was
tweaked several decades later in the underrated 1998 romantic comedy *Sliding Doors,* in which a young woman's
fortunes completely change depending on whether she
catches or misses a London Underground train. Written
and directed by Peter Howitt and beautifully edited by
John Smith, the film echoes *Two for the Road* in the way it
toggles—seemingly effortlessly—between parallel worlds
for its heroine, never sacrificing clarity or creating needless
confusion as it explores its intriguing premise.

The masters of rhythm are Scorsese and his longtime
editor Schoonmaker, who infuse each of their films with
its own beat and singular musicality. (It's clear that Scorsese's love of music informs his approach to constructing
his films, which rise and fall with dramatic, even operatic, highs and lows.) *Raging Bull* and *GoodFellas* are mas-
terpieces of editing and rhythm. The first puts viewers in
the boxing ring to get an immediate, disorienting sense
of what a prizefight is like, its pummeling brutality juxtaposed with soaring operatic music. In *GoodFellas,* Scorsese and Schoonmaker use rising and falling dynamics to
mirror the nascent romanticism and ultimate cynicism of
Henry Hill's criminal career. That tracking shot in the
Copa isn't just great cinematography but also a fine use of
editorial timing, giving the audience a vicarious, even immersive, taste of the excitement and glamour that seduces
Henry's future wife, Karen, against all her better instincts.

Although classical film editing is meant to disappear, in the hands of masters it can be used to powerful
effect by drawing attention to itself. One of my favorite

Scorsese-Schoonmaker moments occurred in one of their most divisive collaborations. For the brutal, chaotic street fight that opens *Gangs of New York*, about nineteenth-century Manhattan, Schoonmaker made her edits to focus not on the blows as they landed, but on the upswing of the men's flailing arms, a choice inspired by Sergei Eisenstein's influential 1925 silent film *Battleship Potemkin*, in which angry sailors revolt against their superior officers on account of the maggot-infested gruel they have to eat. The effect was both unsettlingly exhilarating and oblique, aptly capturing the viciousness of brute hand-to-hand warfare. Later in the film, they cut from a tender love scene between Leonardo DiCaprio and Cameron Diaz to the startling—and terrifying—image of Daniel Day-Lewis's Bill the Butcher sitting stock-still, draped in the American flag. ("The stillness of him is what Marty knew made it frightening," Schoonmaker told me.) Such bold, expressive flourishes notwithstanding, *Gangs of New York* never seemed to cohere as tightly as Scorsese's best work. Some people familiar with the production insist they never had a finished script; others blame a chaotic editing process that wasn't helped by the zealous efforts of executive producer Harvey Weinstein. Whatever the reason, and despite its considerable strengths, *Gangs of New York* ultimately felt over-busy, thematically muddled, and fatally unwieldy.

Rhythm is just as crucial in quiet human dramas as it is in Scorsese's visceral, violence-prone worlds. Some of the best films in recent memory—Kenneth Lonergan's *You Can Count on Me*, Tom McCarthy's *The Visitor* and *Spotlight*—exemplify the art of editing at its most subtle, where effectiveness lies not in complicated time shifts or dramatic juxtapositions but in a shrewd sense of which takes to select and when to get in and out of them. By rights, the experience of watching a bunch of journalists work their phones and clip files to research sexual abuse within the Catholic Church in *Spotlight* should have been about as compelling as watching the proverbial paint dry. But in the hands of Tom McCarthy and his editor Tom McArdle, it takes on the urgent, compulsively forward-moving contours of a thriller (even without the dramatic advantage of a Deep Throat figure in a shadowy parking garage).

In a similar way, Paul Greengrass's *United 93*—about the events of September 11, 2001—begins with the banal routine of people getting on a plane; in an early shot, the camera follows a flight attendant as she makes the same trip down the aisle of a plane that she's surely made thousands of times before. Lulling the audience into the same workaday heartbeat of the characters makes the chaos and murder that ultimately transpire all the more deeply shocking.

Editing for rhythm is especially important in chase scenes, which almost never have dialogue, save for the occasional profane outburst of the people behind the wheel. The ten-minute sequence in *Bullitt* (1968), in which a policeman, played by Steve McQueen (the late actor; no relation to the director), pursues some bad guys, set the standard for constructing not just car chases but action sequences in general. Editor Frank P. Keller adroitly established the position of McQueen's souped-up Mustang in relation to the Dodge Charger he was pursuing, interchanging shots from McQueen's point of view and wider images of the general action to ensure that viewers knew exactly where they were at all times during what amounted to a vertiginous roller-coaster ride through San Francisco's streets.

Although it was difficult to believe that another chase sequence could attain *Bullitt*'s level of clarity, tension, and excitement, it happened just three years later, when Gene Hackman outran an elevated New York subway train in *The French Connection*, edited by Gerald B. Greenberg. The chase scene stands far above current attempts to jack up excitement by way of countless nerve-wracking cuts and ragged close-ups, and the entire movie is a master-piece of editing. Greenberg's work helped to elevate an otherwise ho-hum plot (a police procedural involving a big drug bust) into an engrossing, atmospheric portrait of 1970s-era cynicism. Compared to today's hyperkinetic action films, *Bullitt* and *The French Connection* still hold up as taut, nervy examples of editing at its most rhythmically in-tune and visceral.

The fundamental grammar of movies hasn't changed much over more than a century: films are still composed of scenes, which are composed of shots that tell a story unfolding over time. But norms and expectations have changed quite a bit when it comes to editing those images together. In 1915's *The Birth of a Nation*, D. W. Griffith re-fined the skill of cutting multiple storylines into one nar-rative. Later, Russian filmmakers such as Sergei Eisenstein and Lev Kuleshov showed how juxtaposing seemingly unconnected images could create powerful symbolic and emotional associations in the viewer. In the 1960s, with films like *Breathless* and *Jules et Jim*, the French New Wave introduced freewheeling jump cuts and abrupt transitions that broke with classical rules of continuity and smoothly flowing logical sense; Alfred Hitchcock and editor George Tomasini shocked audiences with the feverishly edited shower sequence in *Psycho*, and the director Sam Peck-inpah, working with editor Louis Lombardo, stunned audiences with heretofore unheard-of splices between, and even *within*, shots of violent shoot-outs in *The Wild Bunch*. Those same values were appropriated and exaggerated by music videos and advertisements to fracture visual language even further.

In 2004, *The Bourne Supremacy* set a new standard by migrating those gestures into the context of a mainstream thriller. The film's jumbled, scattered look is certainly appropriate to its subject (a former secret agent with a case of amnesia), but some of the chase sequences are incoherent, especially the climactic car chase in Moscow. A few years later, in *The Bourne Ultimatum*, editor Christopher Rouse and director Paul Greengrass managed to preserve the distinctive look they had created for the character and his story, but this time it didn't come at the expense of the audience's comprehension; Greengrass and Rouse understood that, after using editing to build to hyperpaced, jumbled climaxes, the film needed to slow down and allow the audience to recover.

In striking that balance between spontaneity and propulsion, most editors strive to leave no fingerprints, content to create an organic, unforced emotional experience for the audience. The finest editors have the confidence to let a scene play if it's working, resisting the urge to edit until it's absolutely needed. But that kind of discipline is increasingly rare at a time when aesthetic expectations have changed, and when editing for its own sake has become accepted by viewers, if not welcome from the professionals. Editors have a word for movies that intentionally draw attention to the editing: "cutty."

More cuts don't mean better editing: one need only compare the chase scene in *Quantum of Solace* (or the equally cutty *Transformers* and *Taken* sequels) with *Bullitt* or *The French Connection*, or simply study the stately, unhurried parallel editing between Michael Corleone attending his nephew's baptism and a series of assassinations he's ordered in *The Godfather*, to understand that. But filmmakers—steeped in the post–New Wave and MTV aesthetic, emboldened by the ease of digital editing, and responding to audiences' increased tolerance for rapid-fire visual assaults—have made the lazy assumption that cutty movies are inherently exciting, when just the opposite is true: in a post-*Armageddon* world, the action movie has become such an incoherent, dizzyingly confusing experience that the viewer emerges feeling assaulted and numb rather than exhilarated. Rather than feeling a part of what's happening on-screen, we're alienated from it.

Obviously, the impact of sped-up editing language is experienced most viscerally—and, to my taste, most unpleasantly—in action movies. There are encouraging exceptions, including the recent action movies *Edge of Tomorrow* and *The Grey*, both of which hewed to classical values of clarity, energy, and spatial logic without resorting to flashy overediting. But the too-cutty-by-half ethic has migrated to other genres, as younger audiences expect and demand movies that simulate their own hyper-distracted, multiscreen experience. Two genres in particular have suffered at the hands of overzealous editing: comedies and musicals. One of the chief pleasures of Golden Age comedies (*Sullivan's Travels*, *Born Yesterday*, *Some Like It Hot*) is the way scenes are allowed to play, giving the jokes time to build and the actors time to finesse their punch lines and establish a comic give-and-take; today, most mainstream comedies are far more chopped up, centering on raunchy sight gags or shocking physical stunts. Happily, such filmmakers as Damien Chazelle are rediscovering the joys of simply beholding two bodies move through space, as he did in his delicious throwback musical *La La Land*, in which Emma Stone and Ryan Gosling were allowed to sing and dance without being interrupted by distracting cuts and gratuitous close-ups.

Overediting has even infected garden-variety dramas. Both 2015's *The Big Short* and 2011's *Moneyball* were based on data-heavy books by Michael Lewis, which meant they both faced the challenge of imparting lots of arcane, conceptually dense information to the audience. *Moneyball* let that understanding come through natural conversations between characters. *The Big Short*, on the other hand, basically delivered a lecture, albeit one cleverly disguised with cameos from the likes of Selena Gomez and Anthony Bourdain and eye-catching montages—quick images of cash, naked women, and other signifiers of decadence, cut together in a rapid-fire collage. It's probably not fair to blame (or credit) the editing of either film—the choices were more likely baked into their scripts—but the dramatically different approaches suggest that the makers of *Moneyball* had enough confidence in their story and the audience's ability to keep up that they had no need of visual gimmicks. That confidence seems to be missing more and more from modern films.

The most masterful editing isn't cutty, but disappears. The 2006 thriller *Children of Men* includes a dazzling scene, in a car that's about to be ambushed, that looks as if it were done in one take (including a bit of business involving Clive Owen and Julianne Moore blowing a Ping-Pong ball back and forth). Editors Alfonso Cuarón (who also directed the film) and Alex Rodriguez went to extraordinary pains to banish the threadwork, making it seem as if the editors never touched it. Cuarón's friend and colleague Alejandro González Iñárritu took that same idea to an extreme eight years later in *Birdman or (the Unexpected Virtue of Ignorance)*, which was carefully edited to appear to be one long, uninterrupted camera movement.

It was an impressive technical feat, yet I was even more awed that year by Sandra Adair's work in *Boyhood.* She and director Richard Linklater wove together moments captured over twelve years of filming the same actors to create an impressionistic tapestry of a boy growing up (and his parents and sister along with him). *Boyhood* could have taken any number of forms, from an episodic, photo album–like memoir to a more avant-garde formal exercise using repeated motifs and scenes. Instead, like *Two for the Road* before it, and thanks to Adair's subtle, practically invisible editing, the film unfolds so naturally that viewers are engrossed in the characters, not the "stunt" of Linklater's multiyear experiment. It's difficult to imagine how any other narrative or editing approach could have put viewers so fully into the quiet miracle of a life being lived in one graceful swoop, its growth and change so gradual as to be virtually imperceptible. We were swept up and taken along, which is exactly what the most seasoned editors want their work to do.

THE TAKES THAT MAKE IT

Were the actors all in the same movie?

Let us now pause to consider the cutting-room floor.

At their best, movie performances feel so real that they seem to have been delivered on the spot, in one perfect pass; everything just looks so *easy*.

Some filmmakers demand just one or two takes from their actors, believing that spontaneity is best served by keeping things fresh. Others, like David Fincher, are notorious for demanding dozens and dozens of takes, the better to wear down actorly affectations and get to the truth of the scene. Most directors capture at least a handful of different versions of a scene, which they mull over later—with their editors—to ascertain which take is best.

"Best," in this case, can mean the version that had the best lighting, or that most aptly served the greater story in terms of pacing and visual information. But it should also mean an actor's finest performance. The audience will never know precisely how many versions of a scene exist, or what the director and editor had to choose from; if actors who are supposed to be madly in love aren't generating the right chemistry on-screen, it could be because their love scenes were filmed early in the shooting schedule, before the actors had a chance to warm up to each other, making it more difficult for the editor to find takes that conveyed passion and connection. Even so, the final cut should show none of this—highlighting only a couple in love.

Or, sometimes, the editor is faced with the challenge of too much chemistry: when she was editing *Raging Bull*, Thelma Schoonmaker was daunted by the scene where Jake LaMotta (Robert De Niro) accuses his brother (Joe Pesci) of sleeping with his wife, an encounter that the two actors largely improvised. "Improvisation is very free form, and when two of the greatest improvisers in the world are given freedom, it becomes really difficult to edit," Schoonmaker recalled. "It was like editing a documentary, where's there's no structure [provided], you have to find it. You have to find a way to get to those guys' great lines and make it feel like a dramatic scene, even though it wasn't shot that way. I had to make it seem like a scripted scene, in a way, even though it was improvised."

Two of my favorite examples of editing for performance share similar DNA: both *The Graduate* and *Michael Clayton* end on long, drawn-out shots of their protagonists, giving the characters and the audience time to allow the preceding events to sink in, and also showcasing amazing feats of great acting. In *The Graduate*, Katharine Ross and Dustin Hoffman, playing, respectively, a young bride on the lam from her recent wedding and a heretofore aimless young man, jump on a moving bus, hurtling into their future; giddy with the sense of transgression and adventure, their laughter quickly gives way to expressions of apprehension, even ambivalence. A traditional rom-com might have frozen the frame before doubt began to play over their faces; instead, Mike Nichols and Sam O'Steen allowed the moment to evolve into vague discomfort, in keeping with the film's tough, uncloying tone. *Michael Clayton* ends similarly, with George Clooney getting into a taxi and setting off into his own unknown world; as the camera settles on his face, his expression goes from tense to wary to relieved as the closing credits begin to roll. It's a one-man answer to Murch's famous question: Where do you end a shot? In the case of *Michael Clayton*, not until the audience has completely internalized your leading man's recent past and tentative, anything but certain, future.

THE GREAT CHALLENGE OF EVALUATING editing—other than knowing whether we feel assaulted by its overuse—is that, as viewers, we'll never know what kind of sow's ear the editing team was presented with in order to create, if not a silk purse, then at least something that could reasonably pass for a purse at all. If a movie has been well-written, acted, and shot, the editor's job of completing the director's vision will be relatively easy and straightforward. If any of those elements experienced trouble, however, editing offers the last chance to solve potentially fatal problems. As Walter Murch explained to me during one of our interviews, "From a surgical point of view, the best-edited film of the year never gets an Oscar nomination, because it was a film that was moved by editing from un-releasable to releasable. . . . And we'll never know which is which."

RECOMMENDED VIEWING ···

Two for the Road (1967)
Bullitt (1968)
The French Connection (1971)
The Conversation (1974)
Into the Wild (2007)
Hunger (2008)

CHAPTER SIX

·············· SOUND AND MUSIC ··············

S o far in this book, I've addressed film as a visual medium. But it's also an aural one. The finest movies
aren't just the result of good stories, impressive acting,
and entrancing images. They provide intensely expressive
experiences, blending dialogue, sound effects, and music
to create a sonic environment every bit as densely layered
and detailed as the one we perceive visually on-screen.

In fact, "environment" may be the best way to think
about sound in movies. Just as production design is a far
more complex matter than merely providing a background
for actors, sound design involves far more than making
sure the dialogue can be clearly heard, or crafting noises
that re-create what is already being shown (technicians use
the term "see a dog, hear a dog" to describe that obvious, literalist approach). In the hands of a sensitive director working with a skilled recording and mixing team,
the soundscape of a movie becomes acoustic architecture,
adding immeasurably to its sense of realism—sometimes
surrealism—and putting viewers into the appropriate
emotional and psychological mindset.

Nowhere is this truer than with music, which exerts an exceedingly powerful effect on the audience: whether by way of a sweeping, romantic orchestral score or minimalist tones that barely sound like notes at all, music can help change a conventional, potentially melodramatic romance into a subtle character study, or a spare contemporary Western into a taut psychological thriller. Walter Murch—who started his career as a sound editor and has often designed sound for the movies he edits—pointed out to me that sound powerfully conditions what we see in a movie, often at an unconscious level. "Sometimes it makes the visual image better," he observed, "and sometimes it makes you see things you don't know are there."

One of the most confounding aspects of film sound is who does what—a confusion reflected in the fact that two Oscars are usually bestowed for sound: one for best sound editing and one for best sound mixing. (Not surprisingly, the awards often go to the same film.) Sound editors compile, create, and assemble everything the audience hears on-screen, including dialogue (recorded during production as well as dubbed in later) and sound effects. Sound mixers decide at what levels those sounds will coexist with each other and the musical score, calibrating that ratio to enhance verisimilitude and emotional impact, as well as the audience's comprehension. The term "sound designer" is a bit fuzzier: Murch was the first person to earn the title, for his groundbreaking contributions to the movie *Apocalypse Now*; since then, it has been used interchangeably with "supervising sound editor" or "rerecording mixer" to describe the person with supervising authority over all aspects of recording and mixing dialogue, sound effects, and music; it can also describe a person who creates brand-new sounds for a film, rather than recording preexisting ones.

Great sound design is never a matter of simply slapping on whiz-bang sound effects after production has wrapped. Rather, it's the result of early and frequent collaboration between the director and the sound team, so that the aural elements in the film will knit together with the visuals in ways that serve and enhance the story. And sound design should never aim simply to make a movie loud; rather, it should always feel specific, well motivated, and variable, both in volume and in terms of the narrative and emotional values it's communicating.

CLEAR AS MUD

Could you hear what you needed to hear?

Did the sound effects drown out the dialogue? Was that an enhancement or a frustration?

Since the movies could first talk, dialogue has been the chief driver of narrative, and their sound designs have reflected that.

For most of the classical era of filmmaking, clarity and coherence—the simple ability to make out what the actors were saying—were paramount while recording and mixing a movie's soundtrack. (Although the term "soundtrack" is often used to refer to the music that appears in a particular film, here it means all the recorded sound—including dialogue, effects, any "source" music that plays within the narrative and is heard by the characters, and scoring and additional music heard only by the audience.) One of the hallmarks of films made in the 1930s and 1940s is their crystalline dialogue, which is discernible because it was mixed at a higher volume than extraneous effects and music.

The primacy of dialogue still holds true today, especially in the dreaded "pictures of people talking" I've been inveighing against in previous chapters. For the most part, mainstream Hollywood motion pictures are recorded competently enough that the audience can hear what's being said on-screen. Even low-budget independent films—which used to be known for their muddy, inconsistent sound recording—now have access to affordable digital equipment that renders their dialogue tracks as clear as those in big-budget blockbusters. Every now and then, however, filmmakers will push the boundaries of dialogue's importance with startling and uneven effects.

The director Christopher Nolan is famous (or infamous) for burying his characters' dialogue beneath thick layers of sound effects and the loud, thudding thwamp-thwamps of bass-heavy musical scores. Nolan has often declared his disdain for the process of additional dialogue recording (ADR), or "looping," whereby actors rerecord their lines after production has wrapped to add volume and clarity. Instead, he prefers the spontaneity of sound recorded on set, even if that means accepting a flub here or there, or less-than-crystal delivery.

The result, in many of Nolan's films, has been provocative at best and unintelligible at worst: *Inception*, a knotty, intellectually complicated 2010 thriller about a man who travels into others' dreams to implant subconscious thoughts and impulses, was difficult enough to understand conceptually without the added strain of trying to hear what was being said in some scenes. The problem was much worse in Nolan's 2014 sci-fi adventure *Interstellar*, which contained entire sequences where it was nearly impossible to make out what Matthew McConaughey's character was saying amid the roar of rocket engines and Hans Zimmer's aggressive scoring.

Many viewers and critics—myself included—took Nolan to task for the incoherent sound in *Interstellar*, but he was unapologetic. "I don't agree with the idea that you can only achieve clarity through dialogue," he told *The Hollywood Reporter*. "Clarity of story, clarity of emotions—I try to achieve that in a very layered way using all the different things at my disposal—picture and sound." Nolan's aims are admirable, but I maintain that, with *Interstellar*, the filmmaker needlessly alienated the audience instead of drawing them further into the story and the imaginary world he so carefully and ingeniously created.

Interestingly, that same year another director tried the exact same thing with far more satisfying results: in 2010's *The Social Network*, about Facebook creator Mark Zuckerberg, David Fincher similarly placed the dialogue far lower in the sound mix than where it usually resides. By accentuating sound effects and music, Fincher strove to mirror the distracted, multitasking world Zuckerberg both inhabits and is helping to create. One scene in particular, when Zuckerberg joins Napster founder Sean Parker for drinks in a San Francisco nightclub, pushes the limits of perception and audience comprehension. As the throbbing music threatens to drown out the actors, Fincher and his sound team make it almost—but not entirely—impossible to discern what the two men are saying as they yell across the table at one another. Rather than a monotonous wash of sound that drives viewers away, though, the mix brings us in closer, as we hungrily eavesdrop on a conversation that's always just on the verge of dropping out entirely. The difference between the frustration of *Interstellar* and the fascination of *The Social Network* embodies the difference between sound designed purely for artistic expression and an approach to sound that doesn't sacrifice consideration of the audience for aesthetic daring.

In Nolan's defense, he's capable of using aural shadings brilliantly: in *Inception*, for example, his sound designer, Richard King, hit on different aural cues to help guide viewers through the film's thicket of competing realities and arcane ideas. For starters, he and composer Zimmer introduced the motif of a ticking watch to remind viewers of how important time was to the characters; King also recorded a low-frequency "boom" that occurs every time one of the characters drops into a dream, helping orient viewers who might be unsure if they are operating in "reality" or not in a given scene. (That's an effect similar to what director Spike Jonze and his sound team used in 1999's *Being John Malkovich*: they subtly, and wittily, changed the ambient sound whenever the film switched to Malkovich's point of view, creating a subjective "in-your-head" soundscape for those scenes rather than the more objective sound of the rest of the film.)

Sound helps coherence in another way, which is to ease transitions between scenes, such as when the rifle fire of the twenty-one-gun salute at Richard Nixon's second inauguration in *All the President's Men* gives way to the percussive tap of typewriter keys, or the hotel desk bell that continues to ring long after John Turturro's title character has made his way to his room in *Barton Fink*. The audience's ears wind up doing most of the legwork in connecting images that otherwise might seem unrelated or awkwardly cobbled together.

HONEST SOUNDS

Did the movie sound "true"?

Part of what makes the nightclub scene in *The Social Network* so effective is that it feels so true to life.

Instead of characters conversing effortlessly in their normal speaking voices within the club's cacophony, they are yelling at each other, as would actually happen in that context. The degree of realism that a soundtrack should convey depends completely on the story the movie is trying to tell, and whether the director is trying to direct the audience's attention simply to his or her characters, or to more symbolic, stylized aspects of their experience.

Realistic sound doesn't mean "real" sound, in the sense that the film only uses sound recorded during production. In fact, some of the most realistic soundtracks are confections, products of production recording, clips from sound effects libraries, and "field" recordings from the real-life place being depicted on-screen.

An elegant example of this approach is Alfred Hitchcock's *Rear Window*, which takes place entirely within the courtyard of a Greenwich Village apartment house. One of the most delightful aspects of the *Rear Window* soundtrack is how sound recordists John Cope and Harry Lindgren expertly layered the noises from individual apartments, "placing" them on the soundtrack so they seemed to emanate from a multitude of directions, echoing differently with each one. The horse in *The Black Stallion* wasn't really fighting against the ropes he was tangled in on the beach of a deserted island; those anguished vocalizations were the product of Alan Splet and Ann Kroeber's meticulous process of gathering and recording just the right snorts, whinnies, and other sounds to convey the animal's terror and desperation.

One of the acknowledged masters of realism in sound was director Robert Altman, who in the 1970s experimented with putting microphones on each of his actors, creating sonic collages of overlapping, sometimes unintelligible dialogue every bit as crowded and jumbled as the ensembles he was filming. After experimenting with this approach in *McCabe & Mrs. Miller* and *M*A*S*H*, Altman perfected the technique in 1975's *Nashville*, wherein he and sound recorder James Webb mic'ed several actors and, with the help of noise-reduction technology invented by Dolby, layered their voices on top of one another in postproduction. The carefully calibrated tapestry subtly directed the viewer's attention to a particular character by bringing his or her lines up in volume within the mix.

Sometimes realism has absolutely nothing to do with reality but rather with established conventions: although it drives ornithologists crazy, playing the screech of a red-tailed hawk while a bald eagle is on-screen is an accepted, albeit clichéd, piece of movie language; similarly, most viewers have no objection to hearing crickets at night regardless of the season, or a thunderclap accompanying a bolt of lightning. When someone punches another person in the face in real life, it rarely makes a cracking sound (in the movies, often achieved by breaking a piece of celery), but on-screen, audiences have come not only to accept that little cheat, but to expect it.

One of my favorite exceptions to the snap-crackle-pop rule of movie-fight sound occurs in James Gray's 2000 urban drama *The Yards*, when friends played by Mark

Wahlberg and Joaquin Phoenix go after each other on a
deserted New York street. Rather than hyping the action
with lots of fake-sounding thwacks and cracks, Gary Ryd-
strom's sound design captured the confrontation as messy
and muffled; the most prominent sounds are the actors'
"oophs" and their shoes scraping on the pavement. (The
scene's authenticity was no doubt heightened by the fact
that Wahlberg and Phoenix actually fought each other
over the course of three or four takes, growing more
black-and-blue with each outing.)

Then there are the filmmakers who proudly dispense
with realism, preferring to underline the weirdness of their
narratives by creating similarly bizarre soundscapes. No
one has been more effective at this than David Lynch, who
with Alan Splet has created some iconic and utterly weird
sonic environments. On *Blue Velvet*, an unsettling journey
past the surface wholesomeness of suburbia into the darkest
reaches of the human psyche, the opening sequence fore-
shadows that trip, as the soporific strains of Bobby Vin-
ton and a spraying garden hose give way to the menacing
munching sounds of insects just under the earth's surface.
Through sound and image, Lynch prepares the audience
for the experience that's about to unfold, which will have
little to do with reality as they know it. As Lynch's rerecording mixer John Ross said of the filmmaker, Lynch is
"definitely not a 'see a dog, hear a dog' kind of guy. He's
more, 'See a dog and possibly imagine what the dog is
thinking.'" Next time one of Lynch's movies pops up on
cable, give yourself a crash tutorial in movie sound: close
your eyes and just listen as an entire world comes to life in
your ears.

OH, THE PLACES YOU WILL HEAR

Where did the sound take you?

Much as production design and cinematography can establish setting, sound can define a specific acoustic space—geographical, historical, and psychological.

For *The New World*, about seventeenth-century figures John Smith and Pocahontas, director Terrence Malick ordered his sound technicians to scour the Virginia Tidewater region for authentic sounds of the area's wind, water, flora, and fauna. Reportedly, around one hundred bird species are represented in the film (all authentic to period and place), including an ivory-billed woodpecker, which Malick included at the very end of the movie as an homage to the rare bird that had been spotted the same year he was making the film.

In *The New World*, as in most of Malick's films, dialogue is sparse to nonexistent, forcing the sound design to do much of the heavy lifting in orienting viewers, as well as immersing them in the film's environment. The same can be said of the 2000 movie *Cast Away*, in which Tom Hanks plays a FedEx executive stranded on an uninhabited island; for one long, forty-five-minute stretch, there is no dialogue or music—just the sounds of crashing waves, creaking palm trees, and Hanks's footsteps in the sand. The challenge for Randy Thom, director of sound design at Skywalker Sound, was to record and then layer lots of specific sounds to create something variable and interesting, rather than a broad swash of beach sounds that would run into each other with no dynamism or depth. (Thom found that wicker baskets were good for those palm tree effects, by the way; whereas the recordists for

The New World used air blown through colanders and vegetable steamers to achieve their variable wind effects.) The key in the sound design of *Cast Away*, as in all movies, was finding specificity within the greater wash of sonic information.

Some of the best examples of sound being used to establish setting can be found in the brilliant sound effects Ben Burtt invented for *Star Wars*. Director George Lucas had extensive conversations with Burtt about the sensibility of the film, which he wanted to be "used" and worn, rather than shiny, computerized, and sterile. For that reason, none of the signature sounds of *Star Wars* are synthesized. Rather, Burtt created them from practical household items; for the sound the light sabers made, for example, he passed a microphone over the screen of a television set. Burtt also used "real motors, real squeaky doors, real animal sounds, real insects" to create the 250 brand-new sounds that became the *Star Wars* library. As important as Lucas's retro-futuristic visual aesthetic was to inviting audiences into a story that felt simultaneously new and familiar and introducing them to its characters, there's no doubt that Burtt's organic soundscape helped viewers accept the filmmaker's wildly imaginary world as real and lived-in.

BUMPS IN THE NIGHT

How did what you hear make you feel?

It's difficult to overstate how crucial sound is in guiding and shaping our emotional reaction to what's on-screen.

We all know how a well-timed moment of silence followed by a creak of a floorboard or the slam of a door can make us jump in fear at a horror movie; similarly, when a scene opens on a quiet, dew-glistened meadow with a stately British mansion in the background, the coo of mourning doves quickly establishes a soothing, reassuring sense of calm.

Sound recordist Ann Kroeber (who collaborated frequently with Splet, her late husband) put things this way: Imagine a couple at night, standing under a streetlight. Depending entirely on what effects the sound editor layers in for the background, the scene can play very differently. "You could make the scene romantic by having sweet little insects, the lovely summer chirp," she told me. "You'd hear the very soft sound of traffic, or a car softly goes by. Or it could be Lynchian. You'd have a low rumble, and the traffic and sounds of the city would have a low sound. The streetlamp would have a kind of buzzing sound, like a fluorescent light. . . . You could give it a completely different feeling just with the sound effects."

Think of the incessant thwap-thwap-thwap as Jack Nicholson's author throws a tennis ball against a wall at the Overlook Hotel in *The Shining*, or the idiosyncratic sound his son's tricycle makes as he wheels it along the carpeted hallways, and how those two sonic moments ratchet up the tension. Or think of the signature scene in *No Country for Old Men*, when Josh Brolin's character awaits the killer Anton Chigurh in a darkened hotel room: Chigurh's muffled footsteps draw closer, stop outside the door, and then move on—until we hear him unscrewing a lightbulb in the hallway. The sound design for *No Country for Old Men* is a masterful example of realism: with very few exceptions, all the sound in the movie is diegetic, meaning it emanates from the people, objects, and spaces seen on-screen; even when effects are added, they underline the sense of spare authenticity, rather than undermining or compromising it. "Joel [Coen] made it clear from the beginning that it would be an experiment in a minimal approach to sound," recalled supervising sound editor Skip Lievsay about *No Country for Old Men*. "So instead of making it as loud and crazy as we can, we tried to make it as quiet and subtle as we can. So we only did the absolute minimum, like just a few footsteps and some ambience, maybe a car [sound] or a gunshot, or whatever was happening on-screen. We wanted to have the appearance that there was literally only the fewest number of sounds possible to convey the information."

No Country also exemplifies why silence can often be far more effective than sound effects in creating unease or wariness in the audience—and there are different types of silence. Most movies feature the sounds of nature, or even "room tones"—literally the sound of an empty room someone has recorded—to provide silent sequences with ambience and dimension (such as in the opening sequence of *There Will Be Blood*). Sometimes, though, a filmmaker uses nothing at all, which conveys a more abstract, airless sense of alienation or dread: William Friedkin used this kind of silence in *The Exorcist*, which goes from loud, demonic sounds to dead quiet, with absolutely nothing on the soundtrack—not even the manufactured sound of nothing. Director Anton Corbijn went for a similar ambience-free effect in *The American*. The opening scene plays against no sound, an almost abstract gambit that accentuates the isolation of George Clooney's lonely assassin and pulls the viewer's attention to his subjective experience.

WHOSE HEADSPACE ARE WE IN?

Did the sound have a point of view?

What we hear from a movie depends on who's hearing it *in* the movie.

Even the loudest, busiest sound designs should embrace a specific point of view—usually the protagonist's. In the 1974 paranoid thriller *The Conversation*, Murch's ingenious sound design re-creates—obsessively, over and over—the often distorted and indistinct voices heard by Gene Hackman's character, a surveillance expert named Harry Caul. The film's echoey acoustic architecture mimics the brutalist San Francisco office building and warehouse space Harry visits and works in as well as his own inner state of isolation and ruminative self-recrimination.

The sounds of a subway train building to a screeching halt when Michael Corleone assassinates two rivals in a restaurant in *The Godfather* not only help create the tension of the scene, but powerfully reflect his own moral ambivalence and pain. For Jake LaMotta's fight sequences in *Raging Bull*, sound designer Frank Warner made sure that every punch and camera flash had its own sound (he used everything from rifle shots to melons breaking for the effects), and occasionally dropped the sound out entirely, to better allow the viewer to get inside LaMotta's embattled psyche.

In *Secretariat*, about the champion racehorse, director Randall Wallace and his sound team devised a sonic signature for their equine hero—whose nickname was Big Red—that reproduced not only the sound of his hooves and the sound of his breath but also the sound of his heart beating. (They achieved the effect by augmenting real-life

horse heartbeats with powerful Japanese taiko drums.)
The filmmakers strived for specificity even within the
crowded, chaotic race scenes: Secretariat's specific sound
signature helped the audience know when he was pulling
up alongside another horse during a race; in one sequence,
amid the roar of the crowd, an alert listener can hear a
child shout, "I saw Big Red!" as Secretariat walks by.
(To this day, *The Black Stallion* and *Never Cry Wolf*, both
directed by Carroll Ballard with sound design by Splet,
are heralded as breakthroughs when it comes to animal
sounds, both for their naturalistic, physical detail and for
their avoidance of anthropomorphizing their subjects with
"humanizing" effects.)

Characters don't have to be sentient beings in order
to be represented on a film's soundtrack. In Peter Weir's
Master and Commander: The Far Side of the World, for example, the ship on which the movie takes place has just
as much of a voice—the creaking, clanking, billowing
sounds of a tall ship in motion—as the humans who toil
on it. Similarly, in the action-adventure *Unstoppable*, a
runaway train groans, grunts, and shrieks with improbable but effective expressiveness, becoming a vibrant player
alongside Denzel Washington and Chris Pine. (For the
first *Star Wars* film, Burtt combined his own vocal sounds
with electronic keyboard sounds to create the robot R2-
D2's voice, which arguably has just as much personality
and character as the movie's animate players.) The often
playfully bizarre soundtrack in the Coen brothers' *Barton Fink* largely mirrors the solipsistic, disoriented mental
state of the title character, a blocked writer played by John
Turturro, whose complete desolation is reflected in hyper-
accentuated sounds of electric fans, squeaky shoes, and
scraping luggage against the silence of his tomb-like hotel.

Lievsay, who designed the sound for *Barton Fink*, recalled one of his favorite creations. It was for a scene where
the beleaguered Fink is sent to a studio screening room
to watch wrestling movies, and he becomes increasingly
uncomfortable in the knowledge that he won't be able to
deliver his promised script. Lievsay used recordings of explosions to accentuate the wrestlers' bodies hitting the mat;
a rock-crushing machine to create "a random crunching
sound"; a chainsaw, whose noise he lowered by a few oc-
taves; and finally, a European train whistle, which came
in at the end of the scene, distorted so that it sounded like
a siren—at which point Fink blacked out. "To me, that's
a good example of sound design," Lievsay said. "You're
finding components that aren't literal, but that heighten
the subjective experience. It's a component that you don't
understand, but it helps deliver the dramatic idea."

Of course, the masterpiece of sound design with a
point of view also happens to be a masterpiece of sound
designed for realism, setting, and mood: Murch achieved
the apotheosis of the form with Francis Ford Coppola's
Apocalypse Now, which begins with a black screen and the
sound of an electronically synthesized helicopter propeller,
whose muffled whir eventually blends with Jim Morri-
son singing "The End." As a helicopter's struts come into
view—followed by a green jungle, then slow-motion, sulfuric orange explosions—the sequence becomes a sonic
and visual collage that not only accurately refers to the
physical and temporal setting of the Vietnam War, but also
captures the conflict's numb, distorted psychic context and
the dreamlike mental state of the film's protagonist, played
by Martin Sheen. (Murch called the rotor effect his "ghost
helicopter," whose sounds changed and "began to bend

reality" as the movie went on.) In contrast to *No Country for Old Men*, much of the sound in *Apocalypse Now* is non-diegetic, meaning it doesn't emanate from what we're seeing on-screen or have a literal connection to it; instead, it's heavily stylized and symbolic. Still, in Murch's perceptive hands and in keeping with the film's psychedelic, end-times context, the sound design never threatens the film's sense of immediacy or realism.

With the *Apocalypse Now* soundtrack, Murch and his team also revolutionized the theatrical sound experience, which had mostly been a matter of sound and music simply emanating from a speaker located behind the movie screen. Murch and his colleagues invented a multichannel recording and playback system that allowed sounds to "travel" from one speaker to another in various locations throughout the theater; like Sheen's dazed army captain, the audience became enveloped in the sounds of the chaos and cacophony of war. (Murch's system was called 5.1 sound, reflecting the five speakers that were placed throughout the theater, and the ".1" being a channel specifically utilized for frequencies so low they could only be felt in the gut, rather than heard audibly—especially useful for explosions and, later, *T. rex* chases in *Jurassic Park*.) Still, Murch frequently reverted to plain-vanilla mono sound throughout the movie, so that viewers wouldn't become exhausted or overstimulated. The result was an aural environment for *Apocalypse Now* that, even at its most bizarre and distorted, never felt incoherent or fatally disorienting. Rather, as director Coppola intended, the sound design draws the audience into the world meticulously created on-screen.

BIG BOOMS AND GUT PUNCHES

Did you feel assaulted or embraced?

Sound can plunge us further into the imagined world on-screen, or it can alienate us from it.

Murch's 5.1 sound system for *Apocalypse Now* eventually became standard in the industry, which has also embraced various versions of "surround sound," where dozens of discrete channels of sound can emanate from the many speakers in the theater. At a time when the theatrical experience is constantly threatened by sophisticated home entertainment systems and ubiquitous iPhones, studios and theater owners have responded by engaging in a technological arms race to produce the biggest, loudest, most overwhelming audio experience with which to lure audiences back into the multiplex.

Just as visual features like 3-D and high-frame-rate digital cinematography are meant to wow viewers with their uncanny realism, surround sound is supposed to engulf them in the kind of all-encompassing experience Coppola was going for in *Apocalypse Now*. But without the sensitivity of a Walter Murch, the result is too often simply a more-is-more ethic of exponentially busier and louder movies, with none of the specificity or dynamic range that the best designers have devoted their careers to refining. Rather than "collapsing and re-stretching" the sound from speaker to speaker, as Murch did in *Apocalypse Now*, many of today's sound mixes are nonstop onslaughts of noise from all directions, leaving viewers feeling assaulted rather than immersed.

Even in the most complex sound mixes, typically only one sound needs to stand out in every scene, with perhaps two or three subordinate sounds to provide depth and context; any more than that, and it becomes an incoherent mishmash. Similarly, even if a theater announces the latest state-of-the-art sound system, it means nothing if its speakers aren't in proper working order, or if the volume is lazily left too high or too low between screenings. (It happens more than you think.)

The next time you're watching a movie—especially a cacophonous action film or comic-book spectacle—ask yourself to what extent the film's sound is organic and useful, rather than bombastic and contrived simply for sensational effect. As with 3-D and other visual gimmicks, the question is whether the quest for greater immersive engagement and sensory experience sacrifices such core values as narrative, character development, and emotion. As Randy Thom told me during one of our interviews, "If everything is loud, then nothing is loud."

THE SOUND OF MUSIC

Were you humming it when you walked out of the theater?

I can't watch *The Bad and the Beautiful* without humming its hauntingly beautiful music for days afterward. If I hear even a few notes from the score for *Cinema Paradiso*, I start to weep. The soulful guitar strains of the music Mark Knopfler composed for the winsome 1983 comedy *Local Hero* spark the same fond memories and longing that the title character succumbs to by the end of the film.

Music affects viewers so strongly, and creates such a potent emotional experience, that its importance to a film can't be overstated. To consider some of the great composer-director collaborations through film history— Ennio Morricone and Sergio Leone; Maurice Jarre and David Lean; John Williams and George Lucas and Steven Spielberg; Bernard Herrmann and Alfred Hitchcock; Carter Burwell and the Coen brothers; Terence Blanchard and Spike Lee—is to understand the essential role that music plays in helping build a convincingly immersive imaginary world.

Ideally, music shouldn't merely repeat or amplify story elements and feelings that are already being communicated visually or through dialogue. It should be additive, never mimicking the action or putting quote marks around it, but giving it more depth and meaning, usually entirely subconsciously. Perhaps most crucially, music should be used sparingly, so that the film allows viewers to make their own associations and connections, rather than continually prodding and poking them toward a particular feeling. The best score watches the movie with the viewers, not for them; it's baked into the film, rather than being slathered on top like too much sugar icing.

The proper use of music mirrors, and works in tandem, with the proper use of sound effects and dialogue, helping achieve the same ends, whether in providing a thematic through-line that strengthens a film's cohesiveness or conveying an emotion that a character can't readily articulate. But, unlike nearly every other craft area of filmmaking, a film's score has the potential to exist as a separate aesthetic product, as a piece of music that can be enjoyed in and of itself, without the attendant images. Although it's gratifying when movie music aspires to and achieves this kind of greatness, it's not required; the composer's first responsibility is not to write something that can be performed later, but to serve and support the story unfolding on-screen. Like a well-meaning friend, music should help that story in any way it can, without intruding, barging in at inopportune moments, or overstaying its welcome.

We can all name snippets of film scores that have become as beloved as the movies themselves: Morricone's lonesome, coyote-like flute notes in Leone's *The Good, the Bad, and the Ugly*. The transporting strains of Jarre's "Lara's Theme" throughout *Doctor Zhivago*. Williams's triumphalist anthem at the beginning of *Star Wars*. Nino Rota's romantic, melancholy theme for *The Godfather*. Magnificent scores, all of them, demonstrating how music can both work for the film it's in and also transcend that role to become iconic in its own right. (Thomas Newman's xylophone riff for *American Beauty* might have even inspired a ringtone.)

Not every film score has to be as instantly recognizable as those compositions to succeed. In fact, some of the strongest film music doesn't stick with the audience after they leave the theater, but nonetheless adds exponentially to their experience while they are in it. Although an appealing, affecting melody is always nice, film scores don't have to be "pretty." The sad, romantic theme that Carter Burwell wrote for the Coens' *Miller's Crossing* is one of the most beautiful pieces of film music ever written. (For a while, it was the go-to score that movie companies would use on their trailers for stirring romantic and historical dramas.) Jonny Greenwood's minimalist electronic score for *There Will Be Blood*, as a counterexample, is forbidding and dissonant. Both work perfectly for the stories they're telling.

When Burwell was honored for his work at Virginia's Middleburg Film Festival in 2015, I asked him how he had managed to come up with so many memorable themes; he told me he plays the piano every day, and when a compelling riff or potential idea occurs to him, he makes sure to record it. He now has around 1,500 such snippets cataloged for future use. "This is one of the things that lets me sleep at night when I have a deadline," he said only half-jokingly.

I'm a music lover, so I tend to notice a movie's score, especially if it's particularly lyrical or when it strikes me as over-the-top or misplaced. Some purists would suggest that if we're noticing a film's music—even to note how lovely it is—then the composer has failed. I disagree: whether the music should stand out depends on genre—a lush, attention-getting orchestral score might be clichéd for an old-fashioned melodrama or period piece, but provide an added layer of lyricism or ambiguity to a tough urban thriller. And it depends on the filmmaker. By now, we've come to expect movies by Martin Scorsese and Todd Haynes to feature "big" musical moments; indeed, their soundtracks and scores are a big part of what makes their work distinctive and hugely enjoyable.

COHERENCE

Did the music help tie the whole movie together?

The musical score can be just as useful as sound design in tying a movie together, especially during transitions; recurring themes and motifs allow characters—and the audience—to access memories or recall crucial plot points without spelling them out in dreary dialogue or clunky exposition. A recent and ingenious example is Antonio

Sanchez's all-drum score for *Birdman or (the Unexpected Virtue of Ignorance)*, Alejandro González Iñárritu's backstage drama about a former action star trying to make a comeback. Iñárritu filmed and edited the movie to resemble one long, unbroken take—an effect helped along by the incessant percussion that propelled the action at such a compulsively breakneck pace that viewers never had time to notice (or care) whether the seams were showing.

In a wonderful example of sound design and music working in tandem, the score of *Atonement*, Joe Wright's adaptation of the Ian McEwan novel, often features the ostinato-like accompaniment of typewriter keys, a subtle reminder of the story's subtext about the power of storytelling, both for good and for ill. The score picks up on that motif, threading viewers along and unifying a story of disparate time periods and shifting character perspectives.

Similarly, sound effects and music blended with chilling efficacy in Hitchcock's *Psycho* and *The Birds*. Both featured scores by his longtime composer Herrmann, who cannily blended high-pitched string arrangements to create eerie, psychologically harrowing soundscapes. (I've always thought that the genius of Williams's *Jaws* theme was how its one-two rhythm mimicked the sound of legs kicking underwater—so that people literally hear it every time they go swimming.)

MENTAL MUSIC

Did the music have a point of view?

One of the chief roles of a musical score is, to quote the great composer Elmer Bernstein, to "get behind and inside" a movie's characters, especially when they're too reticent, isolated, or emotionally blocked to express themselves fully. Just as sound effects help establish a movie's point of view, so does music.

Bernstein's score for *To Kill a Mockingbird* exemplifies this principle with lyrical elegance, both in his simple, childlike theme for the film's protagonist, Scout, and the more mysterious, melancholy orchestral theme for Boo Radley. In *The French Connection*, jazz musician Don Ellis created a slashing, aggressive musical environment that matched the seedy, trash-strewn New York City where the story was set, conveying the simmering rage that motivated the film's pugnacious antihero, Popeye Doyle, played by Gene Hackman. A few years later, Hackman's character inspired another haunting musical score in *The Conversation*, for whom David Shire composed sad, chromatic piano music that subtly conveyed the protagonist's essential loneliness and inability to connect. (In *Rear Window*, in keeping with the film's fealty to the point of view of James Stewart's character, the only time we hear Franz Waxman's beautiful music—with one or two exceptions—is when it's emanating from one of the apartments on the courtyard; the score, in other words, is almost entirely source music.)

More recently, Trent Reznor created a brilliant musical cue to help the audience understand his characters in *The Social Network*. We're first introduced to Mark Zuckerberg in a prickly, rapid-fire conversation he's having with a girl he wants to date in a Cambridge, Massachusetts, pub; nine minutes later, the rebuffed Zuckerberg runs back to his Harvard dorm, hurt and angry—and Reznor's music kicks in, a plaintive piano melody with a slightly dissonant string arrangement underneath that grows more pronounced as he hurries home. Within two minutes, the music has helped establish Zuckerberg as someone's who's deeply wounded and lonely, but in whom aggression and resentment are welling up, to quote director David Fincher, like "a riptide." Comparing Reznor's opening theme for *The Social Network* to composer Wendy Carlos's adaptation of Berlioz for the opening sequence of *The Shining*, Fincher noted that both pieces of music add crucial subtext to otherwise unremarkable actions. In the case of *The Shining*, he said, "It tells you immediately that there is more to it than a guy driving on a highway traveling to a hotel. There's something larger at work." From its first eerily dissonant strains, Mica Levi's powerful score for the 2016 speculative drama *Jackie*, about the days following the assassination of John F. Kennedy, plunged viewers into the fractured psychological state of the title character as she moved numbly through grief, dispossession, and dread.

One of the most accomplished composers in writing for characters is Burwell, who has provided music for Joel and Ethan Coen since their feature debut, *Blood Simple*, and whose music often provides intimacy, empathy, and even warmth that would otherwise be lacking in their often slightly cynical films. For nearly every film he's worked on with the Coens, Burwell has written an identifiable theme for at least one character, whether it's his magnificent adaptation of the Scandinavian hymn "The Lost Sheep" for William H. Macy's hapless criminal in *Fargo* or, more counterintuitively, his elaboration of the unabashedly sentimental Irish song "Danny Boy" for Gabriel Byrne's ice-cold henchman in *Miller's Crossing*. In both instances, Burwell's music elevated the brutality and cynicism on-screen into a space of serious, even mournful, moral reckoning. For *Carol*, Todd Haynes's love story about two women in 1950s New York, Burwell's unabashedly romantic music swept the film along on a tide of emotion that neither character could fully express, by dint of the times and their own restrained temperaments.

MOOD MUSIC

How did the music make you feel?

If it's true that the first several minutes of a movie teach the audience how to watch it, then the music that plays (or doesn't play) during that time offers the most potent clues.

Think of those playful xylophone tones of the *American Beauty* theme, at first working in a darkly funny duet with Kevin Spacey's sarcastic voiceover, then eventually giving way to a more introspective, unapologetically emotional string arrangement when the story takes a genuinely tragic turn. Or think of Burwell's booming timpani in the stark opening sequence of *Fargo*, lending moral gravitas to the bleak comedy that will unfold, or the way his barely there music for *No Country for Old Men*—more a collection of tonal textures than conventional notes—merges almost completely with the film's quietly watchful sound design. As Burwell himself noted, to have placed conventional music into the film at any juncture would have completely destroyed the values that made it such a tour de force of rawboned realism and anxiety.

Music can accentuate mood or ironically play against it: Earl Scruggs's jaunty banjo music for 1967's *Bonnie and Clyde* might reflect the duo's idea of themselves as rakish, Robin Hood–like celebrities, but it's completely at odds with the destructive path they're cutting through

Depression-era Texas. By the time the movie ends in a
shattering, bloody shoot-out, the score has taken on a
deeply troubling sense of irony. (Burwell and the Coens
would resurrect that musical style for their screwball par-
enting comedy *Raising Arizona*, again ironically, but much
more playfully.) The textures and rhythms of the atonal,
abstract-sounding scores for *There Will Be Blood*, *The Revenant*, and *Jackie* introduce notes of unease and discomfort,
putting the audience on notice that those films won't be
cozy, conventional, or reassuring. Similarly, Hans Zimmer's magnificent cello-and-violin score for *12 Years a
Slave*—which never sounded exactly "on period" in terms
of nineteenth-century classical and folk music—lent the
story a contemporary, even avant-garde resonance that
helped the film transcend its specific time and place. As fascinating as these counterintuitive scores were, sometimes
old-fashioned, on-the-nose emotion can be just as welcome, such as Michael Giacchino's compositions for Pixar
animated movies. Working with live orchestras and lush,
often unapologetically sentimental arrangements, Giacchino has perfected the art of giving the audience valuable
emotional cues without making us feel patronized. His
music adds layers to what's on-screen, rather than simply
amplifying or regurgitating; that three-tissue prologue to
Up, so economical in its storytelling, wouldn't have been
half as heartrending were it not for Giacchino's moving
accompaniment. All movie composers manipulate—that's
their business. Giacchino just does it with exceptional pa-
nache and original style.

Indeed, standards have changed dramatically as to what
audiences will accept when it comes to outright manipulation. A Bette Davis melodrama from the 1940s featured
lots of dramatic underscoring—wherein the orchestra

played almost constantly, under the actors' dialogue—but today's contemporary dramas tend to be sparer and more selective in their use of musical cues.

One exception lies in the genres of action thrillers and comic-book movies, in which otherwise fine movie scores are overused as part of nonstop, wall-to-wall sound design—a symptom, no doubt, of Hollywood's increasing dependence on the foreign market for box-office sales and the studios' nervousness about non-English-speaking audiences "getting" every emotional beat and nuance.

The result is a knock-down, drag-out fight between music, sound effects, and dialogue that is likely to leave viewers feeling like the losers (and just as battered and bruised). Fundamentally, over-scoring in films betrays both a lack of trust in the audience and a lack of confidence on the part of filmmakers who continually tell their viewers what to feel, rather than allowing the story and performers to do so.

Often this kind of insecurity is reflected in one of my favorite pieces of film-business jargon: "mickey-mousing," which composers use derisively to describe music that slavishly follows the action unfolding on-screen. (It's too bad the term has become a pejorative, because the cartoon music to which it refers was so brilliantly written and produced.) Certainly, familiar riffs and key changes can provide helpful cues to the audience in terms of a movie's tone and emotional temperature. But one sure sign of hackwork in a film's score is when it consistently reverts to cliché—testosterone-fueled drums thundering under a car chase, for example, or a string riff I call "syncopated pizzicato" during a playful moment in a comedy. Clichéd music provides redundant commentary on the visual action rather than a counterpoint.

Most of my favorite examples of film scores are the ones that exhibit restraint, not only compositionally but in their placement within the movie itself, resulting in music that's sensed more than heard. David Shire's reflective, observant music for *All the President's Men* doesn't begin to play until forty-five minutes into the movie, and then only reappears when absolutely necessary, usually during transitions. Howard Shore created a similarly meditative, sober-minded piano score for *Spotlight*, which, like *All the President's Men* before it, allowed the emotional impact to arise naturally from the actors and their performances, rather than forcing or milking it by other means.

Another fabulous instance of musical restraint can be found in *Ronin*, John Frankenheimer's 1998 thriller whose centerpiece is a stunning car chase through Paris. For the first four minutes, the scene is accompanied by screeching tires and revving engines; the music kicks in at a crucial point, only when the cars begin to race the wrong way down a one-way thoroughfare. After a few loud notes during which the music announces itself, it tucks back down under the sound effects, creating a sonic tableau that, in its own subliminal way, is every bit as spectacular as the action.

BEWARE THE TOP 40

Did the filmmaker rely on pop songs to "sell" the story?

In his book *Pictures at a Revolution*, Mark Harris brilliantly examined how the Best Picture nominees of 1968—*Bonnie and Clyde*, *The Graduate*, *In the Heat of the*

Night, Guess Who's Coming to Dinner, and *Doctor Doolittle*—exemplified seismic cultural shifts both in the movie industry and the broader American society. One bellwether of how movies were changing was that three of the films relied entirely on country, pop, and jazz tunes, rather than traditional orchestral scores, for their music. This approach would hit its apotheosis in the 1970s and 1980s, when soundtrack albums for *Saturday Night Fever* and *Grease* became huge moneymakers for the studios' parent corporations; soon, movies were being scored not according to their narrative or emotional imperatives, but simply by slapping on trendy Top 40 songs that might draw in young audiences and make a cash cow of the soundtrack album.

In the hands of a master—Robert Altman, for example, or Woody Allen, or Martin Scorsese—the compilation score is a thing of beauty, a carefully curated selection of popular or obscure cuts that fit the mood of the scenes they accompany and act like dog whistles for the filmmaker's personal taste and point of view. The Leonard Cohen songs that played throughout Altman's *McCabe & Mrs. Miller* weren't "on period"—in fact, they were completely anachronistic to the film's early twentieth-century setting. But their wintry, reflective mood worked perfectly with the Pacific Northwest setting and the wistful, unresolved relationship between the title characters, played by Warren Beatty and Julie Christie. By contrast, when *Butch Cassidy and the Sundance Kid* is interrupted by a silly, romantic montage sequence set to Burt Bacharach's improbably sunny 1969 hit "Raindrops Keep Fallin' on My Head," it looks and feels like a jarring non sequitur.

Another way filmmakers use previously recorded tunes is as "source music," which is music that both the characters and the audience can hear. One of the best examples of source music was in *One Flew over the Cuckoo's Nest*: "Charmaine," an anodyne waltz from the 1920s, played over the radio in an asylum dayroom in a patronizing effort to subdue a group of male mental patients; the sickly-sweet tune put viewers inside the dayroom themselves, burrowing into our heads just as insidiously as it did the trapped characters on-screen. On the other hand, in the recent romantic drama *Begin Again*, filmmaker John Carney made a hash of source music. When a grizzled music producer played by Mark Ruffalo shares his iPod with a budding songwriter, the playlist is made up of by-the-numbers standards, like Frank Sinatra singing "Luck Be a Lady" and Stevie Wonder's "For Once in My Life"; Ruffalo's character would be far more likely to be a connoisseur of obscure B-sides and rare, unfamiliar cuts. (Though, in his defense, Carney surely was hemmed in by the often exorbitant costs of licensing popular music for films, which impact soundtracks more than most viewers realize.)

Compilation scores carry the same dangers as their orchestral counterparts in filmmakers' tendency to overuse them to sell a particular scene or emotion. I call these "needle drop" movies, because they tend to play short bits of instantly recognizable pop songs to pander to the audience rather than attempting to deepen what's happening on-screen. Scorsese's *GoodFellas* used every song perfectly to capture Henry Hill's rise and fall—apotheosized by the piano solo from Eric Clapton's "Layla" playing over the bloody aftermath of a series of gangland assassinations. But too often, pop soundtracks feel forced and too eager to impress—a problem shared by Zach Braff's pop-crammed romantic comedy *Garden State* and, more recently, the comedies *Suicide Squad* and *War Dogs*, which trotted out musical snippets so compulsively that the ultimate effect was one of too-cool-for-school overkill and swiftly diminishing returns. On the other hand, it's no surprise that Aimee Mann's songs in *Magnolia* feel so organically of a piece with the movie: Paul Thomas Anderson has said Mann's music inspired him to write it in the first place.

MOVIE SOUND IS COMPOSED OF so many elements—"production sound" recorded on set, additional dialogue recorded and dubbed in after production, sound effects, and music—that it's usually impossible to tease out what's working and what's not during the viewing experience. We do know, however, if we heard what we needed to hear in order to understand what was happening onscreen; we know whether we feel addled and overwhelmed upon leaving the theater, or refreshed from having a genuinely novel, emotionally potent experience. We might already be humming the score, we might not; what counts is that the music contributed to the construction of a complete sonic world, enriched in equal measure by the dialogue, sound effects, score, and musical soundtrack. As Murch said of movie sound in one of our interviews: "If it helped the film, it probably made it 4 percent better. If it was wrong, it would hurt 90 percent."

RECOMMENDED VIEWING ···

Apocalypse Now (1979)
The Black Stallion (1979)
Blue Velvet (1986)
Being John Malkovich (1999)
Cast Away (2000)
No Country for Old Men (2007)

CHAPTER SEVEN

········· DIRECTING ·········

*D*irecting a movie is a very overrated job, we all know
it. You just have to say yes or no. What else do you
do? Nothing. "Maestro, should this be red?" Yes.
"Green?" No. "More extras?" Yes. "More lipstick?" No.
Yes. No. Yes. No. That's directing.

Thus speaks the acerbic costume designer played by
Judi Dench in *Nine*, the filmed adaptation of the Broadway
musical, about a self-involved movie director. The speech
is supposed to wink at and puncture directorial ego, which
François Truffaut immortalized with exasperation in his
film about filmmaking, *Day for Night*. "Questions! Questions! So many questions that I don't have time to think!"

Both Dench and Truffaut playfully address an essential
question: What is it that film directors actually do? Do
they "organize an entire universe," as Ingmar Bergman
famously said? Preside over accidents, as Orson Welles
put it? Are they essentially plumbers, which is how John
Frankenheimer once explained the distinctly unglamorous
problem-solving mechanics of the profession? Or are they

men and women "juggling five balls in the air while a train is running behind them at full speed," as Guillermo del Toro told me?

We know when a movie's been well-directed. It's well-directed when it works—when it looks great, sounds great, features believable performances, and leaves the audience feeling satisfied—or, if it's *really great*, permanently transformed.

But wait: We liked the story, the movie's structure was clever, and that dialogue was hilarious—doesn't that mean the movie was well-written? And the lead actor—he's good in everything, isn't he? The director didn't design the costumes. She didn't operate the camera for that breathtaking tracking shot. She didn't compose the musical score we're humming, or invent the sound effects.

Maybe Dame Judi was on to something—maybe directors *are* overrated.

Er, not so fast, wardrobe lady. Yes and No sound easy enough, until you say No when you should say Yes. Or say Yes to the wrong thing. "A director makes a thousand binary decisions a day," the director Jason Reitman explained. "Now, let's say I get one of those questions wrong. It wouldn't be a big deal. Even if I got 5 percent wrong, it'll probably fly by.

"But let's say I got half of it wrong," Reitman continued. "What if this was a really intimate scene and it didn't feel intimate because the location seemed too modern? Or the background actors brought too much attention upon themselves? All of a sudden, enough questions come up that, for whatever reason, you've stopped believing in the reality of this movie. . . . And all of a sudden, the movie is poorly directed."

Alternatively, as the actor Casey Affleck noted, a director's wise choices can save an otherwise negligible

script or a poor performance. "I've been on set with people who I didn't think were very good," he told me. "And
those people came out looking great. They [made] really
interesting choices in the movie. And I *know* that has to do
with the director's contextualizing the performance and
cutting out shit.

"You can make a great performance nothing, and
make nothing a great performance," Affleck continued.
"You can make bad writing good in the execution. . . . It's
sort of like a stew: there's no way of knowing if the carrots
were good and the garlic wasn't. If it's a good stew, it's a
good stew, and all the flavors are working together."

In many ways, our confusion over what directors do
stems from the attempt to give them the appreciation
they deserve. In the mid-1950s, the French critic and
future New Wave director François Truffaut wrote that
films were incontrovertibly the creation of their directors,
whose creative visions were inscribed on every frame,
even if they didn't write the original scripts. (As examples, he pointed to the instantly recognizable style of films
by Alfred Hitchcock and Howard Hawks.) Truffaut's idea
migrated across the Atlantic in 1962 when the *Village Voice*
critic Andrew Sarris vigorously defended what had come
to be known as the *auteur* theory in the journal *Film Culture*, igniting one of cinema's most legendary debates. Most
notably, the critic Pauline Kael (who had yet to assume her
post at *The New Yorker*) took issue with a cinematic version of the Great Man theory, arguing in *Film Quarterly*'s
Spring 1963 issue that screenwriters, cinematographers,
and actors were at least as influential as directors in the
creation of a film, and dismissing auteurism as deficient
in terms of both aesthetic values and logic. Later, in his
groundbreaking book *The Genius of the System*, the film
historian Thomas Schatz made a persuasive case that the

"house styles" of individual studios and their craft departments during Hollywood's Golden Age had as much to do with their films' visual and thematic signatures as the men (and they were mostly men) who made them did.

Even though giants such as Spielberg, Scorsese, Coppola, and Tarantino have become reliable brands, the auteur argument continues to this day. (Just take a screenwriter to a movie that opens with "A film by . . . ," a particular director, and watch the popcorn fly.) Still, it's rare to cross paths with a director who doesn't take pains to acknowledge that film is the ultimate collaborative medium. As the director Alan J. Pakula once observed, "For some strange reason, I always look the most talented when I'm working with the most talented people."

The issue is made even murkier by the fact that, in America, mainstream directors don't commonly "own" their work; rather, it's the property of the studios or producers who hired them and who can re-edit the picture according to their own judgment, whim, or eagerness to please a wide audience. (In France, directors have long enjoyed *droits d'auteur*, or authors' rights, giving creative control to the creator of the work rather than the financer.)

Directors who have reached a certain level of commercial or artistic prestige or who insist on working independently have the right to "final cut" written into their contracts, meaning that their work can't be interfered with after they've delivered their own version. But not all directors are so lucky. David Fincher and Ridley Scott famously complained about studio interference with their films *Alien 3* and *Blade Runner*, respectively; more recently, Duncan Jones mounted similar criticisms regarding the recut of his film *Warcraft*, as did Josh Trank for *Fantastic Four*. When directors get really mad, they take their names off their films, sometimes substituting the pseudonym "Alan Smithee" (although we don't see Alan Smithee credited on many theatrical films, the directors Michael Mann, William Friedkin, and Martin Brest have all requested the moniker for versions of their films that were edited for television).

Even with all of these conditions and caveats, though, it's true that the director is usually connected to a film project longer than any other crew or cast member: choosing the material, or deciding to accept it from a producer; working with the screenwriter to come up with the final script, or rewriting it entirely; casting and rehearsing the actors; assembling the rest of the creative team; scouting locations; choosing a visual style; deciding on and overseeing the shooting schedule; and supervising postproduction functions such as editing, sound design, and scoring. Somehow, the director must keep passion and focus alive through years—sometimes decades—of following an idea to fruition. (A kind word here for producers, who just as often generate and stick by a film project to the bitter end, and whose involvement can be crucial not just creatively but practically, in terms of acquiring financing. Such producers as Scott Rudin, Bona Fide Productions' Albert Berger and Ron Yerxa, Plan B's Dede Gardner and Jeremy Kleiner, and Killer Films founder Christine Vachon, among others, have become hugely influential in developing scripts and shepherding them to gifted directors and casts.)

It's the director who, if not literally making every creative and technical decision, is signing off on each of them. It's the director who must resolve the myriad unexpected disasters, surprises, and opportunities that inevitably emerge on any movie shoot—and does so in a way that doesn't ruin the movie and might even make it better. And it's the director who takes the blame for mishandling these moments when they go awry.

It's the director who establishes the work ethic and atmosphere of the entire production, creating a safe space for actors to expose themselves emotionally (and sometimes physically), listening to the ideas and suggestions of cast and crew members, inspiring everyone to do their very best work, and exuding enough leadership and confidence that the team feels secure and tightly focused on the enterprise at hand. At every moment, the director must communicate and protect the original vision for the movie, which can be so easily chipped away by indecision, expediency, or lack of conviction. "Directing is the ultimate 'all of the above,'" Richard Linklater told me. "You're the head coach. Every department you're collaborating with, whether you've written the script or even if you haven't, you're . . . [creating] an atmosphere where they can do their best work around a common goal, which is to make the best movie possible from this material." It's the director who is ultimately in charge of the aesthetic experience of the viewers, directing their attention visually and aurally and guiding their emotions.

Green or red? This one or that one? Yes or no? Choices that seem trivial can turn out to have disastrous or downright miraculous results while making a movie. And it's the director who is called a hack in the first instance or a genius in the latter. "I love directors who have an open-door policy and the collaborative spirit and all that," Meryl Streep once said, "but I also love that it's his fault in the end."

CHOPS

Did the filmmaker demonstrate fluency and command with the medium?

Did the movie reflect ambition and vision beyond simply recording performances?

A skilled screenwriter and editor can help establish a movie's setting, rhythms, and "rules of the road," but it's the director who enforces those rules from the outset, firmly announcing the film's intention and making it clear that he or she knows precisely where we're going and how to get there. The director's sure-footedness begins on the set, where he or she must project confidence in leading the creative team, and extends all the way to the screen, in convincing filmgoers to enter a new and unfamiliar world.

That feeling of assuredness—sometimes expressed in nervy, bravura camerawork and crisp, firm editing, other times through the quiet willingness to hang back and let scenes play from a discreet distance—can be conveyed in many ways: technical proficiency, craftsmanship, efficiency, even *cojones*. I use the term "chops" to stand for a deep knowledge of film mechanics and staging—where to place the camera, what lenses to use, how to inspire trust and clarity of purpose, the right time to let a scene play or make a cut—as well as of cinematic grammar. And chops count with actors, too: "When I see a bad performance, I never blame the actor," Linklater said. "I blame the director. You either miscast, and that happens, or you didn't create an atmosphere where you could get the best out of that person."

A movie by a director with chops makes clear from the outset that this person has a direct line not only to the story at hand but also to its intended audience. It's a thrilling sensation, and I've been lucky enough to experience it several times throughout my career.

I will never forget seeing Kathryn Bigelow's *The Hurt Locker* at the Toronto International Film Festival in 2008. It was late in the week after a crammed schedule of seeing four or five movies a day. I was at that point of feeling "square-eyed"—burned out and bleary, seeing everything in my path through the same rectangular screen. Then, the propulsive opening of *The Hurt Locker* unspooled and something shifted. My senses awakened and snapped to.

With the atmospheric, superbly paced genre movies *Near Dark*, *Strange Days*, and *Point Break*, Bigelow had already proven herself adept at capturing characters in extreme, often physically perilous situations. But something here was different. As a team of bomb experts sought to defuse an explosive device on a dusty Baghdad street, the Australian actor Guy Pearce made jaunty small talk with his comrades in a manner that suggested he was the star of the movie. In a series of tense, unshowy moments— filmed by cinematographer Barry Ackroyd with his signature handheld immediacy—the audience was promptly situated in the world they thought Bigelow was creating. So it was all the more shocking when, within a minute or two, Pearce's character was blown up.

It was an audacious move—full of nerve and confidence—and orchestrated by Bigelow with both rawboned intensity and exquisite finesse in pacing and atmosphere. She kept those values at the forefront throughout *The Hurt Locker*, which would win an Academy Award for Best Picture and make her—deservedly—the first woman to win an Oscar for Best Director. *The Hurt Locker* was made from a superb script by Mark Boal (who also took home an award), but it was Bigelow's flawless execution of the concept, her ability to marshal the actors and crew to realize the vision she had for a movie that was simultaneously action- and psychology-driven, both immediate and deeply reflective, that made *The Hurt Locker* a work of exceptional mastery. I picked up similar I-got-this vibes from Barry Jenkins's *Moonlight*, Kenneth Lonergan's *Manchester by the Sea*, and Damien Chazelle's *La La Land*, each of which projected both audacity and understated confidence on the part of their directors, whether in the form of *La La Land*'s extravagantly choreographed opening song-and-dance sequence (staged, filmed, and edited as if captured in one take) or *Moonlight's* and *Manchester*'s quieter but equally impressive telegraphing of characters, atmosphere, and emotional stakes within their first few moments.

It's a cliché, but it's true: the best directors make their jobs look easy. They manage to erase all traces of how the weather prevented them from getting a crucial shot on a certain day, or that one actor was weaker than another in a particular take, or, as is usually the case, that they shot an entire movie out of sequence but somehow kept the through-line clear enough in their head to create a seamless whole from a patchwork of choppy, imperfect scenes. (Directorial mastery is particularly important when it comes to achieving a unified vision for a project that has undergone multiple rewrites with maybe dozens of writers.)

That signature Copacabana tracking shot in *GoodFellas* seems like it was designed from the beginning as an efficient, elegant way of allowing viewers to tag along as Karen Friedman becomes absorbed into Henry Hill's mob life.

Not at all. In fact, it was a stopgap solution that Scorsese and his team employed when they found out they weren't allowed to use the front entrance to the New York club to film. What would have been a standard-issue scene with Henry barging to the front of the line and sweet-talking a maître d' instead became a thrilling, far more emotionally involving centerpiece of the film, all because of Scorsese's ability to think—and think *cinematically*—on his feet.

As often as not, thinking cinematically means preparation, whether in the form of scheduling extensive rehearsals, having detailed storyboards made (that is, rough, cartoon-like drawings illustrating the movie's shots and scenes from beginning to end), or simply making sure the crew is ready for last-minute contingencies. Alfred Hitchcock was a fastidious planner, which shouldn't surprise anyone familiar with his intricate, carefully composed films. But so was John Cassavetes (*Faces, Husbands, A Woman Under the Influence*), whose spontaneous, improvised style belied the fact that most of his films were carefully scripted, as are the seemingly off-the-cuff intimate dramas of our current maestro of that form, Mike Leigh (*Secrets & Lies, Happy-Go-Lucky*).

Rehearsals might include improvisational techniques to help actors pin down their roles. In his book *Making Movies*, director Sidney Lumet recalled using this method when making *Dog Day Afternoon*; Al Pacino and the actors playing bank hostages engaged in hours of improvisation— and more of it ended up in the movie than Lumet apparently expected. But sometimes such detailed preparation is impossible, and the outcome, in the hands of a good director and actor, can still be brilliant: Phil Alden Robinson, who directed *Field of Dreams*, once told me that the famous scene in the film where Ray Liotta's Shoeless Joe Jackson asks, "Is this heaven?," before disappearing into a fog-enshrouded cornfield, was filmed in two minutes, while an actual, shelf-like fogbank rolled in suddenly and unexpectedly. Liotta hadn't rehearsed how he'd move through the scene yet, and Robinson had little time to film before the incoming weather would obliterate the lights; Liotta simply asked Robinson where he should stop to say the line, which he did, then turned and ran into the corn. Such lucky accidents are the stuff of great movies, but it takes chops to know how to recognize and seize them.

Chops should not be confused with competence, although a director can't have the former without the latter. When I think of "chops," I think of Scorsese, Bigelow, Tarantino, and Spike Lee, all of whom put visual values and movement first in their movies. I also think of Paul Thomas Anderson, whose *There Will Be Blood* was playing on cable one night when I turned the TV on. The volume happened to be down, so I watched the film silently—and it was completely understandable. That's chops.

Chops also come into play when managing and guiding actors: For *Michael Clayton*, Tony Gilroy needed George Clooney because he was right for the role, and the involvement of a star of his stature helped get the movie made. But Gilroy also needed to dismantle the glamour and star power that Clooney brought with him like so much dazzling baggage—qualities that didn't serve his character as a middle-management legal fixer. So he threw Clooney into his scenes without rehearsal, making sure that every encounter ended with the other character "taking" the moment. Clooney wound up looking, as Gilroy recalled, "slightly out of his depth" in the film, which fit Clayton's own state of mind. (The desire to subvert Clooney's persona also led Gilroy to cast the late Sydney

Pollack as Clayton's boss, because he was one of the few actors who could credibly exert authority over a movie star at the height of Clooney's fame and influence.) David Fincher, on the other hand, demanded dozens (sometimes hundreds) of takes in *The Social Network* to give the actors time to grow accustomed to Aaron Sorkin's particularly paced, verbally acrobatic dialogue. The result felt offhand and fresh, despite being the product of nearly endless repetition and adjustment.

Chops often takes the form of instinct: one of my favorite pieces of cinematic legend and lore is a story John Frankenheimer often told about filming the World War II action drama *The Train*, which involved two train crashes; when filming one of them, he had six operators manning the cameras, including himself. Almost as an afterthought, he decided to bury a seventh camera alongside the track, with the lens pointing upward. When the scene was under way, the engineer mistakenly went too fast, sending Frankenheimer and his crew scrambling for safety; all the cameras were destroyed except the seventh one in the ground, which miraculously captured the wheel of the derailed train as it spun overhead, resulting in a spectacular shot. That's not just chops—that's luck.

When I think of "competence," however, I think of perfectly acceptable storytelling that gets the job done without much zest or imagination, which in some cases can be enough. I didn't find *The Imitation Game* particularly cinematic from a visually virtuosic point of view, but if we're being fair, its gnarly subject matter, codebreaking during World War II, didn't lend itself to much fancy technical footwork. I'm far less forgiving of the costume dramas directed by Tom Hooper, whose *The King's Speech* and *The Danish Girl* are more beautifully arranged backdrops for attention-getting performances than fully realized exercises in cinema.

And then there are directors I think of as "service-able," Hollywood functionaries whose names are as anonymous as their films, which bear no discernible imprint of technical ambition or artistic craftsmanship. These are directors-for-hire who are given a script, cast a few actors, and simply shoot, allowing the cinematographer and production designer to do their thing with little input or interest. Their films are consistently workmanlike, are released in theaters with a minimum of attention or fuss, and are quickly, blessedly forgotten. These functionaries-for-hire might possess baseline capabilities to get a job done, but they don't have chops.

RED OR GREEN?

Were the aesthetic choices within the movie pleasing, satisfying, appropriate for the material?

Did they ring true?

Why, then, do films like *The King's Speech* and *The Imitation Game* do so well during awards season? The answer, I think, lies in that most ambiguous of catchall terms: taste.

Both films could fairly be described as "tasteful," in that their uplifting stories, attractive production designs, and restrained acting make them engrossingly easy to watch. But taste is more than a matter of decorum and astute visual sense. In many ways, taste in a director is similar to tone in a screenplay; it's ineffable, difficult to quantify, but it might be best described, as George Cukor once did, as "a judicious but never ponderous sense of balance." Tyler Perry is roundly derided for the lack of taste in his broad, vulgar comedies featuring his own cross-dressing performance as Madea. But overweening good taste—such as Hooper's attractively appointed, visually inert parlor dramas, or Rob Marshall's clumsily filmed, overedited musicals—can be even more oppressive.

Filmmakers project their taste through every craft involved in the production, from the actors they cast to the costumes, set décor, and music. "Red or green? This one or that one?" is another way of saying that every decision is informed by the director's likes, dislikes, predilections, instincts, and fetishistic obsessions—or, fatally, the lack thereof.

One sure sign of a poorly directed movie is the sense that it's been extruded, not through an individual's quirky, singular sensibility, but through the anonymous machinery of Hollywood at its most generic, indifferent, and marginally competent. I have my own private Hall of Shame where this is concerned: I've always found comedies directed by the Farrelly brothers to be particularly undistinguished from a technical and visual standpoint, and I think the films of Anne Fletcher (27 Dresses, The Guilt Trip, Hot Pursuit) are sludgy and often unforgivably sloppy. But a glance at the dregs of review websites such as Rotten Tomatoes or Metacritic will reveal the names of directors who were likely hired simply to bring a movie in on time and safely under budget, with no personal flair or expression to speak of.

Taste also comes into play when a filmmaker decides how best to relate a narrative—and, indeed, which narrative to relate in the first place. Will this movie tell a new story, or a classic one in a bold, groundbreaking, or important new way? Does the story "want" to be a movie, in the sense that it lends itself naturally to moving images, immersive environments, and vivid, emotionally resonant characters? Did the finished film feel like the only possible way that this particular story could have been told?

Most crucially, a director must decide early on how visible his or her own style should be: in the case of someone like Wes Anderson, this is no debate at all. His fastidious, fussily curated built environments are packed with colors, textures, and visual details. Rather than spontaneous, unforced naturalism, his taste underlines the stagy, theatrical artifice of his stories, a habit that his fans find charming and that his detractors find impossibly self-conscious and mannered.

Stanley Kubrick—to whom Anderson is frequently compared, thanks to their common love of perfectly symmetrical compositions within the frame—also liked to present his films not as recordings of documentary "reality," but rather its inherently false simulacrum. He not only didn't mind the "movie-ness" of the cinematic medium, he embraced it. Stephen King fans may not have appreciated how Kubrick brought his exacting approach to bear on *The Shining* (the author himself was reportedly not thrilled with the film). But there's no doubt that Kubrick's taste—for strong, graphically bold visuals, stylized acting, and monumental environments—made the movie one that only he could have made. In the case of such similarly visual stylists as Spike Lee, Guillermo del Toro, Todd Haynes, Martin Scorsese, and the Coen brothers, the question isn't whether they go "over the top" (because it's almost certain that, at some point, they will). It's whether their stylistic decisions will help the audience connect with the story and characters on-screen, or keep them at an intellectual, uninvolved remove that the filmmaker didn't intend.

As much as I admire filmmakers with the ambition and technical virtuosity to pull off such bravura pieces of cinema as *The Shining*, I've come to be just as much in awe of those directors with a willingness to virtually erase their artistic signature in favor of restraint and self-effacement—the classical style of no-style, if you will. This kind of filmmaking has virtually disappeared in recent years, but it harks back to Hollywood's Golden Age, when directors like George Cukor, Ernst Lubitsch, Billy Wilder, and Howard Hawks made films in which the camera observed from an objective, discreet distance, never moving or cutting away until absolutely necessary. The action was to be found in the words and emotional interaction of the characters, their interplay so rhythmic and dynamic that the films never felt static or overly stagy. The skill here lies in knowing which stories will be enhanced by the style of no-style.

If there was a masterpiece of such cinematic understatement, it was Alan J. Pakula's 1976 film *All the President's Men*, which looked simple but amounted to a masterfully conceived and well-calibrated collection of canny staging and a wealth of visual detail and bravura—if not obvious—camera moves. For instance, when an overhead camera, observing reporters Bob Woodward and Carl Bernstein as they slog through book slips at the Library of Congress, soars high to reduce them to the size of needles in the haystack they are searching, it invests this quiet scene—one that could have been deathly dull—with verve and visual interest in the subtlest way possible. "A story is told as much by what you don't see, what you don't show, as what you show," Pakula explained. "If you show everything, nothing has importance."

There are certain directors whose personal tastes—in the stories they choose to tell, how they tell them, and the "entire universes" they create on-screen—line up perfectly with my own. I've mentioned several throughout this book: Richard Linklater, Tom McCarthy, the Coen brothers, Sofia Coppola, Steven Soderbergh, Kelly Reichardt, Paul Thomas Anderson, Todd Haynes, and the British director Steve McQueen. With few exceptions, whatever world they happen to be building on-screen is one I'll happily inhabit for as long as I can; whatever journey they're embarking on, I'm eager to jump on board.

Other directors have used their taste to make movies of otherwise negligible interest pop with unexpected vibrancy, intelligence, and interest. I wouldn't count myself as a fan of comic book movies—I'd rather lay asphalt on a 100-degree day than attend Comic-Con—but in the hands of Joss Whedon, Kenneth Branagh, and the brother team of Anthony and Joe Russo, the recent Marvel Comics *Avengers* movies have become showcases for smart writing, nuanced acting, and timely allegory, even in the midst of cartoonish action. Similarly, I would never describe myself as a science fiction aficionado, but when Alfonso Cuarón is at the helm of a movie like *Gravity*, his taste and sensibilities transform what might have been a genre exercise into a sensitive, visually ambitious, improbably meditative reflection on existential solitude and rebirth.

Taste is what makes the Coen brothers' adaptation of Cormac McCarthy's *No Country for Old Men* a taut, technically perfect study in understated realism and control, and Ridley Scott's *The Counselor* a far more vulgar, excessive assault on the senses. Taste is what made Sidney Lumet's 1964 drama *Fail-Safe* a tense, sober-minded thriller about an impending nuclear attack, and Kubrick's *Dr. Strangelove or: How I Learned to Stop Worrying and Love the Bomb* a high-wire act of farce and stinging social commentary.

Taste is what makes the carefully calibrated balance between character development and action in *The Hurt Locker* as thoughtful as it is thrilling, whereas the more recent fact-inspired war picture *13 Hours*, about the 2012 attack on a US compound in Benghazi, devolved into a generic-looking action picture. Taste is what makes Judd Apatow and Nicole Holofcener look at the foibles of middle-aged, upper-class denizens of modern-day Los Angeles in completely different ways: one through the lens of broad, undisciplined indulgence of arrested adolescence, and the other through quieter, more bittersweet glimpses of life at a more restrained (and far less raunchy) emotional pitch. Taste is what makes Quentin Tarantino's indisputable filmmaking gifts—his punchy writing, sense of camera position and movement, swift editing, and superb casting—so often devolve into third-act bloodbaths evoking the B-movies he voraciously consumed as a teenager.

Taste is also what can sometimes get in the way of an otherwise "perfect" film by a director whose technical prowess is virtually unrivaled. Part of what has made Steven Spielberg such an enormously successful filmmaker is that his personal taste coincides so completely with that of his audience. Spielberg's instinctive understanding of the audience has resulted in such enduring classics as *E.T. the Extra-Terrestrial* and *Close Encounters of the Third Kind*. But it can sometimes result in movies that feel redundant and too obvious. Spielberg has a tendency to spell out story elements and emotional beats that more subtle directors would have left ambiguous or open-ended. When I gently pressed him once on his decision to end *Lincoln* with the assassination at Ford's Theatre rather than earlier, when

Lincoln leaves the White House for what we know will be the last time, Spielberg told me, "I felt I needed to take the picture to the conclusion that everybody expects." (Spielberg is, by no means, the only director with a tendency to overexplain: Oliver Stone, Clint Eastwood, and Spike Lee share the same habit, which suggests they either don't completely trust their own actors and story, or they don't trust the audience.) Personally, I would have ended *Lincoln* at the White House, leaving it up to viewers to add two and two. But that's simply a matter of taste.

Taste also expresses itself in what details directors let slide, the aesthetic rules they set up for their movies and then allow themselves to break. One of Woody Allen's most recent films, *Café Society*, was an attractive, well-acted example of the director working at solid, midlevel virtuosity, until a series of strange anachronisms began cropping up, like a scene featuring a piano that hadn't come out in the 1930s, when the film was set. What might have been forgivable shortcuts accumulated until I was "taken out" of the film, increasingly aware of Allen's apathy and wondering why I should care if he didn't. If details make or break a movie, the director's taste makes or breaks the details.

POINT OF VIEW

Whose world were we in? Whose eyes did we see the world through?

Did that perspective change or stay the same?

One of the most important questions a director must ask has to do with a film's point of view: Who will lead the audience through the world on-screen? Through whose eyes and sympathies will we view the story's conflicts, heartbreaks, injustices, and triumphs? Generally this is laid out in the script, but it's the director's job to hold true to that perspective throughout the filmmaking process, ensuring that it remains consistent and motivated from the "page to the stage" (and then the screen).

Think of such classics as *Taxi Driver, Dog Day Afternoon,* or *The Graduate*—or, more recently, *Fight Club, Black Swan,* or *Carol.* Each demonstrates how every decision—where to place the camera, whose perspective it shares, whose sonic environment it reflects, whose unexpressed feelings are being communicated through the musical score—should be filtered through character and point of view. Even if the film digresses briefly from that position, there's never any real doubt through whose experience the story is being told.

When I interviewed her about her 2012 thriller *Zero Dark Thirty,* about the search for and assassination of Osama bin Laden, Kathryn Bigelow discussed how the point of view of that movie differed from her earlier film, *The Hurt Locker.* Although both movies are highly detailed, propulsive thrillers about intelligence and military procedures, she very slightly shifted the perspective from one to the other. In some ways that was accomplished through production design, which favored dusty, desaturated landscapes in *The Hurt Locker* and sleeker, more classically handsome interiors in *Zero Dark Thirty.* But primarily, the difference between the two films is obvious in where Bigelow put the camera in each film.

"The point of view in *The Hurt Locker* was sort of a journalistic eye," she told me. "It was the 'third man on the team.' . . . In other words, that camera was in there with the guys, [it was] very subjective. There was never an omniscient eye." Although the perspective in Zero Dark Thirty wasn't omniscient—the camera never pulled back to a distant, "God's-eye view" of the action on-screen—it was slightly more objective than the one in The Hurt Locker the better to allow viewers to keep track of the main character, played by Jessica Chastain, the multiple members of her team, and the shifting time frames within a decade-long mission. "The thing that was important [with Zero Dark Thirty] was to create a completely immersive, experiential, participatory visual language to tell that story" even within slightly more objective parameters, Bigelow said. "So it still has a significant degree of subjectivity, because it's very alive. It's sort of rough-hewn. It's lit, but it doesn't look lit. So it still feels naturalistic." Throughout Zero Dark Thirty, Bigelow said, she was trying to "humanize the hunt" by making an otherwise complicated and arcane intelligence-gathering procedural more immediate, even intimate.

Similarly, it was Cuarón who decided to tell the story of Children of Men, which was based on a novel by P. D. James, from the point of view of Clive Owen's Theo. Only one scene digresses from Theo's perspective, but Cuarón had to fight for and guard that throughout the film's production. Had the same script been shot by another, more generic filmmaker, the movie might have been a perfectly entertaining action-adventure, but it most likely would not have been a work of art. The same could be said for Romanian director Cristian Mungiu's stunning 4 Months, 3 Weeks, 2 Days, a harrowing portrait of a young woman obtaining an abortion in post-communist Bucharest. A masterpiece of cinematic realism, Mungiu's film is constructed so that there is no discernible barrier between the viewer and the characters on-screen; the director's hand, although present every step of the way, never tips in terms of visual flourishes or moral takeaway.

The film *Selma* had been in development for several years when director Ava DuVernay got hold of the project; in her hands, the script went from being a contentious political mano a mano between Martin Luther King Jr. and Lyndon Johnson to a far more sweeping portrait of the civil rights activists who thought up the titular 1964 demonstration and persuaded King to help lead it. In addition to writing in such pivotal historical figures as Diane Nash and James Bevel, DuVernay worked with cinematographer Bradford Young to create a canvas for the film that was both broader and more immediate than what had been suggested in the original screenplay.

David Oyelowo, who played King in *Selma* and had been attached to the film since its inception, observed that he saw the movie "morph into what it should be just by virtue of perspective," from DuVernay's inclusion of women in the narrative to where she put the camera. "You could have had the camera far away, you could have it behind the white soldiers and just see [marchers] in the background and go, 'Oh, here come the black folk,'" he said. "Or, as Ava did, you could be with them, you can slow it down and place you as a human being in the midst of that march."

Paul Greengrass's early experience in documentary filmmaking has made him one of the greatest practitioners of subjective, "eye-level" filmmaking: whether it's the jagged, sometimes discombobulating action of the Jason Bourne movies or such fact-based dramas as *Bloody Sunday*, *United 93*, or *Captain Phillips*, Greengrass has developed both a style and an ethic that keep the camera with his subjects, rather than at a more objective, all-seeing distance. He's dispassionate but not emotionally detached. It's a radically different approach from the aloof, fastidiously centered camera of Kubrick or Anderson, whose films might adopt one character's point of view but at a more objective, ironic remove.

Kubrick and Anderson are what I sometimes call "outside" filmmakers, shorthand for a directorial attitude that assumes a relatively distant point of view and doesn't shy away from artifice. I would also put such contemporary filmmakers as Lars von Trier, the Coen brothers, Pedro Almodóvar, and Todd Haynes in this category, as well as such forebears as Orson Welles, Federico Fellini, and Douglas Sirk. They all share an attitude toward their material that is visually arresting, often exquisitely framed and composed, and unapologetically theatrical.

At the other end of the spectrum are the "inside" filmmakers, directors who strive to create intensely subjective viewing experiences for filmgoers by creating convincingly authentic environments (often filming in real-life locations) and plunging the audience into a singular point of view, allowing for far more immersive experiences and, often, a powerful sense of empathy and understanding.

With his preference for a closely following camera and frequent close-ups of his protagonists, Greengrass is an inside director, as are his countrymen, the British directors Mike Leigh and Ken Loach. In Belgium, Jean-Pierre and Luc Dardenne have spent their careers perfecting an intensely subjective style of filmmaking, wherein they strive for the most naturalistic, unforced visual and acting style possible, so closely following their protagonists that the audience begins to feel less like a silent observer than an appendage of the characters. In many ways, they are the heirs of the French New Wave and Italian neorealism, the postwar film movements that prized roughness and psychological realism over conventional cinematic values like linear narrative and surface sheen.

In America, those principles took hold in the noir films of the 1940s and, later, in such groundbreaking dramas as *On the Waterfront, Marty,* and the films of John Cassavetes. They were all carefully scripted and filmed, but they aspired for a kind of interior truth that felt revolutionary, as if something had broken open and been reinvented (their heirs include contemporary filmmakers such as Sofia Coppola and Ryan Coogler). In the hands of Terrence Malick and David Lynch, as well as such experimental filmmakers as Godfrey Reggio and Jem Cohen, inside filmmaking takes on more abstract dimensions. Their films are more like tone poems of mood, atmosphere, and unconscious feeling than resolved, conventionally "satisfying" stories.

There are deep riches to be found in both inside and outside points of view: films by Kubrick and Anderson are arresting and exhilarating to watch, largely because of their formal elegance, painterly richness, and control of theatrical space. But they can also feel airless, overworked, and detached. There's no doubt that inside filmmaking often results in visceral, profound empathy and connection with characters, but it can also be undisciplined, solipsistic, and self-indulgent, so idiosyncratic that it shuts viewers out from the very understanding the filmmaker was presumably trying to achieve.

Often, the most interesting directorial voices and visions exist in between these extremes, following a path blazed by the filmmakers of the 1930s and 1940s, whose unobtrusive, "classical" approach to storytelling valued clarity over eccentricity, precision over expressiveness, restraint over showmanship. Which isn't to say that the director's hand is invisible in these films. Far from it.

Perhaps the finest example of the classical style, the 1946 wartime drama *The Best Years of Our Lives*, is a masterpiece because of every choice that William Wyler made throughout the film, from casting the real-life veteran Harold Russell as a gravely injured World War II sailor to using Gregg Toland's detailed, deep-focus cinematography. The latter conveyed purely through images the changed, disorienting world engulfing Russell's character and his fellow veterans. This film, with its seamless blend of realism (instead of costumes, the actors wore clothes they had purchased off the rack) and meticulous staging, its epic sweep and moments of unspoken emotion (Myrna Loy delivers a heartbreakingly eloquent performance entirely with her shoulders and back in an early scene), and its tricky balance of sincerity and toughness, embodies the kind of storytelling sense, command of visual language, and tonal control that define movie directing at its finest and most deceptively difficult—intimate, but discreet; objective, but not Olympian; observant, but at a respectful, compassionate distance.

Wyler was in good company during Hollywood's Golden Age, when the studio system both mandated and made possible the kind of lucid, stylish, well-judged movies that were his specialty. Others of the time included Howard Hawks, George Cukor, William Wellman, and Billy Wilder. Those same values would propel such 1970s directors as Sidney Lumet, Alan J. Pakula, Woody Allen, Roman Polanski, and Francis Ford Coppola, and we see them today in the work of Tom McCarthy, Steven Spielberg, and John Crowley, whose 2015 films *Spotlight*, *Bridge of Spies*, and *Brooklyn*, respectively, all evinced a willingness to erase any trace of signature or directorial gesture to deliver old-school, unflashy narratives that were nonetheless absorbing and entertaining, occupying that same objective-subjective space as their classical forebears.

No one mastered the art of point of view more consistently than Alfred Hitchcock, whose early tutelage in silent filmmaking and German expressionism—with its language of shadow and light and clear, legible staging—helped him develop into one of the medium's most fluent visual storytellers. Hitchcock's films were always centered on one character's point of view, but the perspective most privileged was the audience's: more than anything, Hitchcock valued the comprehension and emotional investment of the viewer in what was transpiring on-screen—to "throw them into the picture completely, win them over to [my] way of thinking," as he told Peter Bogdanovich. Hitchcock would do anything to earn and keep the audience's allegiance, even if it meant breaking away from his protagonist to share a piece of information that only the audience would be privy to.

Rear Window, for example, is told almost entirely from the perspective of Jeff Jefferies, a news photographer laid up in his Greenwich Village apartment with a broken leg, with only his neighbors across the courtyard for entertainment. For most of *Rear Window*, which stars James Stewart as Jefferies, the film is an exercise in pure subjective cinema: we see only what Jefferies sees, hear only what he hears—including his neighbors' arguments and the tinkling of a piano. Interestingly, at a moment in the film when Jefferies is sleeping, the camera shows the audience a crucial piece of information that we will have going forward, but he won't. It's a subtle cheat—imperceptible, really—but it adds to the viewer's investment in what's happening on-screen, proof that one must have as superb control of the rules as Hitchcock in order to break them.

Whether directors adopt an intensely subjective point of view of one of their characters, a classically omniscient, neutral perspective, or the distant gaze of a rather disapproving god, when the choice has been made thoughtfully and with commitment, the result is a space that viewers can enter and inhabit, barely aware they've crossed a threshold at all.

IT'S ALL PERSONAL

Was the movie idiosyncratic, risky, strange? Or could it have been made by anyone?

I once asked Paul Greengrass to identify the most important thing about directing. "You have to present a view of the world that's truthful as you see it," he replied firmly. The result, he added, was that the audience would "*feel* how I see the world. And people respond to that or not. That's different than having an agenda. It's an openness, to say, 'Here, this is how I see the world. Do you?'"

A well-directed film feels as if it's been carefully molded, crafted with purpose and intent; a poorly directed one, on the other hand, feels rote, anonymous, and indifferent.

Whether they accomplish it with subtlety or self-conscious flourishes, directors are constantly shaping the audience's perceptions and expectations, guiding our emotions and our eyes through design, the arrangement and choreography of actors within a scene, camera moves, meaningful edits, and sound cues. Every decision they make—from where to put the actors to what musical cue to use at a particular juncture—is conditioned by that governing principle. Poor directors simply shoot coverage—a master shot, a medium shot, and a series of close-ups—and cut it together to get the job done as simplistically as possible: they shoot the script but don't guide the audience. (Or, just as bad, they over-guide the audience through the use of manically edited close-ups that give us no choice where to look.)

Put another way, good direction is always personal, even if the movie in question isn't written by the film-maker, or based on his or her autobiographical experience. There's no doubt that films by such writer-directors as Kenneth Lonergan, Sofia Coppola, Nicole Holofcener, the Coen brothers, and Paul Thomas Anderson reflect the thoughts, tastes, outlooks, and preoccupations of those filmmakers. But there's also no doubt that, even when working with scripts they don't write, such directors as Kathryn Bigelow, Kelly Reichardt, Steve McQueen, and Spike Jonze put their unique imprint on each film they make, resulting in an experience far more powerful than watching a close-up follow a medium shot follow a master and back again. A great example of a director putting his imprint on a project can be found in *Nebraska*, which was written by Bob Nelson and directed by Alexander Payne; it was Payne's idea to shoot in black and white, and to cast Bruce Dern; he also rewrote some scenes, including— perhaps most crucially—the ending. Originally, Nelson had Dern's character, Woody, drive his new truck into a tree, so that his son (Will Forte) would finish the homecoming drive through town. Payne instead allowed Woody to have his proud return, driving slowly down Main Street for all his friends and neighbors to see, while his son hunched down next to him. In the final shot of the film, we see them changing places. A scene that might have sent viewers out of the theater on a downbeat note instead brimmed with compassion, sensitivity, and, ultimately, modest triumph.

So many factors militate against excellence in movies: half-baked scripts, casting mistakes, accidents, unforeseen calamities. Every movie is a reflection of how a particular director responded to those realities, whether he was content to work with a mediocre screenplay or insisted on one more rewrite; whether she was willing to halt the production if the right actor wasn't cast; how he reacted when a bank of fog rolled into the shot, or when the Copacabana withheld permission to film at the entrance.

Whether they call themselves auteurs or plumbers or jugglers, the great directors are grand unifiers, conceiving the ideal form of their movie, protecting that vision from the computer keyboard to the set to the editing suite to the screen, and, if the fates conspire and the angels smile, creating something of permanence, haunting beauty, and, sometimes, lasting worth.

IN MANY WAYS, MERYL STREEP was right: no matter what goes wrong with a movie, it will be blamed on the director. If an actor delivers a poor performance, that really means that the director did a poor job of casting. If the film looks muddy or haphazardly lit, that means the director didn't provide clear guidance to the cinematographer. If the sound is crummy, the director didn't catch it and fix it—or didn't care to get it right in the first place. Most disastrously, if the director's vision for the film differed wildly from that of the studio that employed him or her, then you get a movie that looks like a hastily assembled jumble of spare parts.

But when all of those things come together—when the actors, settings, sound, and music coalesce to create an experience that steeps the viewer in the world of the movie, transcending mere disposable distraction—then the director has done more than just arrange actors in front of a backdrop and point the camera at them: he or she has marshaled knowledge of film history, sensitivity with actors, technical skill, and astute judgment to create an emotional and aesthetic event. If the movie has achieved its thematic goals, that's because the director wove them in, not by way of obvious speeches and ponderous "message" scenes, but with finesse and subtly buried cues. To quote Guillermo del Toro, a movie's been well-directed when you experience it not just with your eyes and ears, but "in your gut and in your brain and in your heart." The director made that possible by guiding and inspiring an entire team of people to create something they could never have achieved alone. Yes or no, red or green: it's the directors who have all the answers, even when they're being guided by pure adrenaline and instinct.

RECOMMENDED VIEWING ··

The Best Years of Our Lives (1946)
Rear Window (1954)
Raging Bull (1980)
Children of Men (2006)
The Hurt Locker (2008)
12 Years a Slave (2013)

·········· WAS IT WORTH DOING? ··········

We've reached perhaps the most crucial point in the critical process, when aesthetic and narrative evaluations have been made, and the filmmaker's aspirations have been ascertained and judged. It's now that viewers must ask themselves if what they've just seen was worth doing.

There are any number of ways to approach this question. If a movie set out merely to be a slick, superficial piece of fluff, it seems unnecessarily churlish to accuse it of not being serious or artistically ambitious enough— although it's fair to point out when the filmmakers took the audience for granted by warming over old plots, creating clichéd, stereotyped characters, or fobbing off a lazy, slapdash production as good enough.

On the other side of the spectrum, just because a film aspires to be sober-minded and philosophically "deep" doesn't make it a better film: I've seen plenty such movies that try mightily to impress the audience with austere statements about the human condition that were reductive, sophomoric, and trite (and all the more irritating because they were so pretentious).

There's nothing wrong with films that want to be either shallow entertainment or serious art—as long as they are rewarding their audiences with work that's honest, original, and reflective of a certain generosity of spirit. It's a terrible feeling to watch a movie and sense that the people behind it hold you in contempt, that they're simply servicing their audience's most undemanding desires and appetites. It's a wonderful feeling to watch a movie and feel lighter, more expansive, and understood—even if it was just a simple comedy or action movie.

Public debates rage on regarding to what extent movies influence the audience—what we believe, what we value as a society. But one doesn't have to buy into simplistic cause-and-effect arguments to acknowledge that, with its realism, aspirational glamour, and enormous reach, cinema has an outsized impact on social norms and assumptions. From the chilling effect on men's undershirt sales after Clark Gable was seen bare-chested in *It Happened One Night* to the trend in menswear chic for women that Diane Keaton jump-started in *Annie Hall*, it's clear that movies can affect how we dress, talk, and act; it stands to reason that the values they embody—either explicitly or on a more unspoken, embedded level—are hugely influential in informing how we see the world and what we expect from it and one another. That influence is all the more consequential considering that movies are one of America's chief exports: for example, as we contemplate yet another bulging slate of expensive comic-book movies, we might ponder whether the big studios are peddling timeless allegories about good and evil, or less benign wish-fulfillment fantasies of potency and overcompensation.

It's within this moral purview that the question "Was it worth doing?" is most profitably posed. When assessing a particular film, one might ask: What values did it celebrate or denigrate? Was human dignity sacrificed in the name of mayhem and depravity? Did the movie inspire apathy and cynicism, or did it awaken a sense of compassion and empathy? Was its stance one of unfeeling, ironic distance, or was it more attuned to the emotional lives and vulnerabilities of the characters? Did it harden the viewer's heart, or soften it?

Make no mistake: this isn't a screed against violence, which has been an element of the cinematic lexicon since the medium was invented. But, as with all such elements, there are gradations and nuances. When graphic violence is thoughtfully staged and edited, it can be a sobering way for viewers to understand the pain and suffering of others; what's more, it can be a potent way to explore our own mortality in a symbolic, safe space. When it's used sadistically, to invite vicarious, voyeuristic thrills, it can be exploitative and soul-killing. When it's used hypocritically—as in movies that linger on sequences of women being raped and killed, the better to set up a male hero's equally gruesome search for revenge—it's not just narratively dubious, it's offensive. Perhaps most destructive is the kind of movie violence that engages in all manner of killing and mayhem without leaving so much as a scratch on the victims, a cartoonish, egregiously dishonest display that might be the most psychically and societally harmful of all.

Nor is this a plea for more movies about unicorns and rainbows. The only thing more annoying than gratuitous cruelty and consequence-free violence is the kind of sentimentalism, sanctimony, and cheap uplift that panders, not to viewers' base desires, but to their most facile notions of virtue and humanism. Patronizing audiences with anodyne morality tales is just as insulting as arousing them with images of torture and savagery.

Just as frustrating as a movie without an idea in its head is a movie whose ideas—however well-meaning—are so obvious and billboard-like that the viewer emerges feeling lobbied rather than edified or entertained. The best movies, the ones "worth doing," exist in that middle ground where audiences are invited to grapple with tough questions, reflect on their own most cherished ideals, experience the world from another point of view, and perhaps experience the singular joy that comes from authentic human connection.

That connection can come wrapped in the guise of a big summer blockbuster or a tiny art-house indie; it can occur while laughing or crying; it can even be the product of gasping at the same time with other audience members. Whether a movie is set in the present-day or in the past, or in a time and place that never existed, it's telling us something about our world—allowing us to see it with new eyes, and move through it in a new way. That's the surpassing power and beauty of a medium that can continually astonish even the most critical viewer: Every single time the theater darkens and the screen flickers to life, we're bearing witness to a unique creation. And by the time the lights come up, we've been shaped anew as well.

DOCUMENTARIES AND
FACT-BASED DRAMAS

ALTHOUGH I'VE USED DOCUMENTARIES AS examples in *Talking Pictures*, I haven't yet addressed nonfiction and fact-based films specifically as genres. These forms are quite different from garden-variety fiction films, and analyzing the final product requires looking through different lenses.

In an era of so-called reality TV and a burgeoning number of cable stations, streaming platforms, and websites seeking to sate the audience's hunger for real-life stories, documentaries, it seems, are more ubiquitous than ever. Add to that Hollywood's enduring appetite for biographical pictures ("biopics"), historical re-creations, and adaptations of history books and news stories, and we seem to be besotted with the "truth," whether it's packaged as a nonfiction film or a dramatized version of actual events.

The attraction is understandable. Some of the finest films of the past several years have been documentaries or fact-based dramatizations, films of formal beauty and sophistication that, thanks to their subject matter, possessed the added frisson of meaning and historical importance. Alex Gibney's Oscar-winning 2007 documentary *Taxi to the Dark Side* gave viewers a scrupulously reported portrait of the use of torture during the wars in Afghanistan and Iraq that was every bit as engrossing as a fictional procedural thriller. Not only did *Spotlight*, which won the Best Picture Oscar in 2016, tack impressively close to actual events when it revisited the *Boston Globe*'s investigation of sexual abuse within the Catholic Church, but cowriters Tom McCarthy and Josh Singer actually uncovered a scoop in their own reporting for the film, when they discovered a regrettable lapse in the *Globe*'s coverage during the 1990s.

In most ways, documentaries and movies based on actual events should hew to the same standards of excellence we apply to any other type of film: their stories should be engrossing and coherent, they should be thoughtfully framed and photographed, and their sound design should be clear and add to the mood and atmosphere they're trying to convey.

But, unlike wholly fictional films, fact-based movies depend to a large extent on how well they support their truth claims, on the viewer's sense of their fairness and accuracy, and on their perceived fealty to events as they actually happened, without putting any undue spin on the ball. We inevitably feel let down, even angry, when we find out later that a filmmaker chose not to include a pivotal episode, or portrayed a particular character in an unjustified or inaccurate light. Such questions can hijack the viewer's experience of the film, making the entire enterprise seem suspect from the start.

These issues are especially vexing for documentaries. The term we use for the genre itself is linguistically related to the Latin *docere*, meaning "to teach." Readers of a certain age will remember growing up in the 1950s and 1960s with "educational films," shown in schools and on public television, that were mostly dreary affairs. While a narrator droned on soporifically, a series of inert archival images would parade across the screen, occasionally interrupted by a rumpled professor or self-described expert in the field lecturing an unseen audience on the topic at hand.

As a genre of filmmaking, the documentary has grown exponentially since those days, achieving new heights in form, content, and popularity with audiences. We now enjoy a plethora of various kinds of nonfiction films, from the straightforward historical surveys of Ken Burns to the muckraking picaresques of Michael Moore. We have the elegant essay films of Alan Berliner (*Intimate Stranger, Nobody's Business*) and Jem Cohen (*Counting*), investigative films by Alex Gibney and Kirby Dick (*The Hunting Ground, The Invisible War*), issue-oriented advocacy pieces such as Davis Guggenheim's *An Inconvenient Truth* and *Waiting for Superman*, and character studies by Errol Morris (*Gates of Heaven*) and the late Albert and David Maysles (*Grey Gardens*). At any given time, in theaters, on cable TV, or on a streaming website, you can see documentaries about food, music, sports, politics, history, art, and people at their most eccentric, provocative, and fascinating.

The form of some of these films—such as those by Burns and Gibney, who often make films about complex, intellectually demanding subjects—is relatively conventional: they use archival material, talking heads, maybe a few eye-catching charts or illustrations, and a stirring musical score to thread viewers through a thicket of arcane facts. Sometimes filmmakers use a more pared-down, *verité* approach, dispensing with music, narration, and obvious editorial flourishes to give viewers a "fly on the wall" glimpse of a story that seems to be unfolding with complete spontaneity and candor. (The Maysles, along with their peers D. A. Pennebaker, Richard Leacock, and Robert Drew, were pioneers in this style; recent examples include the documentary *Weiner*, about former congressman Anthony Weiner from New York, and the US-Mexico border tale *Cartel Land*.)

Whether a documentary is a carefully constructed policy tutorial or a startlingly intimate portrait, viewers should be aware that what they're seeing has been shaped and manipulated by the filmmaker—not with nefarious intent, but because he or she is trying to craft a compelling, emotionally engaging narrative. Although *verité* films, especially, often look "unmade" in terms of their gritty production values and choppy, rough-and-ready editing, they are just as meticulously composed as the slickest episode of *Frontline* or *American Masters*. In both cases, a filmmaker has decided what to film, what to leave out of the frame, what and where to cut in the final edit, and, ultimately, how to portray the subject.

Documentaries aren't scripted in the conventional sense of that term: often, filmmakers embark on an investigation of a story or subject not knowing what they will get in terms of material or even an ending. Most documentary directors approach their projects with at least an outline in mind of what the resulting film will look like and say; but they're at the mercy of circumstances, whether in the form of challenging physical conditions, reluctant or uncooperative participants, last-minute reversals, or other unforeseen developments. Because of this, and because documentaries often involve disparate visual elements, including location shots, talking-head interviews, graphics, and archival material, editing takes on a particularly important role. Documentaries are "written" far more often at later stages of production than their mainstream Hollywood fictional counterparts are.

Formal questions of what to put in and what to leave out in editing inevitably lead to ethical ones when it comes to issues such as access, agendas, and transparency. Did the filmmakers use reenactments along with historical footage to make their film more seamless and compelling? Did they use images from another time and place because they fit their uses better? Did they compensate their subjects—or were they compensated by their subjects—while making the film? If they received extraordinary access, how did they do that, and what were the terms of their agreements? Subjects frequently seek out filmmakers to tell their story, or commission a movie outright; sometimes they assume the role of "producer." But often viewers have no way of knowing the extent to which the subjects themselves had approval or control over the final product.

These are just a few questions that can be fairly posed to nonfiction filmmakers, who choose whether to address them within the body of the film or in the credits, or during personal appearances and in the press.

For documentary fans, there is almost always a tension—sometimes intriguing, sometimes uneasy—between being transfixed by the story on-screen and wondering how the filmmaker went about telling it. Over the years, I've learned to become more skeptical of filmmakers' relationships to their subjects, and more alert to whether a film is succeeding because of content (a charismatic person at the center, an inspiring story, a breathtaking natural locale), or because it has been ingeniously conceived, filmed, and structured. A number of recent films have married form, content, and transparency to a remarkably artful degree, including Sarah Polley's *Stories We Tell*, Joshua Oppenheimer's *The Act of Killing*, Penny Lane's *Nuts!*, and Keith Maitland's *Tower*, which variously used fictional elements, reenactments, heavily annotated websites, and animation in ways that both drew the audience into their stories and pointed up the filmmakers' use of artifice to achieve that engagement.

Issues of disclosure, artistic license, and critical distance are just as germane in the area of fact-based dramas, which in a world of Google and Wikipedia are now subject to more fact-checking than ever. When Oliver Stone directed *JFK* in 1991, he came under scorching attack from historians who accused him of irresponsibly distorting John F. Kennedy's assassination, especially the role of Lyndon B. Johnson. In recent years, such films as *Zero Dark Thirty*, *Selma*, and *Lincoln* have been criticized for shading historical truth, either to make a political point or simply for the sake of narrative expedience. As a critic for the *Washington Post*, whose local readership of politicians and intelligence, military, and foreign service officials are often participants in or experts on the stories being revisited on-screen, I've become particularly attuned to how the scale, realism, and enormous reach of cinema allow it to meld fact and fiction, and to do it far more persuasively—and problematically— than novels, operas, or plays can with similar subject matter. And I've become more sympathetic to those who feel betrayed and powerless when the movie version of reality strays radically from their lived experience.

As I've thought about how best to assess these interpretive histories, which by virtue of their mass audience so often become our consensus version of history itself, I've found myself returning to a conversation I had with Tony Kushner, who wrote *Lincoln* for Steven Spielberg (as well as the fact-based *Munich*). "The first question you ask is, 'Did this happen?'" Kushner told me. "If it happened, it's historical. Did it happen exactly this way? If your answer is, 'As far as we could possibly tell,' then it's history. If the answer is, 'It happened, but not exactly this way,' then it's historical fiction. Historical fiction is when you have a certain license to make up what happens on the way to what happened."

In other words, rather than expecting journalistic accuracy, it's more fruitful for viewers to look to fact-based films for ways to think about the emotional meaning of the people and events they depict, similar to the way we appreciate Shakespeare's interpretive histories of ancient Rome and fifteenth-century England.

To paraphrase the novelist Kate Atkinson: art isn't truth, but art conveys *a* truth. Whether we're watching a documentary, a carefully researched biopic, or a wildly impressionistic take on a specific chapter of history, it's incumbent upon viewers to consider what we value in these narratives, all the while remembering that they haven't given us the facts. They've told us a story. And every story changes, depending on the teller.

ACKNOWLEDGMENTS

THIS BOOK IS THE PRODUCT of hundreds of conversations over twenty-five years with writers, directors, actors, producers, executives, and academics who have been my unofficial tutors in the art, craft, and business of filmmaking. To Ben Affleck, Casey Affleck, Khalik Allah, Woody Allen, Patricia Aufderheide, John Bailey, Albert Berger, Alan Berliner, Joe Berlinger, Bob Berney, Kathryn Bigelow, Mark Boal, Doug Block, Carter Burwell, Anne Carey, Jay Cassidy, George Clooney, Jem Cohen, Ryan Coogler, Alonzo Crawford, Alfonso Cuarón, Guillermo del Toro, Robert De Niro, Ernest Dickerson, Dennis Doros, Ava DuVernay, Charles Eidsvik, Jeffrey Fearing, Tom Ford, Robert Frazen, Cynthia Fuchs, Rodrigo García, Bob Gazzale, Alex Gibney, John Gilroy, Tony Gilroy, Grace Guggenheim, Amy Heller, Dor Howard, James Herbert, Dustin Hoffman, Nicole Holofcener, Ted Hope, Mark Isham, Arthur Jafa, Barry Jenkins, Jerry Johnson, Michael B. Jordan, Elizabeth Kemp, Richard King, Ann Kroeber, Tony Kushner, Franklin Leonard, Ruby Lerner, Barry Levinson, Matthew Libatique, Skip Lievsay, Richard Linklater, Art Linson, Kenneth Lonergan, David Lowery, David Lynch, Mike Mashon, Anne McCabe, Tom McCarthy, Steve McQueen, Mike Medavoy, Roger Michell, Mike Mills, Montré Aza Missouri, Errol Morris, Larry Moss, Walter Murch, Stanley Nelson, Gary Oldman, Jeannine Oppewall, Alexander Payne, Elizabeth Peters,

Bill Pohlad, Benjamin Price, Lynne Ramsay, Jon Raymond, Robert Redford, Nicolas Winding Refn, Kelly Reichardt, Phil Alden Robinson, Howard Rodman, Fred Roos, Tom Rothman, David O. Russell, Harris Savides, Thomas Schatz, Thelma Schoonmaker, Paul Schwartzman, Martin Scorsese, John Sloss, Steven Spielberg, Paul Stekier, Oliver Stone, Tilda Swinton, Randy Thom, Christine Vachon, Lars von Trier, Randall Wallace, Billy Weber, Michelle Williams, and Bradford Young; and to the late Stan Brakhage, John Frankenheimer, Al Maysles, Michael Shamberg, and Bruce Sinofksy: Thank you for your time and wisdom.

To the publicists, festival and theater programmers, and film professionals who made so many of these encounters possible, especially Sarah Taylor, Gloria Jones, and the staff of Allied Integrated Media, as well as Nicolette Aizenberg, Jody Arlington, Mara Buxbaum, Matt Cowal, Donna Daniels, Leslee Dart, Jed Dietz, Scott Feinstein, Jon Gann, Shirin Ghareeb, Tony Gittens, Stu Gottesman, Rob Harris, Jeff Hill, Todd Hitchcock, Sheila Johnson, Sharon Kahn, Laine Kaplowitz, Susan Koch, Bebe Lerner, Peter Lozito, Michael Lumpkin, Andy Mencher, RJ Millard, Susan Norget, Charlie Olsky, Jaime Panoff, Peggy Parsons, Stan Rosenfield, Jamie Shor, Sky Sitney, Emilie Spiegel, Emilia Stefanczyk, Cynthia Swartz, Renée Tsao, Ryan Werner, Connie White, and David Wilson: Thank you for making my continuing education not just possible, but positively delightful.

I gratefully acknowledge the *Washington Post*, under whose auspices many of these interviews were conducted, and in whose pages I first explored these ideas. To my *Post* colleagues past and present, including Marty Baron, Marcus Brauchli, Chip Crews, Len Downie, Tracy Grant, Deborah Heard, Stephen Hunter, Peter Kaufman, Camille Kilgore, Richard Leiby, David Malitz, Ned Martel, Stephanie Merry, Doug Norwood, Michael O'Sullivan, John Pancake, Steve Reiss, Eugene Robinson, Liz Seymour, Nancy Szokan, John Taylor, and Desson Thomson: Every journalist should enjoy such high standards, skilled leadership, and willingness to pull the taffy. I especially wish to thank Leslie Yazel, who helped conceptualize and edit the original articles that would become the spine of this book.

To Linda Lee, the former film editor of the *New York Times* Arts & Leisure section, who in 1992 accepted a pitch from a cold-calling freelance writer, inadvertently launching a wild and wonderful career: I'm so glad you picked up the phone.

To my friend and first reader Scott Butterworth, who alone knows the precise ratio of sow's ear to silk purse from first to final draft: Let's keep it that way. To my agent, Rafe Sagalyn: I hope this begins to make all the lunches, emails, and atta-girls worth it. To Quynh Do, for her faith in *Talking Pictures*, and for a great title, and to Leah Stecher, Katherine Streckfus, and Sandra Beris, who got it across the finish line with patience, finesse, and care: my grateful and enduring appreciation.

Finally, to Dennis and Victoria Greenia, who so rarely complain when I abandon them for nighttime screenings, weekend reporting assignments, and far-flung film festivals, and whose understanding was tested even more than usual during the year it took to write this book: Thank you. I love you. I'm back.

NOTES

INTRODUCTION

ix **five or six movies per year:** Motion Picture Association of America, "2016 Theatrical Market Statistics Report," March 2017, http://www.mpaa.org/wp-content /uploads/2017/03/2016-Theatrical-Market-Statistics -Report-2.pdf, 13.

CHAPTER 1: THE SCREENPLAY

2   **"can't do it the other way around":** George Clooney, interview with author, February 5, 2014.

10 **"wants to pay attention to them":** Kenneth Lonergan, interview with author, September 12, 2016.

12 **"antithetical to the film, a betrayal":** Jem Cohen, email to author, September 24, 2016.

12 **"medium for lazy readers":** Alfonso Cuarón, interview with author, December 8, 2006.

13 **"screaming to the other characters who that character is":** Guillermo del Toro, interview with author, December 13, 2006.

16 **"allowed into heaven":** Aaron Sorkin, interview with author, October 14, 2015.

19 **"just not sure why":** Mark Boal, interview with author, May 10, 2009.

20 **how his stories will end while he's writing:** Guillermo Arriaga, quoted in Tim Grierson, *Screenwriting* (New York: Focal Press, 2013), 26–36.

25 **"seems to feel good":** Lonergan interview.

29 **"not watching the movie":** Paul Schrader interview, in George Stevens Jr., ed., *Conversations at the American Film Institute with the Great Moviemakers: The Next Generation* (New York: Alfred A. Knopf, 2012), 566.

31 **"like you got there on your own, but you didn't":** Casey Affleck, interview with author, September 12, 2016.

31 **"seen a million times":** Lonergan interview.

32 **"It's about the ideas":** Richard Linklater, interview with author, November 10, 2009.

35 **"in love with somebody":** Jason Reitman, interview with author, November 25, 2009.

CHAPTER 2: ACTING

43 **"no idea he's doing that":** Tom McCarthy, interview with author, October 1, 2015.

43 **"the prick that's in *you*":** Dustin Hoffman, interview with author, November 15, 2012.

43 **"from Barbra Streisand?":** Alan J. Pakula interview, in George Stevens Jr., ed., *Conversations at the American Film Institute with the Great Moviemakers: The Next Generation* (New York: Alfred A. Knopf, 2012), 360–361.

44 **"conflicts even they don't sense":** Larry Moss, interview with author, February 2006.

46 **"real up there":** Michael Caine, *Acting in Film: An Actor's Take on Movie Making*, rev. ed. (Milwaukee: Applause Books, 2000), 90.

47 **"figure the man out completely":** Barry Levinson, interview with author, October 6, 2009.

47 **"your troubles are over":** John Sayles, *Thinking in Pictures* (Boston: Houghton Mifflin, 1987), 45.

48 **"totally offensive":** Roger Michell, interview with author, September 10, 2012.

51   **"indelible sense of competence"**: Pakula interview, in Stevens, *Conversations*, 371.

52   **"I just wasn't thinking"**: Robert Redford, interview with author, October 27, 2005.

53   **"rather than with you"**: Jack Lemmon interview, in Stevens, *Conversations*, 279.

53   **"think it's my world"**: George Clooney, interview with author, February 5, 2014.

55   **"she was pulling us"**: Phillip Noyce, interview with author, July 19, 2010.

55   **"bigger than you"**: Angelina Jolie, interview with author, July 19, 2010.

56   **"it's not a cliché"**: David O. Russell, interview with author, November 22, 2013.

56   **"interest in humanity"**: Arthur Nolletti Jr., "Classical Hollywood, 1928–1946," in Claudia Springer and Julie Levinson, eds., *Acting* (New Brunswick, NJ: Rutgers University Press, 2015), 66.

57   **"and then he moves"**: Anthony Hopkins, quoted in Lawrence Grobel, *Above the Line: Conversations About the Movies* (New York: Da Capo), 151.

61   **"the way the shot is set up"**: Edward Norton, press conference for *Moonrise Kingdom*, Cannes Film Festival, 2012.

65   **"where the real action lies"**: Larry Moss, interview with author, February 2006.

65   **"trying to overcome them"**: David Oyelowo, interview with author, December 12, 2014.

71   **"doing the work for me"**: Gary Oldman, interview with author, November 21, 2011.

71   **"what I've done since then"**: Alec Guinness, speech delivered at the 52nd Academy Awards, April 14, 1980.

CHAPTER 3: PRODUCTION DESIGN

77   **"made it a deeper piece"**: Jared Brown, *Alan J. Pakula: His Film and His Life* (New York: Back Stage Books, 2005), 182.

78   **"work of the property man":** Elia Kazan, *Kazan on Directing* (New York: Vintage Books, 2009), 147.

79   **"information there that he could get":** Jeannine Oppewall, interview with author, Middleburg Film Festival, October 22, 2016.

79   **"middle of the wall":** David Fincher, quoted in Emanuel Levy, "Social Network: Interview with Director David Fincher," in Laurence Knapp, ed., *David Fincher Interviews* (Jackson: University Press of Mississippi, 2014), 160.

80   **"background is as important as character":** Alfonso Cuarón, interview with author, December 8, 2006.

81   **"fat ties and sideburns":** David Fincher, press conference for *Zodiac*, Cannes Film Festival, 2007.

86   **"incredible arsenic green":** Fionnuala Halligan, *Production Design* (Burlington, MA: Focal Press, 2013), 116.

86   **"the beauty as well as the pain":** *Precious* production notes, 2009.

89   **"still get more out of it":** David Thompson and Ian Christie, eds., *Scorsese on Scorsese* (London: Faber and Faber, 1989), 154.

90   **"see what he was going through":** Mike Mills, interview with author, May 5, 2011.

93   **"it all came together":** Michael Douglas, interview with author, *Premiere*, April 1988, 30.

93   **"basically says, 'Fuck you'":** Ellen Mirojnick, interview with author, *Premiere*, April 1988, 30.

94   **"expression of the character's soul":** Kazan, *Kazan on Directing*, 271.

95   **soft-edged baby-boomer teens:** Ang Lee, interview with author, May 18, 2009.

99   **"I put it in the background":** Steven Spielberg, interview with author, June 7, 2002.

101   **"the comfort blanket of the past":** Jane Barnwell, *Production Design: Architects of the Screen* (New York: Wallflower Press of Columbia University Press, 2004), 83.

CHAPTER 4: CINEMATOGRAPHY

115   **"talking against walls":** Jeannine Oppewall, interview with author, Middleburg Film Festival, October 22, 2016.

116   **"too much like television":** Spike Lee, quoted in Stephen Pizzello, "Between 'Rock' and a Hard Place," in Cynthia Fuchs, ed., *Spike Lee: Interviews* (Jackson: University Press of Mississippi, 2002), 108.

117   **"no longer 'bedroom perfect,' as De Niro calls it":** David O. Russell, interview with author, November 22, 2013.

123   **"punch in [for a close-up] when we needed it":** Tom McCarthy, interview with author, October 1, 2015.

124   **"a little chamber drama":** Paul Thomas Anderson, interview with author, September 9, 2012.

125   **"face-off,** *epic***":** Tilda Swinton, interview with author, September 10, 2011.

126   **"hemmed in to himself":** Barry Jenkins, interview with author, October 25, 2016.

126   **"in the moment with them":** Kelly Reichardt, Sundance Film Festival, January 21, 2011.

126   **"touched or manipulated":** *Son of Saul* production notes, 2015.

128   **"increasingly confined hours":** Sidney Lumet, *Making Movies* (London: Bloomsbury, 1995), 81.

130   **"eyes of 'strangers'":** Jim Jarmusch, "Some Notes on *Stranger Than Paradise*," 1984, reprinted as a booklet in *Stranger Than Paradise*, Criterion Collection, Director-Approved Double-Disc Set, DVD, September 4, 2007.

134   **"feels like something made up":** Michael Mann interview with John Patterson, *The Guardian*, June 25, 2009.

135   **"the new gaffer":** Nicolas Winding Refn, interview with author, August 25, 2011.

136   **"the way a cloud looks in Story One":** Jenkins interview.

CHAPTER 5: EDITING

148   **"and it flowed":** Albert Berger, interview with author, October 23, 2016.

152   **"explain it to me clearly":** Sean Penn interview with Jean-Paul Chaillet, *Le Figaro*, August 19, 2011.

155   **"tend to putrefy":** Michael Ondaatje, *The Conversations: Walter Murch and the Art of Editing Film* (New York: Alfred A. Knopf, 2002), 267.

162   **vulnerability would be more clearly established:** Thelma Schoonmaker, interview with author, April 2009.

162   **"pushing together one last time":** Berger interview.

162   **"mowed people down with an AK-47?":** Billy Weber, interview with author, March 11, 2009.

163   **"about a look rather than a line":** Anne McCabe, interview with author, March 12, 2009.

163   **"awakening":** Mike Nichols, quoted in *Becoming Mike Nichols*, HBO documentary, directed by Douglas McGrath, 2016.

166   **"knew made it frightening":** Schoonmaker interview.

174   **"even though it was improvised":** Ibid.

175   **"we'll never know which is which":** Walter Murch, interview with author, March 11, 2009.

CHAPTER 6: SOUND AND MUSIC

178   **"things you don't know are there":** Walter Murch, interview with author, October 2010.

181   **"things at my disposal—picture and sound":** Christopher Nolan, interview with Carolyn Giardina, *The Hollywood Reporter*, November 15, 2014.

185   **"'imagine what the dog is thinking'":** John Ross, quoted in Jay Beck with Vanessa Theme Ament, "The New Hollywood, 1981–1999," in Kathryn Kalinak, ed., *Sound: Dialogue, Music, and Effects* (New Brunswick, NJ: Rutgers University Press, 2015), 115.

186 **no dynamism or depth:** Randy Thom, interview with author, September 3, 2010.

187 **"real animal sounds, real insects":** Ben Burtt, quoted in Jeff Smith, "The Auteur Renaissance, 1968–1980," in Kathryn Kalinak, ed., *Sound: Dialogue, Music, and Effects* (New Brunswick, NJ: Rutgers University Press, 2015), 102.

188 **"different feeling just with the sound effects":** Ann Kroeber, interview with author, September 3, 2010.

189 **"convey the information":** Skip Lievsay, interview with author, November 4, 2016.

192 **"deliver the dramatic idea":** Ibid.

192 **"began to bend reality":** Murch interview.

194 **"collapsing and re-stretching":** Ibid.

195 **"then nothing is loud":** Thom interview, 2010.

198 **"when I have a deadline":** Carter Burwell, interview with author, Middleburg Film Festival, October 24, 2015.

199 **"get behind and inside":** Elmer Bernstein, quoted in David Morgan, *Knowing the Score: Film Composers Talk About the Art, Craft, Blood, Sweat, and Tears of Writing for Cinema* (New York: Harper Entertainment, 2000), 3.

201 **"something larger at work":** *The Social Network* production notes, 2010.

208 **"it would hurt 90 percent":** Murch interview, 2010.

CHAPTER 7: DIRECTING

210 **"running behind them at full speed":** Guillermo del Toro, interview with author, December 13, 2006.

210 **"all of a sudden, the movie is poorly directed":** Jason Reitman, interview with author, November 25, 2009.

210 **"flavors are working together":** Casey Affleck, interview with author, September 12, 2016.

211 **one of cinema's most legendary debates:** Andrew Sarris, "Notes on the Auteur Theory in 1962," *Film Culture*, Winter 1962–1963, 1–8.

211   **aesthetic values and logic:** Pauline Kael, "Circles and Squares," *Film Quarterly* 16, no. 3 (1963): 12–26.

212   **"working with the most talented people":** Alan J. Pakula interview, in George Stevens Jr., ed., *Conversations at the American Film Institute with the Great Moviemakers: The Next Generation* (New York: Alfred A. Knopf, 2012), 362.

214   **"the best movie possible from this material":** Richard Linklater, interview with author, November 10, 2009.

214   **"it's his fault in the end":** Meryl Streep interview, in George Stevens Jr., ed., *Conversations at the American Film Institute with the Great Moviemakers: The Next Generation* (New York: Alfred A. Knopf, 2012), 652.

215   **"get the best out of that person":** Linklater interview, 2009.

218   **Lumet recalled using this method:** Sidney Lumet, *Making Movies* (London: Bloomsbury, 1995), 27.

219   **recognize and seize them:** Phil Alden Robinson, interview with author, June 18, 2009.

222   **"never ponderous sense of balance":** George Cukor, quoted in Richard Schickel, *The Men Who Made the Movies* (Chicago: Ivan R. Dee, 1975), 165–166.

224   **"nothing has importance":** Alan J. Pakula, quoted in Jared Brown, *Alan J. Pakula: His Film and His Life* (New York: Back Stage Books, 2005), 84.

227   **"conclusion that everybody expects":** Steven Spielberg, interview with author, October 30, 2012.

229   **"humanize the hunt":** Kathryn Bigelow, interview with author, December 5, 2012.

230   **"you as a human being in the midst of that march":** David Oyelowo, interview with author, December 12, 2014.

234   **"over to [my] way of thinking":** Alfred Hitchcock, interview with Peter Bogdanovich, *Who the Devil Made It: Conversations with Legendary Film Directors* (New York: Ballantine, 1997), 476.

235 **"'how I see the world. Do you?'"**: Paul Greengrass, interview with author, October 4, 2013.

238 **"in your brain and in your heart"**: Del Toro interview, 2006.

APPENDIX

249 **"make up what happens on the way to what happened"**: Tony Kushner, interview with author, October 30, 2012.

BIBLIOGRAPHY AND
SUGGESTED READING

FOR DETAILED EXPLANATIONS AND ANALYSES of specific film-making disciplines, the author highly recommends three book series: *Behind the Silver Screen*, which currently has nine volumes (a tenth is forthcoming), published by Rutgers University Press; *FilmCraft*, with five volumes, published by Focal Press at Routledge; and *Conversations with Filmmakers*, published by the University Press of Mississippi, with over one hundred volumes to date.

Aufderheide, Patricia. *Documentary Film: A Very Short Introduction*. Oxford: Oxford University Press, 2007.

Barnwell, Jane. *Production Design: Architects of the Screen*. New York: Wallflower Press of Columbia University Press, 2004.

Bogdanovich, Peter. *Who the Devil Made It: Conversations with Legendary Film Directors*. New York: Ballantine, 1997.

Brown, Jared. *Alan J. Pakula: His Film and His Life*. New York: Back Stage Books, 2005.

Caine, Michael. *Acting in Film: An Actor's Take on Movie Making*, rev. ed. Milwaukee: Applause Books, 1990.

Coles, Robert. *Doing Documentary Work*. New York: New York Public Library and Oxford University Press, 1997.

Cook, David A. *A History of Narrative Film*, 5th ed. New York: W. W. Norton, 2016.

Fuchs, Cynthia, ed. *Spike Lee: Interviews*. Jackson: University Press of Mississippi, 2002.

Goldman, William. *Adventures in the Screen Trade*. New York: Hachette, 1983.

Grobel, Lawrence. *Above the Line: Conversations About the Movies*. Boston: Da Capo, 2000.

Halligan, Fionnuala. *Production Design*. Burlington, MA: Focal Press, 2013.

Kalinak, Kathryn. *Sound: Dialogue, Music, and Effects*. New Brunswick, NJ: Rutgers University Press, 2015.

Kazan, Elia. *Kazan on Directing*. New York: Vintage Books, 2009.

Knapp, Laurence, ed. *David Fincher Interviews*. Jackson: University Press of Mississippi, 2014.

LoBrutto, Vincent. *Becoming Film Literate: The Art and Craft of Motion Pictures*. Westport, CT: Praeger, 2005.

Lumet, Sidney. *Making Movies*. London: Bloomsbury, 1995.

Monaco, James. *How to Read a Film: Movies, Media, and Beyond*, 4th ed. Oxford: Oxford University Press, 2009.

Morgan, David. *Knowing the Score: Film Composers Talk About the Art, Craft, Blood, Sweat, and Tears of Writing for Cinema*. New York: Harper Entertainment, 2000.

Murch, Walter. *In the Blink of an Eye*. Beverly Hills: Silman-James Press, 2001.

Ondaatje, Michael. *The Conversations: Walter Murch and the Art of Editing*. New York: Alfred A. Knopf, 2002.

Sayles, John. *Thinking in Pictures*. Boston: Houghton Mifflin, 1987.

Schatz, Thomas. *The Genius of the System*. New York: Pantheon, 1989.

Schelle, Michael. *The Score: Interviews with Film Composers*. Los Angeles: Silman-James Press, 1999.

Schickel, Richard. *The Men Who Made the Movies*. Chicago: Ivan R. Dee, 1975.

Springer, Claudia, and Julie Levinson, eds. *Acting*. New Brunswick, NJ: Rutgers University Press, 2015.

Stevens, George, Jr., ed. *Conversations at the American Film Institute with the Great Moviemakers: The Next Generation*. New York: Alfred A. Knopf, 2012.

Thompson, David, and Ian Christie, eds. *Scorsese on Scorsese*. London: Faber and Faber, 1989.

Thompson, Kristin. *Storytelling in the New Hollywood: Understanding Classical Narrative Technique*. Cambridge, MA: Harvard University Press, 1999.

INDEX

ANN HORNADAY is chief film critic at the *Washington Post* and was a finalist for the 2008 Pulitzer Prize in Criticism. Hornaday lives in Baltimore, Maryland.